AF479185

A SOBER DESIRE FOR HISTORY

A SOBER DESIRE FOR HISTORY

William Gilmore Simms as Historian

SEAN R. BUSICK

University of South Carolina Press

Published in Columbia, South Carolina, by the
University of South Carolina Press

Manufactured in the United States of America

09 08 07 06 05   5 4 3 2 1

Library of Congress Cataloging-in-Publication Data

Busick, Sean R., 1969–
  A sober desire for history : William Gilmore Simms as historian / Sean R. Busick.
    p. cm.
  Includes bibliographical references and index.
  ISBN 1-57003-565-2 (cloth : alk. paper)
  1. Simms, William Gilmore, 1806–1870—Knowledge—History. 2. Simms, William
Gilmore, 1806–1870—Knowledge—South Carolina. 3. Historical fiction, American—
History and criticism. 4. Literature and history—South Carolina. 5. South Carolina—
Historiography. 6. Historiography—South Carolina. 7. South Carolina—In literature.
I. Title.
  PS2853.B875 2005
  818'.309—dc22

                                                                                    2004023546

To Jennifer, Ashley Rose, and Cora

CONTENTS

| ACKNOWLEDGMENTS |

While working on this book I have tried to keep in mind the advice of Cato and Virgil that a small farm well cared for is better than a large one poorly cared for. Nevertheless, this field has proven too large for my hands to manage alone. Thankfully, I have been sustained by the friendship and assistance of many people.

Among those who provided welcome support and assistance are Simms scholars Jack Guilds, Jim Meriwether, and Jim Kibler. Jack Guilds suggested the subject of Simms's historianship and has generously shared with me his knowledge of Simms. I have benefited more than I can say from long conversations with Jim Meriwether about Simms and southern literature and history. Jim Kibler has also freely given valuable advice. I could not ask for better friends than Carey Roberts, Jeff Rogers, Sam Smith, John Devanny, and Alan Cornett. I have learned more from them than I have from any class I have taken. Carey deserves special recognition for reading a draft of this work and offering his counsel. Professors Mark Smith, Owen Connelly, Keen Butterworth, Dan Carter, and Clyde Wilson all read the manuscript and supplied helpful criticism and suggestions. Clyde Wilson has not only served as my advisor in this project but has also long been a mentor and friend. Any good research habits I may have are attributable to his guidance. He has provided me with an example of a scholar and a gentleman. My parents, Russell and Sharon, have given me their love and emotional as well as financial support. Finally, I must thank my wife, Jennifer, and daughters, Ashley Rose and Cora, for their tolerance. They made room for Simms in their lives and our house with little complaint considering he took up more space and stayed longer than is polite for a houseguest. Through it all, Jennifer has been a constant encouragement and a true helpmeet.

Special thanks are due to the students in my historical methods seminar at Kentucky Wesleyan College. Many of the ideas contained herein were sharpened in the classroom through our discussions on the nature of history.

It is a pleasure to thank these individuals. Thanks are due also to the Caroliniana Society and Earhart Foundation for providing financial assistance while I pursued graduate studies.

| INTRODUCTION |

A sober desire for history—the unwritten, the unconsidered, but veracious history—has been with me, in this labour, a sort of principle. —Simms, The Partisan

William Gilmore Simms was the central figure in historical studies in the Old South. He worked with practically every historian writing in or on the Old South, either assisting with research or in his capacity as magazine editor and book reviewer.[1] He was far and away the leading southern interpreter of the Revolution. He was one of the nineteenth century's most accomplished, popular, and prolific writers of historical romances. He wrote more history of high quality than anyone else in the South. His biography of Francis Marion is one of the best historical biographies written in the Old South and still contains much to reward curious historians. His school history of South Carolina influenced generations of children. He accumulated one of the finest private collections of historical manuscripts relating to the Revolution in the United States. He was a thoughtful and important commentator on the nature of history and its relationship with fiction.

Though Simms has been the subject of renewed interest, he has, up to now, seldom been studied as a historian. Part of this relative neglect is due to his being better known as a novelist. Part is also due to a more general neglect of southern intellectual history. Before the last few decades historians generally dismissed southern intellectual life "as shallowly conceived and narrowly obsessed with slavery," writes Drew Gilpin Faust.[2] It is "a ruling assumption of American scholarship," adds Michael O'Brien, that the mind of the Old South "was superficial, unintellectual, obsessed with race and slavery, enfeebled by polemic."[3] Among postbellum historians, Henry Adams and William Peterfield Trent popularized the view of the Old South as an intellectually barren and closed society. In the twentieth century W. J. Cash gave wide circulation to this interpretation through his influential *The Mind of the South.* Later, historians William Freehling and Stephen Channing told us that whatever thought may have existed in the Old South was dominated by a paralyzing fear of servile insurrection.[4] According to the fashionable view the freedom of inquiry necessary to intellectual achievement did not exist in the Old South. All southerners were required to close ranks in defense of slavery. "Dissenters were driven out or forced to remain silent," wrote William L. Barney in a typical assessment.[5] No criticism of southern society was allowed.

Yet this dogma has increasingly been subject to revision by scholars led by Richard Beale Davis, Eugene Genovese, Michael O'Brien, and David Moltke-Hansen.[6] They and numerous others have shown that the Old South was in fact intellectually vibrant, if not always in the same ways as the North, and aware of the latest thought from Europe. And earlier John Welsh had shown that Simms himself was an important critic of southern society.[7]

The present study is written in the belief that Simms can only be understood when he is understood as a historian. He certainly thought of himself a historian. Many of his contemporaries also thought of him as a historian. Most of what he wrote, whether novels, dramas, poetry, biography, or reviews, he would have classified as history. We can truly understand Simms only when we understand him as a historian.

Simms deserves study as a historian for several important reasons. First, he was one of the most popular, widely read historical writers of his day. Second, like all of Simms's writings, his history provides us with insights into the elusive mind of the Old South. Third, nearly all of Simms's writings are deeply influenced by his understanding of history. Any attempt to come to terms with Simms, therefore, will be incomplete if it does not take into account his work as a historian. Yet this aspect of his work has been relatively neglected in the accumulating Simms scholarship because most of those who write about him are literary scholars, not historians. Fourth, he thought long and deeply on the nature of history and its relationship to fiction, epic, and myth—problems that all thoughtful historians must grapple with. And finally, at a time when Americans were struggling to define themselves, he staked claim for South Carolinians to the Revolutionary heritage.

The chapters that follow will address Simms's ideas on the relationship between history and fiction, his efforts at collecting and publishing historical manuscripts, his relationship with other historians, his encouragement of other historians and his critical reviewing of history, his work as a biographer, his history and geography textbooks for young South Carolinians, his treatment of history in fiction, and his controversial northern lectures on South Carolina in the Revolution. Some readers may question the lack of attention given to Simms's *Sack and Destruction of the City of Columbia, S.C.* An unquestionably important historical document, his account of the burning of Columbia nevertheless lacks the retrospective viewpoint necessary for writing history. As a historian, Simms sought to put on record as much of America's past as possible, to blend history with fiction, and to instruct Americans in the virtues necessary for citizenship by celebrating the virtuous actions of autonomous individuals.

A SOBER DESIRE FOR HISTORY

| ONE |

Art, Patriotism, and Moral Progress
The Foundation of Simms's Historical Writings

All thinking is indeed Art. —General Carl von Clausewitz, ON WAR

We should not be surprised to learn that, in his day, William Gilmore Simms was widely recognized as one of America's foremost historians. The most important man of letters in the Old South, he was also the central figure in historical studies in the Old South. Author of a history and a geography of South Carolina, book-length biographies of John Smith, Francis Marion, Nathanael Greene, and the Chevalier Bayard, as well as a vast number of shorter pieces either contributed to periodicals or delivered as lectures, and editor of collections of the writings and speeches of John Laurens and James Henry Hammond, Simms is remembered today chiefly for his novels. Most of those novels were historical romances, and he put as much research and concern for accuracy into them as he did into his histories. Today, as people accustomed to the specialization (or, perhaps, compartmentalization) of labor, we expect the writers of fiction to stick to the writing of fiction and historians to stick to history. Consequently, Simms's work is little appreciated as history, and he seldom receives much attention from those who write about American historians.[1]

Simms scholars themselves give little notice to his work as a historian, tending to focus instead on his fiction, poetry, or overtly polemical writings. Even his lone modern biographer, John Caldwell Guilds, in the fullest treatment of Simms to date, considers him primarily as a novelist and poet. Of the other major book-length studies of Simms, Mary Ann Wimsatt's *The Major Fiction of William Gilmore Simms,* as the title suggests, is concerned solely with his fiction, while Jon L. Wakelyn and Charles Watson limit themselves to his political writings. Only William Peterfield Trent, in his justly maligned biography, gives much serious attention to Simms's historical writing. Despite its many shortcomings, Trent's biography deals with Simms's work as a historian at greater length and more seriously than most subsequent works. Perhaps because Trent was writing in 1892, he was still close enough to the era of the great amateur historians to appreciate their work despite the professional training he received at Johns Hopkins University. Yet even Trent devoted fewer than ten pages in a 332-page biography to Simms's work as a historian and failed to recognize that many of his novels and poems were merely history written in a different form.[2]

Before the age of professional historians, it was not thought the least unusual for a novelist to write history or vice versa. Indeed, before late-nineteenth-century professionalization, history was simply one of several genres that constituted literature. As a type of knowledge about humanity, history resembled philosophy, poetry, and other humanistic pursuits.[3] Homer and Herodotus, Shakespeare and Gibbon were all colleagues within the republic of letters. All wrote history, only their manner of presentation differed.[4]

The influential eighteenth-century Scottish intellectual Adam Smith clearly expressed the belief that history was a literary pursuit when he posed the question: "For what is it which constitutes the essential difference betwixt a historicall poem and a history? It is no more than this that the one is in prose and the other in verse."[5] Narrative and poetry were simply different ways of expressing historical knowledge.[6] According to Smith's view, the history differed from the historical poem in style, but not necessarily in substance or historical accuracy. Simms would have heartily agreed with Smith. "Authorship is an art," Simms believed, "having numerous relations and departments," with history, poetry, drama, and novel writing numbered among them.[7]

Not all historians, however, would agree with Smith and Simms. A number of influential historians have been more concerned with achieving supposed dispassionate objectivity than with writing readable narrative. To these scholars, history is (or at least should be) more akin to science than it is to literature.[8] Historian Simon Schama has imaginatively described his colleagues as marshaled into "opposing platoons commanded by Herodotus or Thucydides." In Thucydides, scientific historians "have seen an early paragon of objectivity, of critical use of sources, of dispassionate analytical investigation." Others have admired Herodotus for the literary quality of his writing, "his relish for gossip, his intuitive understanding of the idiosyncrasies of climate and geography, his primitive ethnography, his unabashed subjectivities, the winning mishmash of hearsay and record, real and fantastic."[9] The professional historians have been putting to rout Herodotus's phalanx in the United States since at least 1884, when the American Historical Association was founded, and the reputations of nonscientific historians have suffered accordingly. The university-trained historians who organized the AHA traced their intellectual ancestry to the German universities and thus tended to overlook the contributions of earlier generations of American historians, who had not been trained in their profession and who used seemingly unscientific methodologies.[10] Neglect of earlier historians has been due to both ignorance and design. This is neither surprising nor a recent phenomenon. Historians have always thought that their own work was an improvement over that of their predecessors. Some have even considered ignorance of their predecessors a virtue: it freed them to view the past with fresh eyes. The Roman historian Livy long ago noted that "every writer on history tends to look down his nose at his less cultivated predecessors, happily persuaded that he will better them in point of style, or bring new facts to light."[11] And so it goes.

The employment of scientific methods in the researching and writing of history should not be confused with attempts to discover a science of history, sometimes called historicism.[12] The former seeks exactness in conclusions. The latter seeks to locate the formula that will make the past logical and the future predictable. Historicism is based on a progressive theory of history, in which the future toward which we are being inevitably propelled by forces beyond our control is always better than the present, if not utopian. In terms of ethics, historicists believe that whatever is becoming, is right. Although it is quite common for professional historians to champion the application of scientific methods, few thoughtful students of history realistically expect to find a science of history pointing to humanity's bright future.[13] The problem, as Leo Tolstoy rightly pointed out, is that, until free will is abolished, human actions will never be as predictable as the observations of Copernicus and Galileo made the movement of the planets.[14] Karl Popper has likewise argued that because human nature is unpredictable, advocates of historicism can only predict the future by controlling human nature. Therefore, Popper thought, historicism must eventually lead to totalitarianism.[15]

Yet in the nineteenth century the search for a science of history that would unite the past, present, and future in one grand logical system was in full swing. In the late eighteenth century J. G. Herder, an early proponent of historicism, argued that forces such as climate, culture, and tradition play deterministic roles in history. These forces, along with humanity's striving after perfection, drove history in a progressive, if not always unilinear, direction.[16] G. W. F. Hegel, who wrote in the early nineteenth century, was more progressive still. For Hegel history was developmental, and its deterministic force was spirit. "History in general is therefore the development of Spirit in *Time*," he wrote.[17] The external manifestation of spirit, as well as the manifestation of the general will, was the state. Thus the state was the agent of progress, and higher levels of development could be attained by bringing laws and individual will into unity with spirit. This type of German romantic thought quickly crossed the Atlantic, found expression in some forms of southern romanticism, and motivated American historians like George Bancroft to try to locate the American national spirit.[18]

In the mid–nineteenth century the search for a science of history was given fresh impetus by the writings of Charles Darwin and Karl Marx. The writings of both men seemed to demonstrate that society, and even mankind itself, naturally evolved to some higher, or more perfect, form. "Those of us who . . . in 1859 read the Origin of Species and felt the violent impulse which Darwin gave to the study of natural laws, never doubted that historians would follow until they had exhausted every possible hypothesis to create a science of history," wrote Henry Adams.[19]

In general, Simms, like most American historians, Bancroft included, accepted the idea of progress. He was familiar with contemporary European thought, and his writings indicate that he was influenced by ideas about the deterministic power of both national spirit and material factors such as climate and geography. In his biography of Francis Marion, for example, he discussed how material factors influenced the spirit of the Huguenots, which in turn influenced Marion. But on the whole, Simms's writings show that he was far more interested in the power of autonomous personal character than in impersonal forces. Furthermore, though Simms recognized that impersonal forces could influence history, such forces do not play a deterministic role in his writing. Individuality, he wrote to James Henry Hammond, is a Christian principle "that seperates [*sic*] man from the mass, and lifts him into a responsible personality, crowning him with a will which is based on new considerations of his own importance." Because of this, men must be considered individually, not as members of "castes, professions, or parties." Therefore he regarded Christ as an exponent of democratic principles for freeing mankind "from the shackles of an hereditary priesthood." Hammond thought this doctrine sounded a lot like John Milton's essay "The Readie and Easie Way to Establish a Free Commonwealth."[20]

Likewise, while he had faith in progress, unlike Bancroft he rejected any notion of its inevitability and carefully distinguished moral from material progress. He certainly did not adhere to the morally relativistic position that whatever is becoming is right. Nor did he believe that God marched with the big battalions. The notable exceptions to his rejection of the inevitability of progress were his faith in the certainty of American expansion, which he sometimes called progress, and his faith in man's capacity for technological innovation. In Simms's thought the road to higher levels of civilization was fraught with danger that could lead to regress and there was no guarantee that moral and material progress went hand-in-hand. Simms also denied the perfectibility of mankind. Because he separated moral from material advancement, he viewed progress as being more like a rolling hoop than an ascent up a slope.[21] Morality might spin in revolutions between progress and decline while wealth and technology continued to flourish. This was a commonly held tenet of the Jeffersonian faithful, who believed that England, the wealthiest and most industrialized nation on earth, was morally bankrupt.[22]

The possibility of moral regress can be seen throughout Simms's writings. In his history and romances of the Revolution, he accurately rendered South Carolina's temporary decline into the barbarity of civil war. His romances and stories about the colonization of America depict the death of Indian civilizations and show how European civilization sometimes took an initial step backward when transplanted to the New World. His border romances present the savagery of the frontier, where civilization was continually starting from scratch.

In fact, his depiction of civilization beginning afresh on the frontier brings to mind Frederick Jackson Turner's frontier thesis. In the West, "the absence of the compensative resources of wealth leads to a singular and unreserved freedom among the people," Simms wrote. But the absence of the restraining influences and institutions of the East also created a society that "sanctions promptly the fierce redress—that wild justice of revenge—which punishes without appeal to law."[23]

Professionally minded historians have argued that history is useful only when it is accurate. In that they agree with the proponents of history as art—leaving aside arguments about the utilitarianism of history. They diverge from their artistic brethren in their conception of specifically how an accurate history should be written, believing that, in the words of historian J. B. Bury, "All truths . . . require the most exact methods."[24] The most exact methods are the most scientific. History thus improves in accuracy and therefore utility as its methods approach those of a laboratory science. Accuracy, scientific historians contend, is a measure of factuality. By using objective, systematic methods, they believe, historians can uncover incontrovertible facts. These bare facts should then be compiled and presented to readers without allowing the historian's biases to taint them through any narrative tricks.

Advocates of history as art, on the other hand, contend that historical accuracy cannot be measured by the same standards of exactness that are applied to the physical sciences. Unlike the sciences, history is unsystematic. Historical knowledge is incomplete and often unquantifiable. Historians work with circumstantial evidence instead of scientific facts. According to Carl Becker, what we refer to as historical facts are not really facts at all in any ordinary sense. Instead of being observable or measurable, historical facts are merely symbolic representations of vanished past events.[25] History neither unfolds in nor is written in a laboratory. Because "the conclusion of an historical enquiry cannot be confirmed or falsified by comparing it with the conclusions of any other kind of enquiry, and it cannot be tested against independent criteria of credibility," history is not subject to the same rigorous standards of exactness as the physical sciences.[26] In the words of novelist Cormac McCarthy, "In history there are no control groups."[27] Historians generally have no way in which they may objectively test their hypotheses. Not only are there no control groups in history, but historians are usually not even firsthand observers of their subjects. Because of this limitation on the historian's investigation, R. G. Collingwood, who believed history a science, conceded that it is a "special kind" of science. "It is a science whose business is to study events not accessible to our observation, and to study these events inferentially," he wrote. If history can in any sense be considered scientific, observed Frederic W. Maitland, "it is only in the sense in which the method of a Sherlock Holmes would be scientific."[28]

Moreover, proponents of literary history believe that because facts can be arranged so as to either mislead readers or guide them toward historical truth, the arrangement of facts is at least as important as their discovery. In arranging facts, historians are engaged in a creative enterprise to reconstruct in words vanished events—they are telling a story. Thus, the writing of history is an imaginative engagement with the historical record. It is, according to Michael Oakeshott, "an engagement to infer, to understand discursively and to imagine the character of an historical event."[29] Accurate history must not only be correct in its details as far as that is possible working with an imperfect historical record, it must also correctly convey the character of past events to readers. Historians can achieve this wider degree of accuracy only by paying as much attention to how they write as to what they write.

In most essentials, this is the same argument for history as art that Simms laid out in his essay "The Epochs and Events of American History, as Suited to the Purposes of Art in Fiction," published in the first series of *Views and Reviews in American Literature, History, and Fiction* (1845). He recognized that raw facts, no matter how carefully assembled, never truly speak for themselves: "Dates and names, which, with the mere chronologist are every thing, with us are nothing."[30] Facts are given meaning by the artist-historian, who must first sort the relevant from the irrelevant facts, next arrange these facts so that they work together toward a common purpose. Finally, he or she must fill in the gaps in the historical record, interpreting and giving meaning to the facts by making use of an informed imagination carefully regulated by the dictates of truthfulness.

Of course, even the best historians occasionally fall into error. Simms was no exception. But it was always his goal to present accurate history after carefully weighing the available evidence.[31]

The historian acting as an artist "gives shape to the unhewn fact, . . . yields relation to the scattered fragments, . . . unites the parts in coherent dependency, and endows with life and action, the otherwise motionless automata of history." The hand and imagination of the artist give coherence to the seemingly unrelated facts through their proper arrangement. In the end history is "a story, a causally connected story tested and proved at every point," explained Maitland. By drawing relationships between events the artistic imagination constructs a story out of raw facts. Thus, Simms can write, "It is the soul of art, alone, which binds periods and places together."[32]

"But in history it is particularly important that your fancy shall be regulated severely," Simms cautioned. Imagination and the skills of the artist could appropriately be employed by the historian to fill in the gaps in the historical record, to describe scenery, and for "heightening the force of his picture." But the privilege of being able to enliven history with art did not extend to "lessening the value or altering the character of his facts."[33]

Simms's belief that history should be enlivened with art was misunderstood even in his own day. Reviewers accused him of claiming the right to alter history to suit his purposes. "I am not disparaging the history which is known," he insisted, "but [am] suggesting the free use which the imaginative mind may make of that which is unknown, fragmentary & in ruins."[34] William H. Prescott, thought Simms, through the "judicious use of the fanciful in his descriptions" provided a good example of how history could be enlivened with art.[35]

Prescott and Simms held substantially similar ideas concerning the proper relationship between romance and history. In considering the merits of Sir Walter

Scott's writings as history, Prescott advanced the proposition that the romancer has much to teach the historian about writing picturesque descriptions. Scott "understood, better than any historian since the time of Livy, how to dispose his lights and shades so as to produce the most striking results." A fine example of this is the manner in which Scott animated battle scenes in both his romances and history. Here was an instance of "borrowing something from romance" that in the end "improved history by the embellishments of romance." Scott's writings show how fiction can be made to "minister to history, and may, in point of fact, contain as much real truth"—especially in the delineation of character.[36]

Thus far, Prescott's views differ little from Simms's in *Views and Reviews*. But Prescott believed history and romance could never be completely blended together. This is exactly what Simms tried to do. "The fact is," wrote Prescott, "History and Romance are too near akin ever to be lawfully united." Fact and imagination would be too indeterminate in the resulting hybrid. "It is enough for the novelist if he be true to the spirit; the historian must be true, also, to the letter."[37]

Simms, on the other hand, believed it was not only possible but desirable to write romance that was as true to the letter of history as research could make it. Altering the character of facts would be dishonest. This was an unpardonable transgression because for Simms all history, indeed all art, bears the responsibility of "the elevation of man through the presentation of an ideal, moral, or truth."[38] Like Aristotle, who in the *Poetics* observed that poetry is more philosophical than history because it deals with what might or should have been instead of what actually has been, Simms recognized the potential of fiction to correct the moral judgments of history.[39] The artist must be faithful to the known facts. Yet where the historical record is imperfect, Simms claimed, "It is really of very little importance to mankind whether he is absolutely correct in all his conjectures." It is enough if his narrative teaches a moral truth that "awakens our attention, compels our thought, warms our affections, inspirits our hopes, elevates our aims, and builds up in our minds a fabric of character, compounded of just principles, generous tendencies and clear, correct standards of taste and duty."[40] This, according to Simms, was the highest purpose of the artist. He could aspire to no loftier goal than the moral training of his readers, and American history was full of tales of virtue just waiting to be told. Nevertheless, Simms managed to avoid falling into didacticism because, like all good storytellers, he adhered to the realistic method of storytelling and tried to *show*, not *tell*, his story. Simms believed that history is philosophy teaching by example. By this, it should be understood that he believed history should teach, but that history's teaching should be by example, not through preaching. History should *show*, not *tell*, moral and civic lessons.

The potential of history to provide moral instruction helps explain why Simms thought history was so vitally important. In his thought, history was intimately linked with ideas of nationalism and progress. In order to be truly great, a nation needs to progress morally. The way to progress morally was by learning the moral lessons of history. "It is an argument addressed to all that is hopeful and proud in the hearts of an ardent and growing people," Simms wrote. Unless Americans were content to be "a mere nation of shop-keepers," they needed to cultivate "qualities of soul and genius, which if not yet developed in our moral constitution, are struggling to make themselves heard and felt." The national character "must receive its higher moral tone from the exigencies of society, its traditions and its histories." Familiarity with America's history would produce "those vigorous shoots, of thought and imagination, which make a nation proud of its sons, . . . and which save her from becoming a by-word and reproach to other nations."[41] Americans would truly be able to boast of their national greatness only after their national morals, and not just their political institutions, had progressed beyond those of Europe.

Like many of his fellow southerners, Simms clearly distinguished moral from material progress. As Christians, southerners tended to define moral progress largely in terms of the spread of Christian teachings. Material progress, on the other hand, was evident in the rising standards of living and astonishing technological innovations that accompanied the industrial and transportation revolutions —a kind of cash-register evaluation of life. As Eugene Genovese has astutely observed, "slaveholders displayed deep ambivalence toward that material progress which the overwhelming majority of them saw as inevitable: Literally, they loved and hated it." Southerners welcomed the comfort and convenience that accompanied material progress. Simms, like other southern intellectuals, did not repudiate material progress. Rather, he repudiated "the cult of progress . . . and the moral and political decadence of a modernity run wild."[42] As a defender of what Richard Weaver has called "social bond individualism," Simms feared the atomization of society by rampant individualism. Simms was certainly no foe of individual rights, but he believed our rights could be secured only within the social context.[43]

According to James Kibler, "Simms above all advocates an inspired way of seeing, not bounded by the utilitarian or empirical but, rather, open to the deepened mystery of the world around. Certainly not the reduced and impoverished materialist's way of seeing the world as real estate or resources to exploit for profit."[44] He recognized that the only truly practical pursuits are those that profit one's spiritual and moral nature. Simms chided his contemporaries for their excessive materialism and their lack of attention to their own history. He wrote, "Novelties of invention do not establish the fact of moral superiority." Such novelties merely satisfy our "economies" or "gratify [our] animal passions."[45] Advances in transportation, "the capacity to overcome time and space, are wonderful things—but they are not virtues. . . . I do not believe that all the steam power in the world can bring happiness to one poor human heart. Still less can I believe that all the railroads in the world can carry one poor soul to heaven."[46] Nathaniel Hawthorne similarly ridiculed the notion that material progress inevitably led to moral progress in "The Celestial Railroad." All those who were preoccupied with material advancement were glutting their passions to the neglect of their soul. "The soul requires its own food," wrote Simms. "There must be special provision made for its nurture and its life, even as we make it for the pleasures of the body. . . . It can be fed only upon the fruits of immortality." To ignore the needs of the soul is to endanger it. The soul needs to be nurtured upon the virtues of "Faith, Love, Charity, Beauty, Taste, Genius, Art, [and] Society"—the virtues of citizenship and Christianity that the utilitarian scorns as "childish" and "unprofitable."[47] Yet, Simms argued, it is only through such seemingly impractical virtues that our social, moral, and spiritual condition can be enriched. And history, when written as he felt it should be, was a vast source of moral instruction and thus an engine of progress.

The very qualities of Simms's historical writings that earned him admiration in his own day have led to his neglect as a historian by later generations. Simms's ability to write fast-paced, "fascinating narration," and his skill in the "dramatic development of character," which was not infrequently employed to romanticize history or to draw moral lessons from the past, won him a wide readership and the esteem of his contemporaries.[48] Even some proponents of history as science during Simms's day saw no contradiction in recognizing that history also displayed some of the characteristics of an art and therefore could perhaps forgive him for writing as if history were an art. For example, after defining history as a science, Francis Lieber's 1835 *Encyclopædia Americana* goes on to admit that "in investigating [man in all his social relations], . . . and dispersing the clouds which often envelope truth, history is a science; in exhibiting its treasures of truth, an art."[49] Simms's scientifically inclined peers could be more generous than moderns in their estimate of his history because antebellum Americans held a broad definition of science that included any sort of critical inquiry.[50] As late as 1946, Charles Beard broadly defined the "humanistic sciences" to include any organized body of "knowledge and thought pertaining to human affairs."[51] Theodore Roosevelt and Frederick Jackson Turner likewise recognized history as ideally being scientific in regard to research but requiring an artistic touch to communicate the results of research. Today, as a result of the professionalization of history and our holding a narrower definition of science, those same artistic qualities that once won Simms praise are as likely as not to be counted against his merits as a historian.[52]

Whether Simms fits our notion of what a historian should be, it is clear that he always regarded himself as a historian, as did most of his contemporaries. Simms seems always to have been interested in history. Born in 1806 in Charleston, he would from a young age have heard tales of the Revolution from those who remembered and had participated in the war. His grandfather John Singleton served as a captain under Francis Marion, and his great-grandfather Thomas Singleton was imprisoned by the British in St. Augustine after the fall of Charleston. After Simms's mother died in 1808, his father moved west, leaving young

Simms in the care of his maternal grandmother. While out west his father volunteered under Andrew Jackson in the Seminole War.[53]

The experiences of Simms's family and his native city helped fuel his lifelong interest in history. Later in life he fondly recalled how, as a boy, he learned the Revolutionary history and lore of his family and state.

> There was scarcely a personage, British or American, Whig or Loyalist—scarcely an event, mournful or glorious—scarcely a deed, grand or savage—occurring in the history of the low country of South-Carolina, which has not been conned, for his benefit, . . . by venerable friends and loving kinswomen, now voiceless in the dust.[54]

These stories and his interest in history found expression in Simms's earliest writings. Even when he took up his pen to write poetry, drama, or fiction, his writing seldom wandered far from historical themes. As a result, most of Simms's fiction, most notably his series of eight novels set in Revolutionary South Carolina, and much of his poetry have historical settings and are based on solid research.[55] Many of his poems contain historical footnotes.[56] In fact, some of his earliest efforts at verse were written in commemoration of the Battle of New Orleans and American naval victories in the War of 1812 when he was just eight or nine.[57]

Historian Frederick Jackson Turner noted, in *Rise of the New West,* that the 1820s began with a spirit of exuberant nationalism and ended with a foreboding sense of sectionalism.[58] The 1820s began in the so-called Era of Good Feelings. The decade then witnessed a wave of patriotism inspired by the fiftieth anniversary of the Revolution and the passing away into myth and history of the generation of heroes who had steered the nation to independence. The deaths of both Thomas Jefferson and John Adams on July 4, 1826, caused many Americans to pause and reflect with pride upon both America's past and anticipated glory.

In Charleston the passing away of the Revolutionary heroes coincided with the loss of the city's leading literati of the first two decades of the nineteenth century. The deaths of locally well-regarded authors, such as Edwin C. Holland (1824), William Crafts (1826), and Henry Tudor Farmer (1828), cleared the stage for the emergence of a new generation of aspiring literary talents. Chief among these was William Gilmore Simms, who was destined to become not just Charleston's but also the South's leading antebellum man-of-letters.

Although only twenty-four years old when the decade ended, Simms published an impressive amount during the 1820s. We know that his poetry first began appearing in the pages of local newspapers at least as early as 1823, while he was still in his teens. His first known poem, "Sonnet—To My Books," published when he was just sixteen, declared his intention to write history. "Then let me foster with a filial care, / Your . . . historic scenes," he wrote to his books.[59] In July of 1824, Simms's first known prose piece, "Light Reading," appeared in the *Charleston Courier.* Then in 1825, at the age of nineteen, the Charleston firm of Gray and Ellis published Simms's *Monody on the Death of General Charles Cotesworth Pinckney* as his first separate publication in book form. About the same time he wrote ten or twelve chapters "of a novel called 'Oyster Point' founded on the early History of Charleston."[60] Before the decade ended, Simms had published three more books of poetry, scores of short pieces in journals, and had served as editor of at least two literary journals—the short-lived *Album* and the *Southern Literary Gazette*. In these early publications, produced during a period of fervent nationalism, Simms began exploring three themes that would engage much of the rest of his incredibly productive career: nationalism, progress, and the relationship of history to fiction.

Southerners' sense of nationalism has often been misunderstood by those who wish to divide them into opposing camps of nationalists and sectionalists.[61] The sentiments that we call nationalism and sectionalism have never been mutually exclusive. Indeed, the seventeenth-century German political philosopher Johannes Althusius described how, in federal states where national authority derived from local associations, loyalty to one's nation was grounded in particularism. Likewise Edmund Burke, in *Reflections on the Revolution in France,* argued that local attachments strengthen rather than weaken allegiance to one's nation. And sociologist John Shelton Reed has documented how, among twentieth-century southerners, loyalties to locale, state, region, and nation "cumulate and reinforce one another." The same could be said of early New Englanders, whose political universe revolved around the town meeting. Historians such as David Potter and David Waldstreicher, who have studied nationalism in the early republic, have come to similar conclusions.[62]

In *The Political Economy of Slavery,* historian Eugene D. Genovese rightly observes that antebellum southerners' sense of nationalism and their "protestations of love for the Union were not so much a desire to use the Union to protect slavery as a strong commitment to localism as the highest form of liberty. They genuinely loved the Union so long as it alone among the great states of the world recognized that localism had a wide variety of rights."[63] Simms, like the southerners Genovese describes, was a nationalist who saw no inherent contradiction between a strong commitment to localism and a love of the Union. He sincerely loved the Union because it had effected the independence of South Carolina as well as for the protection it afforded her, which he was confident would allow future unhindered development. "In a sense," Mark Kaplanoff has noted, "South Carolina's nationalism was always conditional—not a commitment to abstract principles but an expedient to protect and promote perceived economic interests."[64]

However, one must always be careful to avoid anachronism when discussing nationalism in the context of the early American republic. The very word "nationalism" did not appear in English until 1844. What we call nationalism in early America is often more akin to patriotism, a word which appeared more than a century earlier in 1738. Patriotism, as explained by George Orwell and John Lukacs, is an essentially defensive love of country or devotion to a particular place and way of life. Indeed, Edward Gibbon wrote: "That public virtue which among the ancients was denominated patriotism, is derived from a strong sense of our own interest in the preservation and prosperity of the free government of which we are members." Nationalism, on the other hand, grew out of German romanticism and the French Revolution and is more of an abstract principle expressing a wish to expand national power and prestige.[65] As late as 1857, Simms himself called his guardianship of South Carolina's history a "jealous Patriotism," and further explained that patriotism is born of "a just sense of what is really great and noble in the deeds of our ancestry."[66] Therefore his nationalism should be understood as love of his locale and his country, not as an abstract desire to optimize American or even southern wealth and military power or to impose his way of life upon others who live elsewhere.[67] Recall that during the Nullification Crisis Simms and fellow Unionists organized themselves into the States Rights and Union Party; the party name serving as an acknowledgment of their dual loyalty. Similarly, John C. Calhoun hoped to preserve the national bond by protecting local rights through nullification and the application of the concurrent majority.[68]

American nationalism in the early republic is usually best described as loyalty to a national government that balanced a variety of diverse interests and sections. When southerners began to feel that their interests were endangered by the federal government, they began developing their own sense of nationalism expressed as a desire to form a separate nation that would protect their particular interests.[69]

In an 1829 address to the Palmetto Society marking the anniversary of the Battle of Sullivan's Island, Simms gave voice to this dual commitment to nationalism and localism. Eventually, he predicted, the anniversary of the battle (sometimes referred to by Simms as the Battle of Fort Moultrie) would cease to be celebrated in Charleston: "The proximity of the 4th of July, a day generally celebrated in the country, will in a great measure render unnecessary, a distinct anniversary of any one achievement, however prominent in our history."[70] As long as the national holiday incorporated the celebration of local accomplishments, observances of local exploits were superfluous. "Every event, of course," explained Simms, "being included in the general celebration of our National Independence." Local exploits should not be ignored, rather they should be celebrated for contributing to the more glorious national achievement—independence and the formation of a federal union. Even though, as Simms acknowledged, love of Union "should equally be the sentiment of all," South Carolinians should not forget that "there are some points where prejudice is a merit, and selfishness the best of virtues. Such are the duties we owe to ourselves, and our own local interests."[71]

Because Simms believed that history served the purposes of nationalism and moral progress, it should come as no surprise that much of his writing during this period of intense nationalism had a historical theme. Nor should we be surprised that his historical themes were often drawn from local subjects. As has already been mentioned, his first published book was the *Monody on the Death of General Charles Cotesworth Pinckney.* His three collections of poetry published in the 1820s contained such historical poems as "Death of King Philip," "Benedict Arnold," "Major Andre," "On the Legislature of South-Carolina, Appropriating Ten Thousand Dollars, for the Benefit of the Heirs of Thomas Jefferson," "Epigram, on Reading a Fourth of July Address to Freedom," and "The Vision of Cortes." Simms also contributed numerous historical pieces to the magazines he edited. Among his contributions to the *Album* were the story "Moonshine" (which eventually evolved into Simms's first Revolutionary War romance, *The Partisan*), and the poem "The Rebel Flower." His most significant historical piece in the *Southern Literary Gazette* was "Battle of Fort Moultrie."[72]

In "Battle of Fort Moultrie," Simms attempted to seamlessly blend history and fiction in order to make the past live for his readers as it did for him. A firm believer that history held moral lessons for the present, Simms also believed that "the most rational, the most noble, and the most important duty imposed on man by his Creator . . . [is] contributing by every means in his power, to promote the welfare and happiness of his fellow beings, . . . [which] may, without presumption, be said to constitute the very essence of genuine Religion."[73] Simms hoped to serve his country by instilling the moral lessons of history in his readers. Oftentimes he attempted to accomplish this by fusing history and fiction. Simms believed that the artist could breathe life into the dry bones of history. It was through the application of art "that the past lives to the counselling and direction of the future, and if she breathe not the breath of life into its nostrils, the wires of the resurrectionist would vainly link together the ricketty skeleton which he disinters for posterity."[74] Once history had been enlivened by art, "the big, blind, struggling heart of the multitude may rush" to history "in the humility of its conscious baseness, and be lifted into gradual excellence and hope!"[75]

This particular piece of writing was unsigned by Simms, but S. Austin Allibone attributed it to him in *A Critical Dictionary of English Literature and British and American Authors,* and Simms's biographer, John C. Guilds, has said it was "probably" written by him. On the basis of this scholarship, the fact that Simms served as editor of the *Southern Literary Gazette,* and internal evidence, Simms can confidently be credited with authorship of this piece. "Battle of Fort Moultrie" contains themes that are important in Simms's later work. Also, the author of "Battle of Fort Moultrie" used imagery to describe the calming sounds of wind and ocean remarkably similar to that which appears in a known Simms contribution to the *Southern Literary Gazette* a month and a half later.[76]

The piece begins when, after viewing a painting of the Battle of Fort Moultrie, Simms decides to take a packet out to Sullivan's Island to visit the scene of the battle. Relaxing on the beach and contemplating the successful defense of Charleston Harbor against the British, "the eternal, low and monotonous rolling of the waters—the soothing and mysterious breeze of evening, and the graduated lights and shadows of the clouds, together with the high and romantic associations of the *Genius Loci*, . . . wrought upon me a total forgetfulness of time, place and circumstance, and lifted me into those regions of romance, so ludicrous to the matter-of-fact animal," writes Simms.[77] Gradually, Simms's surroundings undergo a metamorphosis. Unconscious of the change in his circumstances that had taken place, he suddenly finds himself in the midst of the famous battle.

Simms joins in the battle and fights shoulder to shoulder with those men who were "fighting for their homes" and to "prove themselves worthy" of the affections of their parents, wives, and children, who were anxiously watching the battle from Charleston. As a participant in the battle, Simms is able to give an account of it with all the excitement and immediacy of a first-person narrative. But Simms understood that we have to live in the present, and it is for the present that history's lessons are useful. So, after the British fleet has been repulsed, Simms wakes from his nap to the realization he has missed his packet back to Charleston.

In an earlier, June 28, 1825, address commemorating the anniversary of the Battle of Sullivan's Island, William Crafts had associated the idea of genius loci with Fort Moultrie. "In the mythology of imagination," said Crafts, "there exists what is called the genius of place." This genius of place was a Roman concept that had been resurrected by the romantics. It was, according to Crafts, the "power of natural scenery to retain, keep alive and impart something of the spirit of departed deeds, which occurred in the vicinity, and to rekindle the ardour of virtuous action, and the admiration of noble conduct for time immemorial." The mysterious power that constituted a site's genius of place, or genius loci, had the capacity to make the reflective passerby sensible to "moral beauty." If any place near Charleston possessed genius of place, surely it was Fort Moultrie, which had been sanctified by the blood of patriots and martyrs contending for liberty. "Let us listen to the genius of that place," Crafts encouraged his audience, "as it recalls the triumph of Carolina and the valour of Moultrie."[78]

Simms would have completely agreed. It was just such lessons as the selfless valor of Moultrie and his band of patriots that he hoped to teach his readers. By enlivening his history with art, Simms tried to make the moral lessons of the past as real for his readers as they were for him when he visited Sullivan's Island. Describing the action as a participant also allowed him to present history, with all its potentiality, from an indeterminist point of view. Here, wrote Johan Huizinga, is the basic difference between social scientists and historians.

> The sociologist, etc., deals with his material as if the outcome were given in the known facts: he simply searches for the way in which the result was already determined in the facts. The historian, on the other hand, must always maintain toward his subject an indeterminist point of view. He must constantly put himself at a point in the past at which the known factors still seem to permit different outcomes. If he speaks of Salamis, then it must be as if the Persians might still win.[79]

By maintaining an indeterminist point of view, the historian avoids falling into the whig fallacy. As a believer in free will, Simms frequently used fiction and the artist's touch to show the potentiality of history. "Only by recognizing that possibilities are unlimited can the historian do justice to the fulness of life."[80]

If we truly wish to know Simms as he saw himself and as his contemporaries understood him, then we must recognize that he was not only a prolific and gifted novelist and poet, but that he was also a serious historian. In Simms's mind these were never really separate occupations. History, he thought, should provide the subject matter for poetry and novels, and the writing of history was always a literary endeavor calling for the artistic skills of the novelist and poet. Consequently, Simms's poetry and novels contain historical footnotes and his history was written with an artistic flair. At the time, readers appreciated the literary quality of his history and realized that its artistic merits did not necessarily detract from its accuracy. The ritualistic slaying of their elders by subsequent generations of historians should in no way obscure Simms's achievement.

| TWO |

Simms and Other Historians

One of the most energetic historians of his era, Simms was almost always engaged in promoting history, and not just through his articles, books, and lectures. He was consistently supportive of other historians who turned to him for advice. And the innumerable book reviews he contributed to southern periodicals provided a platform for promoting history while encouraging an American literature. A look at these reviews and his relationship with other historians of his day shows two important things about Simms. First, that he occupied a more central position among mid-nineteenth-century American historians than has heretofore been supposed. And second, it shows how he thought history should be written.

Between April 1847 and March 1848, Simms carried on a correspondence with Albert J. Pickett, who was soliciting advice for his *History of Alabama, and Incidentally of Georgia and Mississippi, from the Earliest Periods* (1851). His responses to Pickett's queries form Simms's most lucid exposition on how history should be written. He recommended to Pickett more than a score of sources for researching early southern history, suggested where these sources might be located, if in manuscript, or purchased, if published, and offered advice for writing his book.

When it comes time to begin writing, Simms advised, Pickett should first make sure of his facts and study them "so as to conceive [*sic*] the general effects of one event upon another." Then the facts should be arranged in proper sequence, "then throw them together in the simplest & directest form & and then polish and perfect your paragraphs." Throughout this process, the "books ought to be at hand, from which you quote." Pickett must be careful to properly acknowledge his sources. To avoid plagiarism, do not "take anything [from an author] without acknowledgment which is peculiar to himself." Yet, no matter how carefully arranged, the facts do not speak for themselves. They require the artistic touch of the historian to give them life. "Undoubtedly, the historian has the privilege of heightening the force of his picture by the adjuncts of imagination & art, whenever he can do so without digressing too greatly or lessening the value or altering the character of his facts." But, Simms cautioned him, in history it is important that the author's imagination be severely regulated. As regards the tedious task of revision, Simms advised Pickett that he should rewrite his manuscript two or three times if he desired a good reputation. If, however, he aimed to make money writing, he had time for no such luxury. In general, though, beginning writers "should rewrite every syllable before publishing." Finally, he should keep his book as brief as possible. One volume is preferred over two. Big books merely collect dust on store shelves. In appreciation of Simms's assistance, Pickett dedicated the book to him and to the other people who took an interest in his "literary enterprises."[1]

In addition to Pickett, Simms carried on correspondence with several other historians, including George Bancroft, William Henry Carpenter, James Fenimore Cooper, Henry B. Dawson, Elizabeth Ellet, Peter Force, Charles E. A. Gayarré, Francis Lister Hawks, Joel Tyler Headley, John Pendleton Kennedy, Benson John Lossing, Henry Stephens Randall, William James Rivers, Lorenzo Sabine, Henry Rowe Schoolcraft, William Bacon Stevens, and William H. Trescot. With these and other historians, Simms sought and gave encouragement, shared advice on facts and interpretation, and discussed the good and bad of American historical writing. He truly was the central figure in historical studies in the Old South.

Simms and Bancroft shared opinions on recent books, and he allowed Bancroft access to portions of his manuscript collection. He answered Lossing's questions on South Carolina's military history. He suggested to Ellet that she write a book on women in the Revolution, which she did. He corresponded with Schoolcraft on Indian history. He exchanged books with his "old friend," Peter Force. He received books from Henry Stephens Randall and counseled him on his *Life of Thomas Jefferson* (1858). He helped get his neighbor David Flavel Jamison's *The Life and Times of Bertrand Du Guesclin: A History of the Fourteenth Century* (1864) published—a book dedicated to Simms and written at Simms's suggestion. He encouraged Stevens, frequently contributed to Dawson's *Historical Magazine* and offered help with Dawson's own research, and solicited articles and reviews from Gayarré for the *Southern Quarterly Review*.[2] After Simms's library was burned in 1865, Gayarré sent copies of his own books to replace those Simms had lost, inscribing the *History of Louisiana* from "one who is so sincerely attached to you and who so fully appreciates your literary labors."[3]

Some of Simms's finest, most thoughtful writing on the nature of history and its relationship to fiction appeared as book reviews. As one of the antebellum South's most energetic magazine editors, Simms noticed or reviewed most of the important, as well as the not-so-important, works of history published during his prolific writing career. From brief notices of the republication of classic works of history such as Edward Gibbon's *Decline and Fall of the Roman Empire* to lengthy reviews of significant new books such as William H. Prescott's *History of the Conquest of Mexico,* few published works of history escaped Simms's critical attention.

As further evidence of the breadth of Simms's reading in history, his reviews are sprinkled with references to still more historians, such as Thomas Carlyle and Barthold Georg Niebuhr. Taken as a whole, these reviews and notices constitute a thoughtful extended commentary on the notable works of history published during the mid–nineteenth century, punctuated with frequent forays into the trivial. Although Simms never set forth in any single essay a systematic philosophy of history, the astute reader can discern from this body of critical writings what Simms thought constituted good—and bad—history, and how it should—or should not—be written. Though of unquestionable importance, *Views and Reviews* presents what might more accurately be termed Simms's philosophy of historical romance than his philosophy of history. He was careful to insist that his comments about enlivening history with art were intended only for instances where the facts were vague or unknowable, that is, what he called *"unwritten history."*[4]

For Simms, the writing of history is always a double-edged endeavor. First and foremost the historian must be accurate. This is what separates the historian from the novelist. The novelist only has to concern himself with being truthful, while the historian has the added burden of being factual. But Simms recognized that the writing of history is also a creative enterprise calling for the imaginative arrangement and presentation of facts. Facts, no matter how extensively compiled, do not speak for themselves. It is up to the historian to give voice to the facts of history by organizing and interpreting them. As Shelby Foote has explained, novelists and historians both aim to recreate the past: "Whether the event took place in a world now gone to dust, preserved by documents and evaluated by scholarship, or in the imagination, preserved by memory and distilled by the creative process, they both want to tell us *how it was.*"[5] Historians, therefore, can learn much from novelists about how to tell a story. Merely being factually correct was only half of the equation. A book that was creatively deficient would be unreadable regardless of its accuracy. One that suffered from a factual deficiency, on the other hand, was not worth reading because it was misleading and could improperly influence the unsuspecting reader. The books that received Simms's praise, therefore, were those that he found to be both factually correct and aesthetically pleasing.

Although accurate, well-written books generally met with Simms's approval, these were not the only qualities that he hoped to find in the histories he reviewed. The object of history should be to teach moral lessons. Like his eighteenth-century precursors, Simms considered history to be philosophy teaching by example and believed that like causes always produced like results. Not that he believed as fervently as his predecessors did that Newtonian laws governing our social and political relations awaited discovery in the dusty annals of history, but Simms did strongly believe that the lives of past heroes and villains, saints and sinners contained practical moral lessons for the living.[6] Good historians, Simms thought, taught these lessons to their readers.

Good historians also realized that the tapestry of history contained more than just the stories of kings and generals. Simms understood that decisions made in wigwams and cabins were often as important as, if not more important than, those made in salons and courts; therefore history should be more than simply a chronicle of edicts and battles. Common men and women played significant roles in the lives of republics, so Simms felt that they should be represented in history books. What the United States needed was a peoples' history. Though not exactly a call for social history as it developed in the twentieth century, he did have in mind a more democratic history than nineteenth-century Americans were accustomed to.[7]

What the United States also needed was good history written by Americans. As a literary nationalist who preferred history to be patriotic, he believed that books written by foreign historians might display unwelcome biases more than books by native historians. He also believed that it was difficult enough to represent faithfully in writing the region in which one lived. To attempt to represent a region other than one's own presented added difficulties. Oral traditions, for example, were most readily available to persons who resided in the region about which they were writing. Therefore the cause of American letters would be best served and the United States could best hope to be represented fairly and faithfully by American historians writing about the regions they knew best. In this chapter, we will look at Simms's reviews of the works of several historians, to see how and by what criteria he evaluated their work.

One of Simms's most interesting pieces is on Mason Locke Weems, a writer whose talents he thought had never been justly evaluated.[8] Weems is best known as the author of popular, highly idealized biographies of George Washington, Francis Marion, Benjamin Franklin, and William Penn. Simms discussed Weems's historical methods at length in his own *The Life of Francis Marion.*[9] In his biographies, "Parson" Weems, like Simms himself, has been charged with overly romanticizing the narrative, with letting a good story get in the way of the facts. In the case of Weems, who is famous for inventing the story about honest young George Washington barking one of his father's cherry trees, the charge is not entirely unjust. Like Simms, Weems believed that history should teach moral and patriotic lessons. Unlike Simms, Weems apparently considered historical facts less important than the lessons he sought to impart.[10]

Although the majority of historians have found little to praise in Weems, Simms judges Weems's biographies to have value despite their obvious faults. Less evenhanded critics, or those holding a narrower definition of history, would hardly deign to call Weems a historian. "Some of your big-wigged gentry," wrote Simms, "will take it in high dudgeon that we should dignify with the title of historian" Parson Weems. "History, with this sort of persons, is a matter of very solemn concern. It is not your light romances—your irreverent poetry." These critics, as Simms imagines them, regard history as merely a compilation of facts, and the more obscure those facts, the better. "You must delve, you must drudge . . . in order to be a historian after the modern acceptation. You must discuss problems, however insignificant, with a corresponding minuteness." Neither Weems nor Simms was temperamentally suited to such an enterprise.[11]

Simms was usually careful to distinguish between facts and the truth. According to Simms's understanding, facts were the substance of truth. Historical truth was composed of individual facts creatively arranged and given significance by the historian. Part of the historian's job was to decide which facts were necessary components of the greater truth and which facts were not. So despite Simms's conviction that history must be factually correct, he recognized that this left historians unfettered by facts in two instances: first, when the facts in question did not contribute materially to the truth and, second, when facts were unknown or nonexistent. Unnecessary facts simply cluttered up the narrative and got in the way of the truth. Where the facts were unknown, historians were free to supply the want using their imaginations, as long as they did not violate truth. Simms felt strongly that historians should neither fear the use of imagination where facts were lacking nor should they be "solicitous in mere minutiæ, toiling after the fact, though the fact be no ways important to the wholeness and the perpetuity of the truth." None of this, however, gave historians liberty to purposely violate facts. Such a history contributed to partisanship rather than the truth and was contrary to one of the purposes of history—teaching moral lessons.[12]

Despite Weems's acknowledged looseness with facts, Simms judged him, perhaps generously, to merit the title historian because in Simms's estimation he was always faithful to the greater truth. As a historian, Weems never lost sight of the truth that was his goal. Weems "never plodded—never could plod,—scratched no bewildered head,—never was at a loss—never hesitated in his progress, but went forward with a promptness and singleness of vision, that never allowed itself to linger at details." Sure of the truth, Weems never allowed himself to become bogged down in seemingly inconsequential facts: "If a small fact suited not his great fact, he shoved it aside as unfitted for his purpose. It was enough for him that, satisfied of his hero and his results, he made all things tributary to the glory of the one, and the proper finish of the other." Accordingly, Weems's books were hagiographic and sometimes unreliable in their details. "Certainly, Weems was not a [Barthold Georg] Niebuhr," conceded Simms. "There can be no mistake about that." Weems had not the temperament "to pursue the cold and cruel analysis by which the learned German acquired his renown." But Simms does not find Weems lacking in *all* the essentials of a good historian. When the imaginative and artistic qualities of history are taken into account, it is Niebuhr, better known for his investigative than his narrative skill, who suffers from comparison with Weems. The popular biographer excelled at writing enthusiastic, imaginative books that reached a large audience. Indeed, his books were early best sellers, and both Abraham Lincoln and Woodrow Wilson can be counted among his admirers.[13]

Even though Weems's historical methods were at times uncritical and unscientific, Simms believed that "with all his extravagance, his fondness for colouring, his episodical anecdote, (most probably, in half the number of cases, invented for the occasion,) his books are yet faithful to all the vital truths of history." More critically inclined historians might disapprove of Weems's methods because of the artistic liberties he took with the minor facts of history, but his books reached a "vast circulation," teaching the moral lessons of history's vital truths, and exercising "a wondrous influence over the young minds of the country." "That his notions of the privileges of the historian were rather loose, is not to be denied," Simms acknowledged. Nevertheless, Weems's transgressions were no greater than those of others whose claim to the title historian was undisputed. Simms merely "claimed for him the rights of an artist,—such rights as were exercised by Livy and by [Jean] Froissart."[14] Such rights as were exercised by Simms as well. More recent critics, such as Marcus Cunliffe and Richard M. Weaver, have praised Simms's fairness and arrived at similar assessments of Weems. They contend that the criticism that has been leveled at him over the years has been too harsh. Weems was unquestionably successful at what he did. Weaver even dubs Weems "beyond doubt one of the greatest rhetoricians which this country . . . has brought forth."[15] That Weems's books are uncritical of their subjects (or heroes) and unreliable in some of their details is not denied. However, Weems was no more careless with the facts than better respected historians. His reputation has suffered because his inaccuracies are glaring and famous, not because they occur more frequently than in comparable histories written by his contemporaries. Recognizing that Weems intended his books to serve as popular biographies of American heroes suitable for young readers rather than as serious scholarly histories, and that he succeeded in teaching some essential truth to a large number of readers while keeping them entertained, Simms forgave his offenses and allowed Weems greater liberties with the facts than he allowed most historians whose books passed under his critical eye.[16]

Simms examined the work of another popular historian in a review of Joel Tyler Headley's *The Life of Oliver Cromwell* (1848).[17] One of the nineteenth century's best-selling and most prolific historians, who is best remembered for his superficial books *Napoleon and His Marshals* (1846) and *Washington and His Generals* (1847), Headley received lukewarm praise from Simms for his artistic presentation of facts. But Simms held Headley, as well as most historians, to a stricter standard of factuality than he did Mason Weems. Like Thomas Carlyle, Headley attempted to dramatize his history. This was, Simms judged, a perfectly valid method of writing history as long as the author remained faithful to the truth: "It seems necessary that the narration of facts should be as simple as possible;—yet there is such a thing as, so grouping them together in the narrative, as to make them assume a dramatic attitude, which, without in any degree disparaging the truth, shall impress it with tenfold effect upon the imagination of the reader." This was the method employed by Carlyle, whose historical narrative was more natural and less formal than earlier historians'. Carlyle succeeded in this, Simms thought, by achieving "that perfection of art, which places the [historical] actor in the position of the writer, and makes the narrative rather conversational than oratorical,—which was, hitherto, but too commonly the character of history." Inasmuch as Carlyle and Headley were able to present history in a more accessible and engaging style, they were able to make history come alive for their readers.[18]

Yet, the historian could go too far in dramatizing his narrative. Headley was occasionally guilty of this trespass, and Simms took him to task for it. In taking artistic "privileges" with the facts "for which there is no authority, our author passes beyond the province of the historian." According to Simms, one instance where Headley committed this offense was in his melodramatic description of General Cornwallis at the battle of Camden: "It may be that Cornwallis smiled with grim delight as he beheld Gates, rushing blindly into the toils at Camden; but where is the evidence that he did so?" asks Simms. "Were *we* to say that *our* authorities assert on the other hand, that he did not *smile,* but *sneezed* on this very occassion, . . . it would be difficult for Mr. Headley to refute us." The taking of such liberties in his descriptions may seem like a trivial offense, but Simms felt it was contrary to the purpose of history, which was to present the past as truthfully as possible. Nevertheless, Headley's book, "though loosely written, is a very readable one" and should satisfy "the great body of readers."[19] Despite its shortcomings, *The Life of Oliver Cromwell,* like Headley's better known books, Simms judged not too bad for popular history and thought it should be suitable for general readers.

In a critical notice of the first two volumes of Richard Hildreth's *History of the United States of America, from the Discovery of the Continent, to the Organization of Government under the Federal Constitution* (in three volumes, 1849), Simms found another opportunity to discourse on the necessity of history being both well written and well researched. Unlike Weems and Headley, who were better stylists than researchers, Richard Hildreth has been more respected for his reliance upon and faithfulness to primary sources than for his prose style.[20]

Simms hoped that Hildreth's volumes would fill a need for "an honest and well written history" of the United States, written by an American. As to the honesty of Hildreth's *History of the United States,* Simms withheld judgment until completion of the third and final volume. He had read enough though to be discouraged by its lack of literary merit: "It is written with a pretension almost amounting to insolence, and in a pert and vulgar style which is particularly unsuited to the dignity of the historian." Simms found Hildreth's prose far from elegant: "At best, his sentences can lay claim only to an intelligible distinctness." But he conceded that "our author may improve as he proceeds." If Hildreth was engaged in writing an honest history, Simms certainly hoped his writing would improve so as to win his volumes a wide readership. If he is not an honest historian, "the colder and clumsier his narrative the better. So shall he fail in those arts which might beguile the simple and confiding into belief."[21]

In "Domestic Histories of the South," a lengthy review of two pamphlets in the April 1852 issue of the *Southern Quarterly Review,* Simms addressed what he considered some shortcomings in histories being written at the time.[22] Most historians and biographers, Simms thought, held an inflated view of both themselves and their subjects. Thus elevated in their own minds, they go about searching for facts as if walking on stilts: "He raises himself, accordingly, so very high above the ground upon which he walks, that he can behold no objects but those which are lofty like himself. The humble things of the earth escape him entirely." The common man and woman and their everyday concerns are thought unworthy of attention, for history is made only by great men (and sometimes women) engaged in heroic actions involving the fate of nations. "He sees only the stately and the grand; the big and the portentous; fierce warriors, golden crowns and principalities, swords, sceptres, the scaffold, and the axe!" He is oblivious to the plight of the masses, on whose shoulders the princes and warriors stand. "Our stately historian is apt to see nothing of these, and to say nothing of them, except when he reports ten, twenty or thirty thousand subjects slain, fighting the battles of his hero, and shovelled into the earth without leaving name or memorial behind them."[23]

These "stately historians," overlook the most salient features of American history. The hardy pioneers who boldly settled along the frontier, thus sowing the seeds of American civilization across the continent, were generally too humble and inconspicuous to draw the stately historians' attention. Yet theirs is the true story of America. In language anticipating Frederick Jackson Turner's famous frontier thesis of 1893, Simms asserted that

> ours is a curious history of a perpetual colonization—new shores, new forests, opening daily—new foes and necessities encountered;—fresh discoveries in hourly developments, and fresh accessions of strength to the whole, resulting from the continual multiplication of the parts;—a history of incessant transition, . . . the due consequence of the hourly recurring conflict between art and nature, civilization and the savage!

If this story could be properly told, giving due attention to the countless brave pioneers and to America's progress from humble beginnings to more elevated levels of refinement and civilization, it would teach moral lessons of courage and self-reliance to the young and provide grist for the patriotic poet. Therein lay the value of the ephemeral pamphlets under consideration. Their authors were attempting to tell what Simms thought was an unjustly neglected portion of American history, and for this he praised them.[24]

In a lengthy review of Elizabeth F. Ellet's *The Women of the American Revolution* (1850), Simms criticized other historians for ignoring this group of Americans. Little read today, Ellet was moderately popular in her day and was the first American historian to devote herself to the study and writing of women's history. Her largely anecdotal *Women of the American Revolution* drew upon both published and unpublished primary sources as well as family recollections. She described the wartime experiences of over one hundred fifty women in a lively style that undoubtedly entertained while informing a wide audience of readers.[25]

Simms had high praise for both the content and the style of Ellet's history. "As history has usually been written, it is the history rather of princes than of a people," Simms wrote. Not so *The Women of the American Revolution*. Ellet's book was representative of an increased interest in the stories of common men and women. This interest in the stories of the masses was a result of the democratic realization that leaders held no monopoly on virtue. Common men and women were at least as likely as their leaders to exhibit virtue; thus their lives could be profitably studied. "The great moral triumph of recent times is the recognition of the race as well as the individual. . . . We now read *human* histories," observed Simms.[26]

He had one bone of contention with Ellet: "She tells us, in her introduction, that the leading spirits of our Revolution derived the sources of their power from the sentiment pervading the great mass of the people. This is a great mistake, and one which is too commonly made in our recent histories." Undoubtedly influenced by his knowledge of the intense civil war that characterized the Revolution in South Carolina, Simms asserted that the great mass of the people really had little sympathy with the independence movement at first. According to Simms's estimation, "in one-half of the States, if not in all, [Loyalists] were nearly if not quite as numerous as those who originated and maintained the contest for independence." If not for the large numbers of Loyalists, the conflict would have been favorably resolved much sooner and without the bitter civil strife. Contrary to what Mrs. Ellet believed, Simms thought the leading figures of the Revolution derived their power not from the sympathy of the masses, but in large measure from their wives and mothers, who served as guardians and cultivators of virtue within the domestic sphere. Yet he believed her right to insist that American women played a vital but unheralded role in steeling patriot men for battle. Later generations could benefit from their example. Therein lay the value of Ellet's study of American women during the Revolution.[27]

An avid collector of Revolutionary era manuscripts, who made a point of editing and publishing some of the more notable materials in his possession, Simms well understood the importance of preserving primary sources. It is not surprising then, that Simms applauded the appearance in 1848 of a less expensive edition of Jared Sparks's *The Writings of George Washington* (originally published in 1834).[28] "No work more amply deserves to find its way to every American library, to meet with fond and eager welcome in every American homestead," wrote Simms, hoping this new, cheaper edition would enjoy a wide distribution.[29]

Even though it would fail to measure up to the editorial practices of our own day, Sparks's twelve-volume edition of Washington's writings stood for many years as one of the standard works of American history. Sparks frankly admitted in his introduction that "in preparing the manuscripts for the press, I have been obliged sometimes to use a latitude of discretion." Although he has subsequently been criticized for the practice, most people at the time were apparently not the least bit disturbed by his correcting of Washington's spelling and grammar or even his omitting "unimportant passages" without in any way identifying the omissions and corrections for readers. Indeed, consistent with the literary practice of the day, Sparks considered it an important duty of a "faithful editor, to hazard such corrections as . . . a cool judgment dictated." It would be an injustice to any writer to publish his private compositions, never meant for the public eye, without "subjecting them to a careful revision," he decided.[30]

On this matter he consulted with the Massachusetts Historical Society, John Adams, John Marshall, Noah Webster, and Edward Everett. All of them advised him to correct Washington's writing. In 1851, when Sparks's editorial practices came under attack by English historian Lord Mahon, Peter Force and Washington Irving, among others, rushed to his defense.[31] As late as 1893 Herbert Baxter Adams, who more than any other individual is responsible for the professionalization of American history, could write in his biography of Sparks: "It is still regarded as an open question whether the proper method of editing for publication the writings of men who have passed away should be in all cases the same."[32] Whether an editor omitted supposedly unimportant passages and corrected spelling and grammar or faithfully transcribed a dead man's papers was more a matter of taste than of professionalism. So Simms was in good company when he applauded Sparks's edition of Washington's writings in 1849. Still, there is no reason to suppose that Simms or other readers were initially aware of the full extent of Sparks's corrections to Washington's writings. Sparks's sin lay not in correcting Washington but in his failure to fully apprise readers of his corrections and their extent.

Edited volumes of the papers of historic figures such as Washington were, Simms thought, even more valuable than biographies. Washington's own letters revealed the private, inner man in a way that no biographer could ever hope to do: "Here we have the written record of his almost daily thoughts, emotions, opinions: . . . the wisdom, virtue, sagacity and energy, with which he bore up manfully through all, to attain the most perfect triumph in the end."[33] But the letters revealed not only Washington's character, they also contained a wealth of information for anyone interested in the Revolution and the political history of the early years of the Republic. Hence, Sparks had done a great service to future American historians by collecting and editing Washington's papers. Simms had in his possession several of Washington's letters not included in Sparks's collection. As a further help to future historians he transcribed and published four of these letters, addressed to Henry Laurens, president of the Continental Congress, and dating from November 1, 1777, to December 9, 1778, as a supplement to his review.[34]

One of Simms's favorite historians was William H. Prescott.[35] He published lengthy, complimentary reviews of Prescott's *History of the Conquest of Mexico* and *History of the Conquest of Peru*. These reviews were more descriptive than critical, but his review of *History of the Conquest of Peru* is noteworthy because in it Simms describes what he considered the two major classes of historians. Most historians, he wrote, could be described as either narrative or philosophical. Narrative historians are characterized by "fidelity and closeness of detail, a rigid regard to the regular order of events, a respectful and constant attention to authorities, clearness of style and simplicity of statement." Additionally, any narrative historian worth reading also possessed an artistic concern for the quality of his prose. He considered Prescott a superb example of this type of historian.[36] "His secret," Simms wrote, "consists chiefly in the exercise of the appropriate degree of art."[37]

The philosophical historian, on the other hand, is more interested in uncovering motives than in describing actions and "is not so much after details as principles. He disdains minutiæ in his search for generalities." Despite this disdain for details, Simms thought the philosophical historian more accurate than the narrative historian. Using what he called "the general laws of evidence," philosophical historians subject their evidence to more rigorous tests than do narrative historians. The philosophical historian tests his evidence with the methods "of the lawyer and philosopher. He cross-examines with the one, and dilates into generalities with the other." He does not simply narrate the successes and failures of people and governments but attempts to "correct the morals of history" by showing the how and why of past events. Simms held up Guizot and Michelet as good examples of philosophical historians and thought that Gibbon and Thierry successfully united the best qualities of both classes of historians.[38]

Simms's reviews of history books show not just his wide reading in history, but also his thoughtful understanding of how history should be written. In each of these reviews, and in almost countless others, Simms holds the author accountable for a book's artistic merit as well as its truthfulness. Both accuracy and fine prose were necessary components of good history. Simms's reviews also show that he realized the important role played in the nation's history by extraordinary but unsung "common" men and women, and as evidenced by his review of Sparks, Simms and other nineteenth-century historians clearly understood the importance of primary sources.

That Simms considered the writing of history an artistic undertaking may set him apart from most modern historians, but it makes him highly typical of his own time. Simms wrote in the tradition of the great romantic historians of the first half of the nineteenth century—George Bancroft, John Lothrop Motley, Francis Parkman, William Hickling Prescott, and their European counterparts. Even though Simms and other of the better romantic historians of his day have, at times, been accused of being uncritical, of not relying heavily enough on primary sources, of being careless with facts, and of only being interested in the stories of so-called great men and events, such was not really the case. At the very least, this charge of carelessness exaggerates their faults while overlooking what they got right. To borrow from Shelby Foote's description of how he wrote *The Civil War,* they "employed the novelist's methods without his license."[39] Simms's reviews exhibit a constant concern for accuracy, an awareness of the importance of primary sources, and an interest in social history and in the stories of common men and women, who under trial acted with uncommon virtue. By writing history that is both readable and accurate, Simms and a few other romantic historians have set an example that stands as an indictment of much of what passes for history today—written by professional historians with no regard for history as art or as meaningful narrative.

In Simms's day, it was understood that the application of art to history did not necessarily mean the fictionalization of history. It simply meant a concern for how ideas were expressed. Therefore, before the professionalization of history, Simms was regularly recognized and cited as an authority on southern history by historians and political writers alike. Diplomatic historian William Henry Trescot spoke highly of his work. Historian Benson J. Lossing cited the work of "William Gilmore Simms, the distinguished South Carolina scholar," in his books *Our Country: A Household History for All Readers, . . .* and *The Pictorial Field-Book of the Revolution.* The latter book makes extensive use of *The Life of Francis Marion,* citing it as the only source for Peter Horry's valuable memoir. Lossing, along with George Bancroft, also invited Simms to lecture in the North on South Carolina's history. Henry B. Dawson, editor of the *Historical Magazine* and author of a number of works on American history, made heavy use of Simms's *History of South Carolina* in his exhaustively documented *Battles of the United States, by Land and Sea.* Massachusetts Historical Society member William H. Whitmore likewise found *The History of South Carolina* useful in his research into early American history and quoted liberally from it in his *Essay on the Founders of the Thirteen Colonies.*[40]

Simms did as much research for his historical fiction as for his history and doubtless, therefore, would have been pleased that investigators into the American past also found valuable material in his historical romances. William H. Venable, for instance, in his 1872 *School History of the United States,* referred interested readers to *The Cassique of Kiawah* as one of his sources for early Carolina history. George R. Fairbanks, vice president of the Florida Historical Society, also gathered material from Simms's romances. In both his *History and Antiquities of the City of St. Augustine* and his *History of Florida,* he quotes from Simms, whom he acknowledges as the "writer who has . . . done more to rescue from oblivion the historical romance of the South than any other."[41]

Among politicians, Alexander H. Stephens, vice president of the Confederacy and a talented historian, quoted at length from the work of the "gifted and accomplished William Gilmore Simms, LL.D." in his apologia, *A Constitutional View of the Late War between the States.* Even Massachusetts Senator Charles Sumner paid Simms the ironic tribute of inaccurately citing *The History of South Carolina* in a speech castigating the South for supposedly being enervated by slavery during the Revolution.[42]

Simms can deservedly be considered the central historian of his era working in the South. Every important historian writing in or on the South came to Simms for advice and/or received his encouragement. Many of them cited him in their work. "I have never withheld myself, in respect to applications . . . when the subject of inquiry . . . contemplates our American Biography & History,"

Simms wrote in November 1860. The advice he gave was the same as his criteria for judging history in his reviews: write honestly and write well. He recognized, as has John Lukacs, that "facts are not more important than words; indeed, they are inseparable from words, because we speak and think in words." Therefore, "the historian must be master of his words as much of his 'facts,' whatever those might mean."[43]

Simms as Collector and Publisher of Manuscripts

Like many another nineteenth-century historian, Simms's interest in history also found expression in the collecting of manuscripts. With public archives few and far between, the importance of such private collections cannot be underestimated. His impressive manuscript collection provided him with ready access to a large archive of important primary material to draw upon whenever he wrote history. We will never know the full extent of Simms's collection since there is no record of precisely what perished when Sherman's army burned his library in 1865 and the surviving material was divided up. In 1862, before Northern troops destroyed his home, he estimated that if published his manuscript collection would fill fifty volumes and his library, which included many published primary sources, stood at over 10,000 volumes.[1] Some of his manuscript collection was saved from the flames only to be scattered when postwar poverty forced him to sell it. But there is reason to believe much of value was lost.

Fearing for the material's safety, in 1862 Simms asked William J. Rivers in Columbia to keep "four folio volumes, [of manuscript material] which I had interleaved & bound, with notes, and a large mass besides." A visitor to Woodlands in 1848 estimated that it must have cost between ten and twenty thousand dollars to put together the material in Simms's library and that it was "made up of rare and well selected works in almost every department of literature." Although he is writing about his own letters rather than the correspondence of Revolutionary heroes that he had collected, Simms wrote to William Hawkins Ferris, on February 8, 1867, that "what is lost [when Woodlands burned] is much greater than I had imagined. Many packets, of superior value are missing." And earlier, on July 28, 1866, he had written to Evert Duyckinck: "Among the books lost in the destruction of my Library, were sundry of the Congressional publications." These were "of peculiar interest to the Historian, the student and the man of Letters." This was not the only disaster that cost him part of his library. He also lost "some 150 vols . . . and a bundle of MSS" to fire in 1833. Here again, we do not know exactly what burned.[2]

Though we will never know the precise extent or contents of Simms's library or how much of it was lost, it is clear that the collection was immense and historically important. The largest surviving portion of the collection consisted of nearly 1,200 items of Laurens family papers, which Simms sold to the Long

Island Historical Society in 1867 for $1,500 to pay for rebuilding his home. He chose to hold on to, give away, or sell separately as individual pieces or lots the remainder of his manuscript collection, such as the bundle of George Washington's letters he sold in 1866 for $250.[3]

From what we can reconstruct of his collection, it is clear that it was vast and consisted not merely of autographs and inconsequential ephemera. Simms began his collection of historical manuscripts sometime around 1835, when he was twenty-nine years old, and added to it throughout the remainder of his life, intending it to serve as an archive for serious historical research. To that end he carefully arranged and annotated his Laurens family papers, and other manuscripts that he once owned bear his annotations as well.

Building this collection of historical manuscripts "had cost me great painstaking and research, and some money," he wrote. Just when he was forced to sell the largest portion of the collection to rebuild his home, Simms confided to Duyckinck, "I had been looking forward to a period of repose & quiet when I could address myself to the grave labours of Historian & Biographer, building largely on this material."[4] The material he had on hand before the fire included letters, journals, and other documents from many of the major figures of the American Revolution, especially in the South. Among those persons known to have been represented in the collection were George Washington, Patrick Henry, John Adams, John Jay, Arthur Lee, Richard Henry Lee, Francis Marion, Thomas Paine, John Rutledge, General Horatio Gates, Baron de Kalb, Baron von Steuben, Christopher Gadsden, William Moultrie, Henry Laurens, Colonel John Laurens, Governor Jonathan Trumbull of Connecticut, Governor Francis Nash of North Carolina, and Samuel A. Otis.

Recognizing the historical value of the manuscripts in his possession, Simms edited and published many of these documents. To prepare his Revolutionary manuscripts "as biography & History, has been with me a leading idea for many years," Simms wrote to Evert Duyckinck in December 1866.[5] His Revolutionary manuscripts were so dear to him that "it was actually in saving these manuscripts, that I lost my dwelling House at Woodlands," he wrote.

> I hurried away with them, on the approach of Sherman's army, to Columbia, to put them in safety. My communication was cut off, by the car trains ceasing to run; I could not return; and the House was destroyed by the Invader, (as a general rule) because of the absence of the proprietor. That absence cost me House, furniture & Library—more than $50,000 in gold, and that absence was solely occasioned by my desire to save my MSS Collections. You can readily concieve [*sic*] how greatly I should value them.[6]

Ultimately he parted with his precious collection only after his home was burned, selling it to help fund construction of shelter for his family.

In addition to his own manuscript collection, he also had access to others' libraries and manuscript collections, including the impressive collection of Robert

Wilson Gibbes, who published a *Documentary History of the American Revolution* (1853–57), and the "very extensive collection" of his "friend [Israel Keech] Tefft of Savannah," which he thought included Pulaski and Marion letters. "To his collection, have I had, scores of times, to resort, as to a joint record, for the materials which I could nowhere else discover, and for the matter illustrative of that which I already had in my possession," Simms wrote.[7]

So dedicated was Simms to the gathering of important historical documents that he even at one point encouraged his friend James Henry Hammond to seek appropriation from the South Carolina legislature for an official state "Historiographer." As he envisioned the office, the historiographer would "go to Europe and ransack the Colonial Offices for documents relating to our Ante-revolutionary periods." This matter had been brought to Simms's attention earlier by Robert Barnwell Rhett's younger brother Albert Moore Rhett, who shortly before he died had asked Simms if he would accept appointment to such an office if the legislature could be persuaded to fund it.[8]

Simms now urged the subject upon Hammond's attention. Appointing an official historiographer "would be quite as legitimate as the Geological Survey," Simms reasoned. Other states had already sent agents to Europe to collect and copy their colonial documents. Simms's friend Charles E. A. Gayarré, for instance, used his position as Louisiana's secretary of state to build the state's collections by copying and purchasing materials from Europe. "A State never arrives at her true dignity until she is in possession of her own facts," Simms wrote.[9] Nor was this the first time Simms had considered traveling abroad to collect historical material. In 1845, when angling for a diplomatic appointment from President Polk, he wrote to Armistead Burt that one of the benefits of a foreign post was that it would give him the opportunity to record material for use in history and fiction.[10]

Simms was far from unusual in his enthusiasm for publishing historical documents. Many of America's important records had been lost or scattered during the war. With few public repositories, publication of primary materials was the best way to preserve and make accessible what remained, and the effort to collect and publish American records was already well underway before the close of the eighteenth century. Ebenezer Hazard brought out his *Historical Collections* between 1792 and 1794, and 1797 saw the publication of Jedidiah Morse's *American Gazetteer.* The trend continued with increased urgency in the nineteenth century as the Revolutionary generation passed away. In 1822 Hezekiah Niles published his *Principles and Acts of the Revolution in America,* followed by Morse's *Annals of the American Revolution* (1824), Jonathan Elliot's four-volume *Debates, Resolutions, and other Proceedings in Convention on the Adoption of the Federal Constitution* (1827–30), Jared Sparks's twelve-volume *Diplomatic Correspondence of the American Revolution* (1829–30) and *The Writings of George Washington* (1834), Elliot's valuable five-volume *Debates in the Several State Conventions on the Adoption of the Federal Constitution* (1836–59), Peter Force's monumental *American Archives* (1837–53), and R. W. Gibbes's *Documentary History of the American Revolution*.[11] "It is our policy to collect and bind together as many of these old documents, relating to our country and its early history, as we can procure," Simms wrote.[12] At the same time many veterans of the Revolution sent their memoirs to press to put their version of events on record.

In the absence of a national archive and of many state archives, state and local historical societies advanced the collection and publication of America's historical documents. These societies, open to anyone with an interest in history, were places where members gathered for intellectual companionship, to talk about history, and to promote scholarship and the collection of historical documents. The first historical society in America was the Massachusetts Historical Society, founded in 1791 by Jeremy Belknap. Soon nearly every state and most cities of any consequence had their own. At least 111 historical societies had been organized by 1860.

In these state and local historical societies, according to George H. Callcott, "more than in colleges, was the origin of historical association and professionalism" in the United States.[13] Simms was an active member or supporter of several such societies, including the South Carolina Historical Society, the Georgia Historical Society, the Maryland Historical Society, the New-York Historical Society, and accepted election to the Wisconsin State Historical Society at the invitation of the great collector Lyman C. Draper. Simms believed the gathering, preservation, and publication of manuscript material should be the primary object of such societies. He advised John Pendleton Kennedy of the Maryland Historical Society that "accumulating MS.S." should be "a chief concern" of the Society. Building an impressive library of books was less important than preserving "private letters which, I am persuaded, are still to be dragged out of old chests & old wives closets. I have now a very valuable & numerous collection, thus obtained, the existence of which was totally unsuspected in the community." Upon receiving an honorary appointment to the Georgia Historical Society, he congratulated the members on their efforts in collecting and publishing material. "With large and various materiel among us, worthy of honorable & careful preservation, our people of the South have been quite too remiss in looking after and collecting it," he wrote.[14]

Simms's vast knowledge of documentary materials is evident throughout his writing. His biography of Francis Marion drew heavily from a manuscript memoir of Lieutenant Peter Horry, who served under the Swamp Fox. Simms's quotations from Horry preserved portions of this valuable memoir that today exist nowhere else.[15] His knowledge of documentary materials also shows in important magazine articles on Revolutionary figures such as John Rutledge and the Baron de Kalb. Indeed, many of Simms's articles contain extensive quotations, sometimes amounting to entire letters, from his manuscript collection. Not infrequently he published important letters and documents in toto, adding only brief prefatory remarks and occasional explanatory endnotes. Such was his series of "Revolutionary Letters" in the *Historical Magazine*.[16]

In addition to preserving written records of the past, Simms was also a strong advocate of putting oral history on record. Oral history informs much of his writing, most noticeably his *Life of Francis Marion* and series of Revolutionary War romances. He encouraged Benjamin F. Perry, who had published a series of Revolutionary traditions and anecdotes under the title "Revolutionary Incidents" in the *Magnolia* in 1843, to continue to "serve the public by gathering up the *disjecta membra* of Revolutionary & traditional anecdotes," in spite of the *Magnolia*'s demise.[17]

Simms was also, most likely, the anonymous editor and compiler of *Selections from the Letters and Speeches of the Hon. James H. Hammond, of South Carolina* (1866). He proposed to John Reuben Thompson with the Virginia State Library on January 16, 1862, publication of a "Library of the Confederate States." Each state should be represented: "We should prepare Histories, in single volumes, of the several States, biographies of Washington, Jefferson, Randolph, Calhoun & others, with selections from their writings." The writings and speeches of his old friend Hammond and the writings of "old Beverley Tucker, of Virginia," could be the first two volumes. "I am now revising Hammond's Essays & Speeches for the press," Simms wrote. Each title, he counseled, should be a single, portable volume, about 400 pages long. The anonymously published book ran to 368 pages without the front matter. Then on January 24, 1865, two months after Hammond's death, he wrote Hammond's son Harry offering suggestions and assistance "for some future volume" of his letters. These two letters, and the fact that the book resembles the format of the volume Simms planned, make it highly probable that Simms was the book's anonymous editor.[18]

Simms's other major effort at documentary editing was *The Army Correspondence of Colonel John Laurens . . . with a Memoir,* published in a limited edition by New York's Bradford Club in 1867. This was his final book-length effort at history other than the unfinished historical romance *Joscelyn*.[19] Most of the 250-page volume consists of Laurens's army correspondence to his father, Henry Laurens, from the years 1777 and 1778, with the memoir only filling forty-six pages.

Simms had long wanted to publish the Laurens correspondence. As early as January 1845 we find him writing to Henry G. Langley, publisher of Simms's *The Life of Francis Marion,* to find out if he had any interest in publishing "valuable Letters . . . of distinguished men during the revolution."[20] In addition to John Laurens, he had manuscripts of Henry Laurens, John Rutledge, Arthur Lee, Patrick Henry, General Horatio Gates, General William Heath, and unnamed others that he proposed publishing with short biographical introductions. Later, in May 1862, he returned to the topic in a letter to Professor William J. Rivers at South Carolina College in Columbia. Afraid that the war would put his beloved library in danger, Simms asked Rivers to accept some of his manuscripts for safekeeping. The collection contained letters of John Rutledge, Richard Henry Lee, Baron von Steuben, Baron de Kalb, Francis Marion, Christopher Gadsden, Hezekiah Maham, and Henry and John Laurens.[21]

"It is my farther idea," he suggested, "and was long since, that you & I, at some future time, more auspicious period, might jointly prepare them for the press. I had proposed Lives of Henry & John Laurens, for example, with selections from their correspondence & a running commentary, in which we might mutually engage."[22] Then a bit later Simms added that the manuscripts would need little commentary, "nothing more than can be done by either of us, with care."[23] Nothing came of either of these early proposals, but they serve to illustrate his longstanding intention to publish some of the Laurens letters in his possession.

Although the collection published only those letters written by Laurens to his father between August 13, 1777, and October 13, 1778, Simms both refers to and quotes from other letters Laurens addressed to "his father, uncle, and others of his family" in his memoir of Laurens, mentioning letters dated as early as April 1772. Other sources known to have been used by Simms in researching the memoir include Arthur Lee's *Memoir* and manuscript letters from George Washington and John Adams to Henry Laurens, all of which are mentioned in footnotes. Additionally, he had references to and quoted in their entirety a letter from John C. Hamilton (Alexander Hamilton's son) and Robert Y. Hayne's speech in the Senate on the bill for the relief of Laurens's grandson.[24]

Laurens, Simms tells us, was "the Bayard of America." He was truly a man who would have agreed with Horace that *dulce et decorum est pro patria mori*.[25] Born in 1754, Laurens joined the Continental Army in 1777 and served on Washington's staff, becoming a close confidant of George Washington and Alexander Hamilton. He secured an assignment to his native South Carolina, joined with the militia under William Moultrie, participated in the unsuccessful attack against the British in Savannah, and was captured in Charleston when General Benjamin Lincoln surrendered the city on May 12, 1780. On every occasion Laurens distinguished himself and displayed that "headlong enthusiastic gallantry, which was sometimes condemned as temerity, but which had the good effect usually of inspiring confidence in his troops." Soon after his capture he was exchanged for a British prisoner, then sent by the Continental Congress as a special envoy to France. Following his diplomatic mission he returned to America and rejoined Washington in time to participate in the capture of Cornwallis's army at Yorktown. Here again he distinguished himself on the field of battle and had the honor of conveying Washington's demand for surrender.[26]

After the British surrender at Yorktown, with the outcome of the Revolution no longer in doubt, Laurens returned to South Carolina and attached himself to General Greene's command. With the British still in possession of Charleston and boldly sallying out of the city on periodic raids, Laurens was "rarely" found "out of the saddle." According to Simms, in these actions he showed himself endowed with that special talent for partisan warfare that made Marion and Sumter famous. "He displayed his wonted gallantry and dash—carrying it sometimes, in the excess of his zeal, to a desparate extent, which provoked alike the rebuke and admiration of his contemporaries." His rashness finally proved to be his undoing. On August 27, 1782, he died leading a small party of men against a force of British foragers that had ascended the Combahee River and that outnumbered his own force by perhaps six to one.[27]

Simms greatly admired Laurens's boldness. In fact, he was far from certain that Laurens was guilty of being overly rash. Audacity may well have been necessary to success in leading the poorly equipped, usually outnumbered American troops. "It is a matter of question," wrote Simms, "whether [his rashness] . . . did not serve as a useful virtue, in the encouragement of his own troops, and the depression of the enemy." Robert M. Weir concurred: "Bravery such as his was doubtlessly functional in the revolutionary army, where an officer's example often had to substitute for discipline among an amateur soldiery."[28]

Simms hoped the collection of letters would prove interesting to the general reader and "a most valuable contribution to the material of American history."[29] Even before their publication, his recognition of the letters' worth led him to make some of them available to other historians, including George Bancroft. Whatever our judgment of Laurens, we know him as well as we do in part because Simms preserved and published his correspondence. His interest in collecting manuscripts was never simply a hobby or an antiquarian's fascination with minutiae. Rather, he recognized the materials he collected as the raw material of both history and fiction. Simms, like Lyman C. Draper, Peter Force, William J. Rivers, and countless other nineteenth-century collectors and historians to whom we owe thanks, wanted to preserve this material and make it available for future use. Without their efforts our understanding of the American past would be far more incomplete than it is.

FOUR

Simms as Biographer

During his lifetime, Simms's most popular nonfiction was in the field of biography. With four book-length biographies and numerous biographical sketches to his credit, it is no exaggeration to view him as the central figure working in the genre in the mid-nineteenth-century South. Perhaps because many of the most notable twentieth-century biographies have tended to be both prurient and (perhaps therefore) enormously popular, it has been easy for scholars to rank biography well below history. Edward Hallett Carr, in *What Is History?*, refused to even consider the study of individual lives as "history," a word he reserved for the study of society and impersonal social forces. And R. G. Collingwood wrote that "howevermuch history it contains, [biography] is constructed on principles that are not only non-historical but anti-historical."[1] However in the nineteenth century, as Scott E. Casper has convincingly shown, biography was an altogether respectable form of history.[2] Through familiarity with classical writers such as Plutarch, Polybius, and Tacitus, Americans were aware of the value to republican citizens of studying the lives of virtuous individuals.[3]

American readers and writers alike flocked to biography in the early nineteenth century. "There is no kind of writing, which has truth and instruction for its main object, so interesting and popular, on the whole, as biography," wrote William H. Prescott in 1838.[4] In the early years of the republic, the most popular biographies were filiopietistic, like Parson Weems's volumes on George Washington and Francis Marion. After the Revolution, biography performed an educative function. It was widely recognized that "the office of biography is to teach by examples."[5] If history was philosophy teaching by example, then the study of distinguished individuals' lives seemed the most practical form of history. People believed that to avoid languishing in immaturity they must learn from those who had gone before them. "If we do not take to our aid the foregone studies of men reputed intelligent and learned," wrote Edmund Burke, "we shall be always beginners." In short, nineteenth-century Americans "believed that biography had power: the power to shape individuals' lives and character and to help define America's national character."[6]

Enlisted in the cause of constructing a national identity, biographies of American heroes taught the spirit and character traits of republican citizenship exemplified by the Founding Fathers to a generation too young to have participated in the Revolution. These earliest American biographies were overtly nationalistic.

They idealized military and founding heroes and moralized while they entertained. "Long before Thomas Carlyle developed the great man thesis readers had learned to love the hero, and authors had learned that there was no surer way of pleasing the public than by catering to its sense of self-identification with a colorful personality," noted George Callcott. The majority of Americans of Simms's generation would likely have been put off by Jacob Burckhardt's formulation of the great man thesis: that history "tends at times to become suddenly concentrated in one man, who is then obeyed by the world."[7] But as long as the great men embodied (or could be portrayed as embodying) republican, and somewhat later, democratic ideals, their lives were fit for study.[8]

In reaction to the overly romantic idealization of American heroes, the next generation of American biographers sought to serve the same instructive purpose with a stricter adherence to facts. Typical of these biographers are Simms, Jared Sparks, and Elizabeth Ellet. As Casper has noted, Simms's "objective resembled that of many other historians working in the 1840s: to chronicle history that had not yet been written, to distinguish truth from faulty memory." Their greater concern for facts in no way diminished their appetite for heroes or their desire to produce history of literary quality. Biographies were still written for the young "who seek for guidance to an honourable fame," as John Pendleton Kennedy wrote in the dedication to his life of William Wirt.[9] In our own cynical age, heroic biographies and the great man thesis seem hopelessly naive to many academics despite their immense popularity with the reading public.[10] Even in academic circles, interest in individuals, as opposed to social and economic forces, as the actors in history has never completely died. In his essay *Historical Inevitability,* Isaiah Berlin argued that individuals rather than impersonal forces play the decisive role in history, as did Karl Popper in *The Poverty of Historicism.* Marc Bloch defined history as the science of men in time in *The Historian's Craft.* And historian George C. Rogers Jr. has reminded his colleagues that history is about names, not numbers. "The proper study of history includes, principally, persons rather than social types," wrote John Lukacs. "A history of science must be a history of scientists, a history of technology of the inventors, producers, and managers of technology."[11]

Simms's first books were poetry collections and novels. The transition from these to biography proved an easy one for him however, as it has for countless other writers. The very popularity of biography enticed many authors better known in other fields to try their hand at the genre. For example, Washington Irving wrote a biography of George Washington; fellow South Carolinian and poet Paul Hamilton Hayne wrote biographies of his kinsman Robert Y. Hayne and Francis W. Pickens; John Pendleton Kennedy wrote a life of William Wirt; and Nathaniel Hawthorne wrote a campaign biography of Franklin Pierce.[12] A biographer and novelist himself, Robert Penn Warren has taught that biography lies closer to "pure literature" than most types of history. Biography "goes beyond ordinary history in that, with its concentration upon an individual, it tends to give a more complete and coherent picture of character in action, and invites, with reference to the character presented, an imaginative involvement that makes for dramatic tension," he wrote. Also like "pure literature," biography tends to explore the problems of human values more fully than "ordinary history."[13]

The Life of Francis Marion (1844) was Simms's most commercially successful work of nonfiction and his first full-scale biography. It was one of the best-selling history books the year it was published. The first edition sold out in less than a week, without any advertising. It continued to sell well, went through three editions in its first three months off the press, and had been through ten editions by January 1847.[14] He followed *The Life of Francis Marion*'s success by preparing volumes on John Smith (1846), the Chevalier Bayard (1847), and Nathanael Greene (1849). Though none of these matched Marion's popularity, they all went through multiple editions in their author's lifetime. As history, the lives of Marion and Greene are better than the others. They display deeper research in primary materials, which is to be expected since Simms's own holdings and the collections to which he had ready access were stronger in the history of the Revolution than in the history of seventeenth-century Virginia or France.

Nevertheless, we know from Simms's letters that he early purchased John Smith's *History of Virginia*.[15] And *The Life of the Chevalier Bayard* was written with footnotes and a page of works consulted. Among the works consulted, Simms lists *Les gestes ensemble la vie du preulx Chevalier Bayard . . .* (1525), by Symphorien Champier; *La très-joyeuse and plaisante histoire, composée par le Loyal Serviteur, des faits, gestes et prouesses du Bon Chevalier, sans peur et sans reproche . . .* translated into English by Coleridge's daughter; and *Histoire de Pierre Terrail, dit le Chevalier Bayard, sans peur et sans reproche* (1822), by Jean Cohen. Additionally, Simms claims to have consulted many other works "which relate to contemporaneous events, as well as to those in the life of Bayard." Included among these, he named the works of Philip des Comines and Monstrelet, St. Palaye's *Ancient Chivalry*, Robert Macquereau, Gaspard de Saulx-Tavannes, Roscoe's *Leo X*, Bacon's *Francis I*, Quintana's *Gonzalvo do Cordova*, Hume's *History of England*, Roberts' *Henry VIII*, and "Sismondi's and other Histories of France." In his footnotes are references to even more sources, both ancient and modern.[16] Though his lives of Bayard and Smith show extensive research in primary and secondary sources, both must nonetheless be considered popular, not scholarly, biographies.

As early as May 1840, shortly after finishing *The History of South Carolina*, Simms contemplated taking notes for and writing Marion's biography as well as the biographies of Thomas Sumter, Andrew Pickens, William Moultrie, and other "worthies of Carolina Revolutionary History." In September 1840 Simms had already begun taking notes for his biographies of Marion and Nathanael Greene. As of late October 1843 he was still taking notes, and in late January of 1844 he reports following up George Frederick Holmes's "hint touching Gen. [David Flavel] Jamison and the Life of Marion, and at your suggestion have just penned him a letter" asking research questions. After spending more than three years taking notes, Simms wrote Marion's biography relatively quickly; he could write to Holmes on May 14, less than five months after the first letter, that "Marion . . . is at length out of my hands."[17]

The Life of Francis Marion was certainly Simms's most scholarly biography. Simms's footnotes point (albeit inconsistently) to both primary and secondary sources he used, and he included a selective bibliography. In his other biographies he also informed readers which sources he consulted, but never as clearly or consistently as in *Marion*. Simms's biography of John Smith, for instance, contains footnotes to Smith's published writings, but it does not display the same kind of original research into primary sources as *The Life of Francis Marion* does. The bibliography in *Marion* includes seventeen sources, with primary sources figuring prominently in the list. Among the published sources consulted are William Dobein James's *A Sketch of the Life of Brig. Gen. Francis Marion* (1822); Mason Locke Weems and Peter Horry's *The Life of Gen. Francis Marion* (1833); William Johnson's *Sketches of the Life and Correspondence of Nathanael Greene* (1822); William Moultrie's *Memoirs of the American Revolution* (1802); Alexander Garden's *Anecdotes of the Revolutionary War in America* (1822); Henry Lee's *Memoirs of the War in the Southern Department of the United States* (1812); John Drayton's *Memoirs of the American Revolution* (1821); Banastre Tarleton's *A History of the Campaigns of 1780 and 1781, in the Southern Provinces of North America* (1797); the late lieutenant in the 71st Regiment Roderick Mackenzie's *Strictures on Lieut. Col. Tarleton's History* (1787); and David Ramsay's *History of the Revolution of South Carolina* (1785). Simms also liberally used "five volumes of MS. Letters from distinguished officers of the Revolution in the South. From the Collection of Gen. Peter Horry" and a "MS. Memoir of the Life of Brig. Gen. P[eter] Horry. By Himself."[18] Unfortunately the valuable memoir of Peter Horry, who served under Marion during the Revolution, has been partially lost. All that remains of some sections are the passages quoted by Simms. In addition, other sources are cited throughout the book in footnotes.[19]

The written sources were supplemented by his extensive use of local oral histories. Simms's generation of American historians was the last that could interview eyewitnesses to the events of the Revolution. Evidence scattered throughout his corpus indicates that he actively sought local histories and traditions from witnesses of and participants in the war, including surviving members of Marion's brigade.[20]

The sources that Simms employed are not used uncritically. Being a lawyer, Simms was practiced at carefully examining testimony. In a biographical sketch of Daniel Boone, he dismisses the 1746 date Humphrey Marshall gives for Boone's birth in his *History of Kentucky*, estimating that 1737 must be closer to the truth.[21] In fact, Boone was born in 1734. When it came to Francis Marion, he judged William Dobein James's treatment "not thorough" and lacking literary merit, and noted Weems's *Life of Gen. Francis Marion* "inspire[s] us with frequent doubts of its statements." Indeed, it was partly to correct these deficiencies that Simms undertook his own life of Marion. In several instances, he points out inaccuracies—or at least inconsistencies—in his sources. For instance, he describes an embellishment found in Weems's account but absent from James's. Finding no other evidence to support Weems's story, Simms concludes that "any attempt at details where so little is known to have been preserved, must necessarily, of itself, subject to doubt any narrative not fortified by the most conclusive evidence." In another case he points out an apparent error in Moultrie's *Memoirs of the American Revolution.* Moultrie placed the date of Marion's first military enlistment at 1761, but Simms thought the evidence conclusive that the correct date was actually two years earlier. Not only did he indicate where his sources could not be trusted, he also did not hesitate to point out where the record was silent instead of simply filling in the gaps without telling readers what he was up to.[22]

Though lacking footnotes, Simms's biography of Nathanael Greene also displays a deep knowledge of primary sources. There is some dispute whether Simms wrote or only edited *The Life of Nathanael Greene.* The title page names him as editor. Some scholars, such as Frederick Wagner, have argued that in preparing the biography Simms "edited" William P. Johnson's 1822 biography of Greene, shortening and enlivening the work.[23] We know that Simms did think highly of Johnson's biography of Greene. Johnson gave him an autographed copy of the book, which Simms later gave to Benjamin F. Perry at a time when his second copy of the biography was on loan elsewhere.[24] In 1847, before publication of his own biography of Greene, he advised Alabama historian Albert James Pickett that it was one of the most important books on South Carolina history.[25] In 1859 he recommended Johnson's *Sketches of the Life and Correspondence of Nathanael Greene* along with several other books, including his own *History of South Carolina,* to Henry B. Dawson, who sought details of the Revolution in the South.[26] And in the preface to his *History of South Carolina* Simms noted that "no work of American biography, could the author have descended to the humbler task of making an abridgment, would have more amply compensated both publisher and reader."[27]

Others, beginning with William Peterfield Trent, have argued that Simms in fact was the author, not the editor, of *The Life of Nathanael Greene.* Trent saw Simms's "ear-marks . . . through the whole of it." In *A History of American Biography,* Edward O'Neill followed Trent's lead and concluded the "style and method of this biography prove" Simms was in fact the author. Jon L. Wakelyn, one of the few historians who has given any serious attention to *The Life of Nathanael Greene,* does not even consider the possibility that Simms may not have actually written the book. But his judgment is suspect because his treatment of the biography is not wholly accurate. In his contribution to *Long Years of Neglect,* "Biography and the Southern Mind: William Gilmore Simms," John McCardell also assumes that Simms was the author of Greene's biography but fails to justify his assumption.[28] The biography does bear a strong family resemblance to his other works on the Revolution in style, design, and argument.

Nor do Simms's extant letters indicate he was simply reworking Johnson's book. To the contrary, they show that Simms had long contemplated a biography of Greene, that he was taking notes for the biography as early as September 1840. "I am . . . taking notes for *my* life of Greene & Marion [emphasis added]," he wrote.[29] Eight years later he wrote Lawson that "I am getting on slowly with the Life of Greene. It costs me more labor than I anticipated."[30]

Further evidence that Simms did more than shorten and enliven Johnson is found in the book's "Advertisement." Here Simms tells readers that he "has consulted nearly all the volumes which promised to have any bearing upon the subject." Among his enumerated sources are many that he also found useful in writing Marion's biography: "The copious biographical sketches of [William P.] Johnson," and the memoirs and histories of Henry Lee, David Ramsay, William Moultrie, John Marshall, Banastre Tarleton, Alexander Graydon,[31] "and others, not forgetting the very graceful memoir of Greene, from the pen of his grandson." For this latter book, Simms had high praise. "Who better prepared than himself to do justice to the great public services and private worth of his grandsire?" Simms asked. There was much worthy of discussion in this book, and Simms hoped to give "to the public a more elaborate performance on the same subject."[32] Simms also undoubtedly found Colonel Otho Holland Williams's narrative of the southern campaign of 1780 useful in preparing Greene's biography. Williams's narrative follows the biography as a thirty-five-page appendix.

A textual analysis of Simms's book and Johnson's biography does indeed reveal Simms's close reliance on Johnson. The book's organization is similar to Johnson's, and Johnson's volume is the source of many of Simms's details. Nevertheless, it is also clear that Simms carefully weighed Johnson's account against others' and wrote the biography using his own words. For instance, internal evidence suggests that Simms was also familiar with Henry Lee Jr.'s five-hundred-page screed against Johnson's biography, *The Campaign of 1781 in the Carolinas*, though Lee's book is not specifically mentioned as a source. A comparison of the three books reveals that Simms corrected or omitted many of the passages where Lee claims Johnson was in error. Often, however, the errors claimed by Lee are nothing more than perceived slights against the reputation of his ancestor Light Horse Harry, and do not warrant correction. Simms rewrote and shortened Johnson and corrected where necessary after consulting all the sources at his disposal.[33] He carefully used the sources available to him, according to M. F. Treacy, author of a history of Greene's southern campaign. Treacy judged Simms's *Life of Nathanael Greene* "accurate within the limitations of his sources."[34] The book's organization and many of its details come from Johnson, but the words are Simms's own. In short, Johnson provided the major source for Simms's biography of Greene, but it was far from the only source, and Simms's rewriting and revising was more substantial than the term "editing" sometimes implies.

Regardless, Simms felt his debt to his sources too great to put his name on the book as its author.

According to John McCardell, the great theme of these four biographies is Simms's longstanding concern with poetry and the practical, art and the utilitarian. In each of them, McCardell sees Simms reexamining the role of the intellectual in society. This is also what Drew Gilpin Faust understands to be the theme of Simms's career. Faust argues that Simms was a frustrated intellectual who sought commiseration within his "sacred circle" of friends, who alone among southerners appreciated the man of genius. "What most united [these biographies], in other words," writes McCardell, "was the way in which they allowed Simms to speak out in a personal way about himself as a writer in Charleston."[35]

Although it can with some justice be argued that all writing contains an element of autobiography, what most united these biographies was not how they allowed Simms to speak about his own experience as an intellectual in Charleston. Nor was it the intellectual accomplishments of their subjects. What most united the lives of Marion, Greene, Smith, and Bayard was that they were all men of action whose moral character Simms admired. Indeed, Simms even cautioned his friend Evert Duyckinck against modeling his biography of Sir Philip Sidney after *The Life of the Chevalier Bayard*. "Bayard's life was wholly military—not so Sidney's," Simms wrote. Unlike a biography of Bayard, one of Sidney must also acknowledge Sidney's literary accomplishments.[36]

Simms unquestionably viewed the subjects he chose to write about as heroic men of action who left their mark on history. But they were not quite depicted as heroes in the Carlylean sense. Nor are they Hegelian world-historical individuals unconstrained by morality.[37] His view of the great man thesis, which he never completely accepted, can be glimpsed in his review of Prescott's *History of the Conquest of Mexico*. Here he admits that were he "in a mood, after the fashion of Mr. Carlyle, to endow a modern Pantheon with Hero-divinities," he would not hesitate to include Hernando Cortés. But his election to the pantheon was merely an expression of the admiration which we "yield" to the man of action. By classifying Cortés as a hero, after the fashion of Carlyle, Simms did not necessarily intend to recommend his moral character. Cortés was a hero, a man of military greatness, a politician, "the man of iron nerves, of inflexible composure and fortitude,—doing without questioning,—prompt, brave, cruel,—resolute to win the game, once begun, at whatever sacrifice, the prize of which is" to become the hero or great man. These were characteristics of greatness, not goodness. "Our eulogium, therefore, is necessarily qualified," he wrote. Though we may yield admiration to the man of purely military distinction, our highest praise should be reserved for those men of superior moral or intellectual attainment or creative accomplishment who contribute to "the great cause of human progress."[38]

Such a man was Daniel Boone, whom Simms characterized as brave and good. He was the type of man who, in a more chivalric age, "would have been a knight errant, equally fearless and gentle." In his own age, he was a discoverer who risked his life to open the West for the advance of American civilization.[39] "The creative mind must always rank very far above the destructive," and therefore, Simms defined greatness as "the ability, in the worst of times, and with the worst means, of achieving the most wonderful results."[40] Judged by this standard Marion, Greene, Smith, and Bayard, as well as most of the people Simms wrote biographical sketches of, were unquestionably great.

Yet they were not all great in the same way. Simms seldom calls Greene a "hero," for instance. In fact, the word "hero" only appears in Greene's biography six times and is usually applied to other people or else used simply to designate Greene as the subject of the biography; rarely does Simms use the word to praise Greene's character.[41] Never does Simms describe Greene as chivalrous. Compare this with Simms's descriptions of John Smith, the Chevalier Bayard, and Francis Marion. Bayard and Smith are portrayed as the very embodiment of chivalry. The word "hero" appears seventy-six times in *The Life of Captain John Smith* and is not uncommonly used in praise of Smith's character.[42] Marion, likewise, is described in romantic terms as one of the great heroes of South Carolina as well as of the American Revolution.[43]

Greene's greatness lay in his eminently "practical" mind, which ideally suited him for the task of leading the Continental forces in expelling the British from the South.[44] He was never flashy, but Greene's practical brilliance was precisely what was needed to achieve the most wonderful results in the worst of times and with the worst of means. When Nathanael Greene arrived at Charlotte, North Carolina, in December 1780 to assume command of the remnants of the Southern Continental Army, the prospect before him was daunting. Lacking clothes, arms, and ammunition, Greene's new command numbered only 970 Continental troops and 1,013 militia, not including a separate command operating independently under General Daniel Morgan. His British counterpart, Lord Cornwallis, possessed all of the major posts in South Carolina and a force in excess of 5,000 well-equipped troops soon to be reinforced with nearly 3,000 more arriving from Virginia under General Leslie. General Horatio Gates had already failed with more favorable odds, "but Greene's mind—calm, equable, well-trained, and executive —quickly rose to the exigency before it."[45] Greene's genius, Simms wrote in *The Scout*, "was eminently cautious" and his "true merit lay in the prudence with which he prosecuted an enterprise."[46]

As his first order of business Greene exerted himself to secure adequate supplies for his troops. Unlike his predecessor, General Gates, Greene recognized the value and usefulness of the local partisan militia leaders to his efforts. These roving bands of guerrillas served several important functions. First, they supplied Greene with intelligence of British positions, strength, and movements. Second, through their constant activity they helped prevent the British from concentrating their numerically superior forces for a decisive strike at Greene. Third, they were useful in disrupting enemy supply lines and gradually wearing down the

British army. And fourth, their successes gave encouragement to timid Whigs, who might otherwise have faltered. "Greene was by no means insensible to these services," and later in the war "he despatched Colonel Lee, with three hundred men, to co-operate with Marion."[47]

Unable to match the British in numbers, Greene adopted guerrilla tactics. He coordinated his efforts with those of the partisans who were intimately familiar with the land and could provision themselves from it. He divided his small army, forcing Cornwallis to do likewise, and he proceeded into battle cautiously, fighting only when the situation seemed advantageous. Employing these tactics, a detachment of the Southern Army under Morgan's leadership routed a portion of the British Army at Cowpens, and Greene forced Cornwallis to give chase across North Carolina before he turned to fight the British at Guilford Courthouse.

Such tactics proved peculiarly well suited to South Carolina. A sparsely settled country, with few good roads and plentiful hiding places in the recesses of forests and swamps, South Carolina provided an ideal theater for the guerrilla operations against a more numerous foe. Simms, like later historians, attributed Greene's eventual success in dislodging the British Army from the colony to his ability to keep an army in the field and wear down the enemy and to his willingness to abandon textbook tactics in favor of those more suited to the situation.[48] Outnumbered "and frequently without provisions and ammunition, we find him steadily waging the conflict—evading the foe whom he could not confidently meet, but ever hanging about his path, watchful to take advantage of all his mistakes, and to dart upon his moments of unwariness and inaction."[49]

Simms clearly felt there was much about Greene worthy of admiration. Like Simms himself, Greene was born into a family of modest means.[50] What little formal education Greene acquired was supplemented by his voracious reading habits and ambition for self-improvement. He grew to be a man with "calm and thoughtful" manners, "a good heart," and a sharp mind.[51] As a military commander, he was "brave without rashness, prudent without fear, bold without temerity, . . . and endowed with a constancy that never lost sight of its object." Simms felt certain that all who read the history of the Revolution and became familiar with Greene's services to his country would admire the character and achievements of this favorite of Washington: "Of all our major-generals of the Revolution, he is universally admitted to be the one who stands nearest to Washington."[52]

The Chevalier Bayard also achieved much in trying times, setting an outstanding example by his character.[53] As depicted by Simms, he truly was the Good Knight without fear or reproach. Of Bayard, Simms wrote: "Foibles and faults may be charged to his account, but it would be difficult to reproach him with any vice." Bayard was honest, pious, faithful, generous, humble, brave, and intelligent, but he had the misfortune to live at a time when chivalry was dying in Europe and "had yielded on every hand . . . to a growth of the grossest passions" and a disregard of honor and pledges of faith. Nonetheless he furnished the greatest example of "those virtues which had made [chivalry] fruitful of good to humanity."[54]

Fighting at times against stunning odds, Bayard proved himself a courageous and resourceful warrior. On one occasion he singlehandedly defended a bridge against two hundred Spaniards.[55] "As a partisan warrior," wrote Simms, "he was, perhaps, one of the greatest captains that France has ever produced." Ever watchful, he was quick to seize the opportunity to surprise his enemy while avoiding being surprised himself. "Considered in every point of view, we are constrained to affirm the spontaneous judgment of his contemporaries," who thought him "the model of a perfect character, with which none among themselves could presume to compare," Simms wrote.[56]

Like Simms's other biographical subjects, John Smith also accomplished much under difficult conditions, but Simms's depiction of him more closely resembles that of Bayard than Greene. Using as his chief source Smith's own writings, Simms portrays him as one of the true heroes of the British exploration and colonization of North America. John Smith, he wrote, was a man whose romantic adventures "lift into heroic dignity a name so little significant in itself as to be commonly a subject for the vulgar jest."[57]

Smith was a man of action. He was blessed with an active mind and an eager, resolute temperament. According to Simms, his blood and brain worked together harmoniously to achieve spectacular results: "With persons thus fortunately constituted, deliberation is rather an obstacle than a help to the right performance. . . . Such are the men who commonly appear to shape and regulate the transition periods in society."[58] In Smith's case, he helped establish the colony of Virginia, and he guided it through the difficult early years when, facing starvation and hostile neighbors, infighting threatened the colony's survival.

Yet what truly made Smith heroic and worthy of emulation was his moral character. A hero should be judged "by what he has forborne of crime and error, and what he has resisted of temptation," Simms wrote. Smith was characterized not only by courage and activity, but also by honesty, benevolence, and mercy. "To have done so much with so little; in the teeth of discontent and faction; . . . with so much provocation to anger and severity, yet with so great toleration and pity for the offender; so much firmness with so much mercy," amply shows Smith to be a hero who compares favorably with any "to be found in the progress of a commercial age and people," Simms wrote. "Considering its date," O'Neill thought this biography "excellent."[59]

Francis Marion is also portrayed as a man of exceptional moral character who accomplished much under the worst of circumstances. Like George Bancroft, Francis Parkman, and many other historians of his day, Simms's history at times betrayed romantic and materialist tendencies. That is, he sometimes accorded deterministic power to national spirit, circumstances, and condition. Marion came from Huguenot stock, and Simms sought insight into his character in the peculiar spirit and circumstances of this people. "The Huguenots were a better sort of people" than the typical Europeans who settled in America. French Protestants who were persecuted and then expelled from France, they were better prepared for the hardships of life in a new country and were more appreciative of the liberties they gained. "They were a people of principle," and "pure habits."[60] Their devotion to principle was proved by the persecution they endured for their faith. The Huguenots arrived in Carolina as poor refugees, and they were distrusted by the English, who had traditionally viewed the French as their enemies. Yet in time the Huguenots would thrive in Carolina and be fully accepted by the English. Their eventual success was the result of perseverance and tireless industry. These virtues, part of the Huguenot spirit, were inherited by Marion.

Typical of Simms's biographical subjects, Marion was a man of action. He was "*par excellence,* the famous partizan" of South Carolina.[61] In terms of his character, Marion was the model of the virtuous republican citizen. Simms even paid Marion the supreme tribute of comparing him to George Washington. In fact, so consistent is the comparison between Marion and Washington that it can be said to be the basis around which the biography is organized. The first reference to a similarity between Marion and Washington appears on page 25. Here, after noting that the two Revolutionary heroes were both born in 1732, Simms continues: "This coincidence, which otherwise it might seem impertinent to notice here, derives some importance from the fact that it does not stand alone, but is rendered impressive by others, to be shown as we proceed; not to speak of the striking moral resemblances, which it will be no disparagement to the fame of the great Virginian to trace between the two."[62] As promised, Simms points out many other similarities between the two.

We learn that as youths both Washington and Marion dreamed of careers in the Royal Navy. Washington's mother convinced her son otherwise; Marion's plans were changed by a shipwreck.[63] After returning from sea Marion took up farming and his self-improvement. Here again, Simms draws a parallel between the lives of the two men: "Equally denied the advantages of education, they equally drew from the great mother-sources of nature. Thrown upon their own thoughts, taught by observation and experience—the same results of character,—firmness, temperance, good sense, sagacious foresight, and deliberate prudence —became conspicuous in the conduct and career of both." Later, Simms remarks on how both men had similar even-keeled temperaments. Marion's expression "never darkened by gloom, it was seldom usurped by mere merriment" either. He maintained a Spartan control over his emotions, never allowing himself to be carried away to excess, whether in triumph or defeat. "The equable tone of his mind reminds us again of Washington." As a young farmer, Marion, the Carolina Cincinnatus, exhibited "quiet and persevering industry" but had not quite outgrown his restlessness. In 1759 his pastoral tranquility was disturbed by war with the Cherokee. Marion left the farm to fulfill his civic duty by volunteering to serve in South Carolina's defense. When the threat had passed Marion again took up the bucolic life of the farmer. In 1775 his peace was disturbed yet again when, with America facing war with England, Marion's neighbors called upon his leadership. Preeminently a man of action, who best served his country on the battlefield, he nevertheless served ably in the Provincial Congress though, like Washington, he was no orator.[64]

We learn from Simms that British officers refused to use Marion's and Washington's official military titles but called them both "Mister": "The very attempt here made to sneer away the official, adds to the personal importance of the individual." The republican simplicity and virtue of "plain Mr. Marion" and "his ragged followers, who, untitled, could give such annoyance to His Majesty's officers," warrants "a degree of respect which his title might not otherwise have commanded." After the war, when his country's hour of danger had passed, Marion, like Washington, retired to the peace and quiet of his farm only to be interrupted by the call of political service. Late in life Marion took a wife, and like Washington's, his marriage produced no heirs.[65]

Marion's moral character made him worthy of emulation; his achievements in battle made him a hero. When South Carolina's fortunes looked bleakest, he struck back at the British and helped to expel them from the state. He did this against overwhelming odds, fighting an enemy more numerous, better trained, and better equipped.

In all his works on the American Revolution Simms stressed that the war in the South was a vicious civil conflict. In *The Life of Francis Marion* he explained how the ethnic diversity of South Carolina's population was one of the factors that tended to divide citizens' loyalties. According to Simms's judgment, colonists of Scots-Irish descent made some of the fiercest Whigs: "The bitter heritage of hate to the English, which they brought with them to America, was transmitted with undiminished fervor to their descendants." The Scots-Irish Carolinians were easily persuaded that the same English government that had tyrannically disregarded their rights in Ireland had similar designs against their liberty in America: "At one remove only from the exiled and suffering generation, the sons had as lively a recollection of the tyrannies of Britain as if the experience had been immediately their own." Settlers of "Scotch" descent along the North Carolina border, on the other hand, Simms counted among the most virulent Tories.[66]

Other important factors that tended to divide the state included backcountry resentment against the lowcountry elite and the heavy-handed tactics of the patriots. Simms made the Loyalists' case sympathetically. "Let us do justice to this people," he wrote. "The loyalists . . . were, probably, in the majority of cases, governed by principle, by a firm and settled conviction, after deliberate examination of the case." Perhaps given time, and had the patriots been "more indulgent and considerate," they would have become good patriots themselves. "Unfortunately, this was not the case; and the desire [of patriots] to coerce where they could not easily convince, had the effect of making a determined and deadly, out of a doubtful foe."[67]

As a result, the war in South Carolina was especially bitter and not only arrayed neighbor against neighbor, but literally pitted brother against brother.[68] The entire population of the colony seemed divided into opposing armed camps. As in a religious war, a civil war works the combatants up into a fanatical passion, Simms wrote. The warfare degenerated into personal feuds. "Motives of private anger and personal revenge embittered and increased the usual ferocities of civil war," leading General Greene to declare that "the participants pursued each other rather like wild beasts than men." The war laid waste to the country. The upshot was that "the revolutionary struggle in Carolina was of a sort utterly unknown in any other part of the Union."[69]

A civil conflict fought in a sparsely settled state with inadequate routes of travel and communication proved an almost ideal theater for the operation of partisans. In South Carolina the militia proved its worth, time and again employing guerrilla tactics against a superior foe that had already driven the Continental Army from the state. In spite of this success, Simms felt the militia's role had been denigrated by regular army officers who complained of the militia's lack of discipline and lack of the proper material of war. Further, its accomplishments had been slighted by historians and a public that preferred to commemorate the victories of the Continental Army on such fields as Saratoga and Yorktown instead of the backwoods victories won by small, ragged bands of partisans. Simms conceded that the poorly equipped militia could never have expelled the British from the state without assistance from the Continental Army. He also insisted, "But for this militia, and the great spirit and conduct manifested by the partisan leaders in Carolina, no regular force which Congress would or could have sent into the field, would have sufficed for the recovery of the two almost isolated States of South Carolina and Georgia." The partisans and militia kept up the conflict while the Continental Army was too weak to take the field. They maintained a constant harassment of British and Loyalist forces, cut off their detachments, endangered their supplies, and forced the British to divide their force, while inspiriting local patriots. Simms assured readers he meant none of this to detract from credit owed the Continental Army. "It is only intended to insist upon those claims of the partisans, which . . . have been a little too irreverently dismissed by others."[70]

Under the command of good leaders familiar with the "native spirit" of their men, the Carolina militia proved a formidable military force. At battles such as Quinby Bridge and Eutaw Springs, Simms noted, Marion's and Andrew Pickens's troops exhibited courage and steadiness under fire that, in the words of General Greene, "would have graced the veterans of the great king of Prussia [Frederick the Great]." With able leadership the militia seldom faltered, and they and their officers are due much of credit for the eventual American victory in the Deep South. "But for these leaders, Marion, Sumter, Pickens, [William Richardson] Davie, [Wade] Hampton, and some fifty more well endowed and gallant spirits," Simms wrote, "the Continental forces sent to Carolina would have vainly flung themselves upon the impenetrable masses of the British."[71] Marion and his fellow patriots were instrumental in the fight for independence in South Carolina.

The Life of Francis Marion is as engagingly written as any of Simms's histories and shows a close attention to fairness and truthfulness. Indeed, Simms paints a far more balanced picture of the Revolution than many historians before or since. Edward O'Neill believed that *The Life of Francis Marion* never received the attention it should have *because* Simms tried to be "accurate and fair." His sympathies clearly lie with the Whigs, but he never hesitates to condemn those patriots who behaved barbarously or to praise those Tories and Englishmen who acted with chivalry. Both Whigs and Tories are guilty of atrocities in his narrative.[72] And even though it is a biography of a military hero, its attention is not focused solely on Marion. Simms was very much aware that the success of South Carolina's patriots was due more to the sacrifices of the humble than to the decisions of the famous. He even makes a point of praising "those great dames of the Revolution, to whom the nation is so largely indebted for the glory of that event."[73] This is, undoubtedly, why he considered the moral education of South Carolinians through the preservation and publication of stories like Marion's so vitally important. In hours of trial, future generations could then recall the selfless patriotism of Marion and all those who fought alongside him. And Simms's own busy generation could be reminded of virtue. Simms concluded his biography with a short verse that stressed for readers one last time the excellence and importance of Marion's example:

> If it be we love
> His fame and virtues, it were well, methinks,
> To link them with his name I' the public eye,
> That men, who in the paths of gainful trade,
> Do still forget the venerable and good,
> May have such noble monitor still nigh,
> And, musing at his monument, recal,
> Those precious memories of the deeds of one
> Whose life were the best model for their sons.[74]

An anonymous reviewer of Thomas Arnold's *Introductory Lectures on Modern History* in the *Southern Quarterly Review* wrote, "History is said to be the biography of society. Society is composed of individuals—and the biography of an individual who has exerted a wide influence in the community of which he was a member is actually the history of that community."[75] Such was certainly true of the four men of whom Simms wrote biographies. Rejecting the romantic notion that national spirit drove history forward, Simms focused his attention on individuals. Bayard, Smith, Greene, and Marion each exerted a wide influence, achieving much under the worst of conditions. Each of them defended their community. Smith, Greene, and Marion, in particular, dramatically influenced the world in which Simms lived. Smith helped found the English colonies in North

America, Greene and Marion were leaders in those same colonies' fight to gain independence. But what made each of these men great and a fit model for posterity was his character.

Here it should be noted that Simms considered Bayard, Smith, Marion, and Greene fit models for all Americans—not just southerners. Though he advocated recording regional history and Smith, Greene, and especially Marion were southern heroes, he depicted them as important figures on the national stage. Smith was important to the New Englander as well as the Virginian. Greene was born and raised in the North. Throughout his biography Simms compared Marion to the preeminent national hero, Washington. At the time these biographies were written, in the 1840s, it was still possible to be regional without being divisively sectional.

Simms did not distort the past to make his point. Like all historians, he sometimes fell into error. But accuracy was always his ideal. Though he thought highly of each of these men and their lives are written sympathetically, he attempted to deal fairly with them as well as the other people who appear in the pages with them. He conducted careful research in the sources available to him and was true to the facts as presented in those sources. Oral traditions and folklore were carefully weighed as evidence. If in most cases his work has been superseded by that of subsequent historians (although there still is no really satisfactory biography of Marion and few biographies of Bayard exist in English), it represented the highest standards of scholarship when it was written. The lives of Marion and Greene can still be read as primary sources, and they preserve other primary sources. *The Life of Nathanael Greene* is one of the few places where Colonel Otho Holland Williams's narrative can be found, and *The Life of Francis Marion* is the only place where portions of General Peter Horry's memoir still exist. Even the biographies of Smith and Bayard, though they should be read as popular biographies, were based on the best sources available to Simms. He was not any less careful in these two biographies; he simply had fewer sources from which to work.

FIVE

The History of South Carolina

In 1840 S. Babcock and Company of Charleston published the first edition of Simms's *The History of South Carolina, from Its First European Discovery to Its Erection into a Republic: With a Supplementary Chronicle of Events to the Present Time*. Simms revised the book in 1842 and the next year published under Babcock and Company's imprint *The Geography of South Carolina*, designed to serve as a companion to the history. Simms again revised his *History of South Carolina* in 1860, bringing it up to date. Between 1840 and 1860 it had grown from 319 pages to 437 pages.

The two main lessons of the book are that South Carolinians ought always to depend on native leadership and that they ought also to present a united front against external foes. These points are driven home in his telling of the story of the American Revolution in South Carolina. Though not strictly limited in scope to the Revolutionary War, *The History of South Carolina* deals extensively with the Revolution and is one of Simms's most important treatments of the war. In the 1860 edition, 237 of the 437 pages are devoted to the Revolution in South Carolina and the events from 1765 leading up to it. The American Revolution is the central theme of the narrative. In fact, the full title chosen for the book indicates that the history of South Carolina culminates in the Revolution and the state's "erection" into the republic; subsequent events were mere epilogue.

As was the case with his other works on the Revolution, Simms sought to represent the war in South Carolina accurately and in a lively narrative to reach as large an audience as possible. In his narrative the Revolution is described as the product of a long progress of social and ideological forces that tempered the nation until it was ready for independence. Simms depicts the Revolution in South Carolina as a civil war exacerbated by ethnic divisions within the colony, and much of the credit for the eventual victory, he emphasizes, was due to the partisan militia. If this history can truly be said to have a thesis, it is that unity is essential in times of crisis and that South Carolina had been fortunate in having native leaders to see it through every emergency.

The History of South Carolina differed somewhat from his other works in that it was conceived as a textbook for the young as well as for interested general readers. South Carolinians, he felt, were regrettably ignorant of their own past: "To say that the great majority of our young people know little or nothing of the history of the state, is to do them no injustice. We may equally charge this deficiency upon the old."[1] So while he always sought to enliven his narrative with art, here he also intended to simplify it in an attempt to reach young or benighted readers. This is also the reason that *The Geography of South Carolina* was published separately. "In separating the political and social from the geographical history of the state," Simms wrote, "the object was to simplify the subject, and so to preserve unbroken the stream of narrative in the former work, as to make its perusal by the youthful reader, a pleasure rather than a task."[2] In the preface to the 1860 edition of *The History of South Carolina,* Simms explained that the book began when he undertook to teach his thirteen-year-old daughter Augusta her state's history. No existing book seemed suitable to his purposes.

It was widely understood in early America that the fate of republics depended upon the education of the young in virtue and character. As Gordon Wood has pointed out, Americans knew that it was "the character and spirit of the people" rather than force of arms that both made the ancient republics great and, ultimately, led to their downfall. "The rustic traits of the sturdy yeoman" and the "virile martial qualities—the scorn of ease, the contempt of danger, the love of valor—" were what made a society strong and a nation great.[3] Many, Simms included, recognized the study of history as the best way to teach the republican virtues. "Examples are better than precepts; and history is the best instructor both in polity and morals," explained the northern preacher Samuel Langdon.[4]

Simms found the existing histories of South Carolina "so cumbrous, and so loaded as they are with prolix disquisition, and unnecessary if not irrelevant detail," that he felt they were unsuited to "the unprepared understanding and the ardent temper of the young."[5] The standard histories of the state by "Hewatt, Drayton, Ramsay, Moultrie, etc.," were long, unimaginatively written, and encumbered by dry discourses on the nature of republican institutions. These histories may have been useful when America's federal government was new, but they no longer held any interest for readers of Simms's day: "To the great portion of the reading community they are entirely useless."[6]

Another problem with the histories of South Carolina then available was that their excessive length made them too expensive. "Books for schools and for the popular reader—the two objects for which the present history is designed—must be cheap as well as compact."[7] Keeping his audience in mind, Simms left out all "unnecessary details" and avoided "prolixity."[8] He also left out footnotes, adding instead review questions for students. Simms believed one of the chief goals of authors and publishers should be the diffusion of knowledge to the poor through the availability of "cheap literature."[9]

> To place the facts in a simple form, in a just order; to give them an expressive and energetic character; to couple events closely, so that no irrelevant or unnecessary matter should interpose itself between the legitimate relation of cause and effect; and to be careful that the regular stream of the narrative should flow on without interruption to the end of its course, have been with me primary objects.[10]

Thus he summed up his method of writing a history that he hoped would appeal to a wide audience within South Carolina.

However, the finished product was somewhat less ambitious in scope and production than Simms's original conception of it. Discussing his plans for revising of *The History of South Carolina* with James Henry Hammond, Simms wrote of his wish to publish a history that "comprise[d] a careful review of the documentary matter & a selection from it, & to include all those portions of the history of the interior & hill country which are now scattered fragmentarily over numerous fields of publication, in pamphlets, periodicals &c. bringing the narrative to the present period." As envisioned, the comprehensive history of South Carolina would be illustrated with maps and plates and could not be compressed into less than two large octavos. The difficulty in publishing such a work, as Simms was well aware, is that it would be prohibitively expensive. And the history of a small state would interest only a small audience. To be feasible he calculated that the volume would have to be subsidized by one thousand subscribers and the state legislature. This was simply outside the realm of the possible in antebellum South Carolina, so Simms scaled back his design, limiting himself to a relatively small one-volume history and a separate one-volume geography of the state.[11]

The Geography of South Carolina draws heavily from the work of Robert Mills, whose atlas is still the most comprehensive source for geographical information on early nineteenth-century South Carolina. It might more accurately be thought of as a natural history of South Carolina; Simms wrote and organized it according to the conventions of natural history. This peculiarly American genre developed out of the need to describe systematically a vast new continent, and it included the writings of Bartram, Jefferson, Filson, and many others with whose works Simms was familiar. Natural history would later engage the talents of writers ranging from Henry David Thoreau to Wendell Berry. Like countless earlier descriptions of America, Simms's geography begins by surveying the state's physical extent, then moves on to enumerate its physical features, its flora, and its fauna, before describing its human inhabitants and their higher attainments.[12]

Simms acknowledged his debt to several authors in *The History of South Carolina*'s preface. Those authors included Bartholomew Rivers Carroll Jr., Alexander Hewatt, John Drayton, David Ramsay, William Moultrie, William Johnson, George Bancroft, William J. Rivers, Banastre Tarleton, "and several others."[13] He quoted freely from these authors, and though the quotes are not cited in footnotes, the text generally makes clear the sources from which he borrowed.

Despite his indebtedness to the standard sources, Simms did not slavishly rely on them. He used his sources critically, pointing out when they were wrong or inconsistent.[14] And he did not hesitate to admit his uncertainty when his researches failed to conclusively settle an issue. "All the clues to argument upon doubtful or disputed points have been indicated," he told his readers.[15] Because of that and of his extensive original research, Simms felt his own *History of South*

Carolina was "in many respects original, especially in the suggestion of clues; and it embodies much material which has escaped other historians."[16] Upon completing *The History of South Carolina* Simms could write "there is no Romance about it"[17]—unlike some of his other books.

His original research involved delving into all the manuscripts he could obtain access to, traveling to all portions of the state, and conversing and corresponding with authorities on local history. One such research trip was planned for the summer of 1847 to familiarize himself with the scenery, history, and manners of the upcountry. Simms wrote in May 1847 to John C. Calhoun that he hoped to take a summer "jaunt" in South Carolina's mountains: "My purpose will be to pick up as much historical material as possible in relation to the events of the revolution in the interior, so that I may make my History of the State more complete, and more satisfactory to the upper country."[18] In planning the trip he sought the assistance of Greenville's Benjamin F. Perry, who was knowledgeable about upcountry Revolutionary history. "I am thinking of a new Edition of my History of South Carolina, in which I propose to incorporate all the matter that can be procured in regard to the up country history," he wrote to Perry. "In this work I shall look to you for assistance."[19] Simms's itinerary included the Cowpens and King's Mountain battlefields, and he desired Perry to share his knowledge of local Revolutionary history and lore.[20] As a result of his diligent research and careful revising he felt confident that impartial readers of the 1860 revised edition of *The History of South Carolina* would agree that he had "suffered nothing, by way of clue, suggestion, argument, or fact, to escape me."[21]

According to Simms, the Revolution in South Carolina commenced in October 1765, when the decision was made to resist the Stamp Act.[22] Before this, South Carolina had little reason for discontent with the mother country: "She had, on the contrary, many good reasons for loving her with undeviating loyalty." She enjoyed the protection of British arms and fleets and profited by her mercantile connection with the mother country. South Carolinians suffered lightly, if at all, under "the array of evils, wrongs, and abuses" that afflicted the northern colonies with more substantial manufacturing and shipping interests.[23] Instead of finding herself in competition with English economic interests, South Carolina benefited from her connection with England. "She provided the raw material which the other manufactured, and she received the manufactured goods in exchange for her productions. The intercourse was simple enough between them, and the occasions for conflict were few and unimportant."[24] Nor had she felt the oppressiveness of British arms. On the contrary, British "men, money, and munitions" protected South Carolina from hostile Native Americans and Spaniards.[25] Her causes of quarrel were not economic; rather she found herself in sympathy with the plight of Massachusetts, and chafing at British arrogance and the denial of a few abstract principles. "The duties on tea and stamped paper were not felt, regarding the amount; but as the assertion of an authority adverse to the rights of the people and the province," Simms explained.[26]

South Carolina and Great Britain were bound not only by self-interest but also by an affection grown from sharing a language, a similar culture, and many of the same traditions. South Carolina's constitution and government were based on British models, and many of her citizens worshiped at Anglican churches and enjoyed reading English literature. South Carolinians, claimed Simms, "were especially fond of British tastes, manners, and opinions; their children had a British education, and they spoke of the mother-country invariable under the endearing appellation of 'home.'" They also inherited "the natural spirit of liberty and right which fills the bosom of an English stock."[27]

South Carolinians considered themselves Englishmen, possessed of the rights of Englishmen. These rights had always been jealously guarded, and they never shrank from asserting them. Indeed, they overthrew the Lords Proprietors in 1719 for abusing these rights. Simms believed that "the whole progress of the province of South Carolina had been calculated to nourish a spirit of independence among the people." Trial and strife had both strengthened them and made them aware of their strength. Most white colonists were freehold farmers who recognized no superiors, and "agriculture had taught them simplicity, hardihood, and a frank, bold, free speech and thought."[28] South Carolinians had no formal aristocracy and knew no constitutional restraints on their exercise of religion. Even slavery tended to make them more jealous of their own liberties while heightening their own sense of dignity. As the colony grew in population and wealth, the colonists grew in local pride and boldness and were less content to be governed by a distant foreign court.

The period that witnessed Carolina's astounding growth and prosperity was an interval of salutary neglect during the reigns of George I and II that had fostered self-government and conditioned her citizens to expect little royal or parliamentary interference in their affairs. However, Simms notes, "The ascent of George the Third to the throne brought with it a change of policy in Britain, and with regard to the province, which awakened the anxieties of the intelligent and aroused the fears of the vigilant and jealous."[29] Unfortunately for the cause of imperial rule, the cessation of salutary neglect coincided with the successful termination of the Seven Years' War, which removed the most dangerous threats to the colony's peace and safety. Free from foreign pressure, South Carolinians could now begin to calculate the cost of union with England. Once this inquiry had begun, they "soon arrived at those convictions of political truth, law, and equity, which learned to question the tenure of foreign authority, and the legitimacy of these relations with the mother-country, which placed the provincials wholly at her mercy." From here, "the summits of republican freedom were not far from sight."[30]

Though they suffered little compared to the people of Boston, South Carolinians actively sympathized with them and saw in Boston's plight a real danger to their own liberty. In no colony, Simms wrote, was sympathy for Boston more passionately felt and expressed than in South Carolina. The unrestrained power that was allowed to subjugate one colony, they recognized, could subjugate them all. Safety was in unity and concerted resistance to tyranny.[31]

What was true for the colonies as a whole was also true for South Carolina. But its ethnic and cultural diversity spoiled hopes of internal unity against an external foe. Building upon the work of David Ramsay, Simms explained that the colony's population contained large numbers of English, Scots, Scots-Irish, Germans, and French Huguenots, who brought their national prejudices to America and who were further divided by economic and geographic interests.[32] Inhabitants of the backcountry, for instance, had little in common with those who lived in the lowcountry. In the backcountry, "a large portion of the people were foreigners, born British subjects, had been only eight or ten years in the country, had no intercourse, no sympathies, with the people of the seaboard, and were particularly jealous and resentful of the superiority which they asserted in arts, refinements, wealth, and education."[33] Having only lived in America for a short period, many of them had not developed local attachments stronger than their ties to the mother country. And they certainly felt little loyalty to the haughty lowcountry Carolinians whom Simms places in the lead of the movement for independence.

In the backcountry also were large Scottish and German communities, which provided many Loyalists. These Scottish communities were not the Protestant or Scots-Irish, who were among the strongest supporters of independence. Rather, Simms explains elsewhere, they were Highland Scots, who settled along the North Carolina border from Cape Fear to the Great Pee Dee.[34] National differences among immigrants were compounded by the fact that they tended to settle in close-knit communities, maintaining their language and customs and having little intercourse with outsiders. "Here, in one place, were Scotch, loyal, intense in their loyalty, and stubborn in their prejudices." In another were Protestant Irish, "more eager, enthusiastic, impulsive, somewhat reckless, and never remarkable for their loyalty to the English dominion." In other places were German, Swiss, and French Huguenot settlements. The Germans were often loyal to the Hanoverian monarch on Britain's throne: many of them having been convinced by Loyalists that rebellion meant the forfeiture of their royal grants of land. The French, like the Scots-Irish, were relatively quick to assimilate and held little sympathy for England.[35]

The antipathy of some colonists in the interior for the coastal leaders of the rebellion furnished another reason for Loyalist sympathies and engendered discord among Carolinians. In fact, backcountry farmers often viewed the lowcountry planters in much the same way that American Whigs viewed the governing aristocrats in London. If America was the periphery to London's metropolitan center, then the South Carolina backcountry could with equal justice be regarded the periphery to the metropolitan center in Charleston. Seeking supporters of the crown in the backcountry, Loyalist leaders successfully appealed to the "natural jealousies" and "prejudices" of poorer settlers "against rank and wealth, the haughty assumptions of the citizens and planters of the seaboard, and their free expenditure of the public money." Whig complaints against virtual representation or taxation without representation did not resonate among those who settled the interior. They had the same complaint against the lowcountry. "The upper settlements had been little considered by the popular leaders, in the whole progress of the revolutionary proceedings; had been, until a recent period, unrepresented in their congresses and public meetings; and, but few efforts had been made to conciliate the more talented and influential of their leading men." Neglect of their interests and fear that cavalier rebel leaders intended to dragoon them and their sons into service earned the Whigs many bitter enemies among those in the upcountry who had not already embraced the Loyalist cause out of affection for the crown.[36] In trying to justify backcountry Tories, Simms may have somewhat overemphasized the degree of Loyalism in the interior. He gives more attention to backcountry patriots elsewhere, for example, in *Joscelyn*.

Opinion in the lowcountry was also fiercely divided. In the early stages of the Revolution, a large portion of the mercantile community attempted to remain aloof out of concern that an active engagement in politics might be bad for business—"trade being always reluctant to peril capital upon the caprices of politics." Nevertheless, when eventually forced to choose sides, "they showed themselves in their true colors, as bigoted loyalists, hostile to all popular proceedings, a danger in the very heart of the commonwealth."[37]

Despite his description of certain loyal merchants as "bigoted," Simms's treatment of the Loyalists is relatively more charitable than that offered by many of his contemporaries. In his assessment, the Loyalists were wrong and stood in the way of progress. Generally they failed to see the full picture. Sometimes this was because they were blinded by their own selfish interests, as in the case of the merchants. Other times, however, their loyalty sprang from conviction. Many colonists were reluctant to sever ties with Britain, not having lived long in South Carolina or fearing a potentially tyrannical power in Charleston more than one in London. Others simply did not feel oppressed and therefore found the arguments for independence unconvincing; "South Carolina had, indeed, been a favorite plantation of the crown, and the reluctance of thousands to sever the friendly bands which had linked them together, was not less honorable to their principles, than natural to their affections."[38]

Simms's analysis of the divisions within South Carolina closely follows David Ramsay's and has been confirmed by later historians. Ramsay wrote, "Country religion, local policy, as well as private views, operated in disposing the inhabitants to take different sides."[39]

There were strong arguments in favor of the Loyalists' viewpoint, and as far as Simms was concerned, adherence to one's convictions did not make one a villain. He doubted not that "many of the loyalists were persons of little principle, . . . but, that the people who were subsequently degraded, under the general and opprobrious term of 'tories,' were, in many instances, moved only by an honest and loyal, if not a wise and just sense of duty, can not well be questioned." They may have been less farsighted than their adversaries, but if their loyalty was based on honest motives, they were no less respectable.[40]

Not only were the Loyalists, as described by Simms, not necessarily men with black hearts, they also did not necessarily have feeble minds. In fact, "the loyalists possessed numerous citizens of talents and real worth, who might have been conciliated, at least, to acquiesce in the movement which they might yet refuse to lead."[41] That they were not conciliated was due to the imprudence and indiscretion of patriot leaders. Unfortunately for South Carolina, individuals of both parties were guilty of indiscretions that made the conflict between them all the more harsh. Consequently, "the gulf through which they had to wade, to sympathy and union in the end, was one that dyed their garments in blood, the stains of which, to this day, are scarcely obliterated."[42] When it comes to the treatment of Loyalists, Simms follows David Ramsay in offering a more balanced approach than George Bancroft and most other nineteenth-century American historians did.[43]

Because South Carolina's heterogeneous population was so sharply divided, within its borders the Revolution more closely resembled a civil war than a war against a foreign foe. South Carolina "became one vast and bloody battlefield, in which nearly all of her sons contended," Simms wrote. "Unhappily, they too often contended with one another; and it is with a sentiment of profoundest melancholy that we record the fact, that the direst issues that ever took place within her borders . . . were those in which her own sons were pitted against each other." The war in South Carolina was especially savage, with both sides guilty of atrocities.[44]

In one of those fortunate catastrophes that sometimes occur in war, South Carolina's defense was left to its militia after the capture of Charleston and the defeat of the Continental Army under General Gates at Camden in 1780. Ill equipped, badly outnumbered, and with the British and their Loyalist allies in possession of the most important posts, the militia fought a partisan war against the enemy. The operation of these small bands of guerrillas was particularly suited to the sparsely settled country.

Simms attributed much of the militia's success to its custom of choosing its own leaders. These leaders, like the citizen-soldiers they commanded, were natives of South Carolina and intimately familiar with the land and people. Local partisan leaders, such as Marion, Sumter, and Pickens, met with greater success than generals who held national commissions, such as Lincoln and Gates, partly because they had "a better knowledge of the temper, character, and interests of those whom they would lead, and a proper knowledge of the soil, the situation and circumstances of the country which they undertook to defend." They were therefore better able to adapt their tactics to their circumstances than were either national or British commanders. Lacking local knowledge, "commanders, otherwise brave and skilful, have led thousands of gallant men to defeat, whom a better judgment and a native genius might have led to victory."[45]

South Carolina's greatest partisan leader was Francis Marion. He boldly yet carefully led his little band of men through the swamps and forests, tirelessly harassing his foe, giving battle only when it was advantageous. By these means he disrupted British communications and supplies, forced the enemy to disperse its forces over the countryside, and cheered independence-minded Carolinians. He extorted from the enemy "a bloody toll at every passage through swamp, thicket, or river." Marion was so successful, Simms argues, because his familiarity with the state and its citizens allowed him to employ tactics "peculiarly adapted to the peculiarities in Carolina, and consequently to the genius of her people."[46] Given adequate supplies and a suitable leader, like Marion, South Carolina's militia showed itself a match for the best drilled European regulars.[47]

The first edition of *The History of South Carolina* says very little about nullification. The narrative concludes with the evacuation of Charleston by the British. The only mention of nullification appears in an appendix "comprising a chronicle of the leading events" since the Revolution, which matter-of-factly states, "South Carolina makes a declaration of state rights and enacts an ordinance to nullify the operation of the act of congress imposing duties, &c. December, 17th, 1830."[48] We know from his letters to Hammond in the 1840s that Simms still thought nullification was nonsense and strongly opposed it, though he believed in the constitutionality of secession. Even in the 1860 edition of the book, his strong opposition to nullification is not readily apparent.

This silence about the nullification issue was perhaps partly calculated. Simms still hoped the state legislature would adopt his book for use in the free schools. There is no reason however to doubt his sincerity when he concluded the first edition by remarking:

One lesson, in chief, may be gleaned, among many others, from this imperfect story of the past. It is that which teaches the citizen to cling to the soil of his birth in the day of its difficulty, with the resolution of the son who stands above the grave of a mother and protects it from violation. This will be a safe rule for the citizen, whatever may be the cause of war or the character of the invader. Opinion hourly fluctuates and changes; public policy is, of all things, the most uncertain and capricious; and the pretexts of ambition suggest a thousand subtle combinations of thought and doctrine, upon which the human mind would depend with doubt and difficulty. But the resolves of a decided majority, in all questions of public expediency or policy, assumed as the voice of the soil, would be the course equally of patriotism and safety. This rule, preserved in memory and maintained as a principle, would unite a people and make them invincible. The thunders and threatenings of the foe would die away, unharming, in the distance. Unanimity among our citizens will always give them unconquerable strength, and invasion will never again set hostile foot on the shores of our country.[49]

Regardless of what he thought of nullification, he considered it a duty of citizenship to stand firm with the majority against outside pressure once the issue had been decided. It is well to recall that Robert Weir found this same consensual approach to politics prevalent in colonial South Carolina. Because of their intense and near universal devotion to the country ideal, colonial South Carolinians developed an especially harmonious political system.

> The essence of politics, as they knew it, involved not the resolution of conflict within the body politic, but a constitutional struggle between extraordinarily able men, representing a unified local society, and the agents of another power. When the actions of such a power seemed to become excessively hostile, the logical response was to withdraw; when internal divisions threatened, the natural response was to extend the consensus.[50]

Believing South Carolina threatened by a hostile outside power, Simms determined to "cling to the soil of his birth."

In 1848 he discussed with Hammond his designs for a new and expanded two-volume state history, done up in a style similar to Prescott's *History of the Conquest of Peru*. He wrote to his former opponent from the nullification controversy that in the proposed book he planned "giving the nullification history without discussing it."[51] But on Hammond's advice, he decided to avoid the subject altogether by bringing the new history only down to the Constitution or the close of the War of 1812. Hammond cautioned him that a fair and accurate history of nullification written by a Unionist might ruffle some feathers. You cannot really conceive how we Nullifiers thought, he warned. And Hammond admitted that now even he altogether doubted the constitutionality of nullification.[52]

"Why not you write" the history of nullification, Simms then encouraged Hammond? "Write such a history for yourself—for your own exercise & gratification, in which you may honorably and, indeed, with peculiar nobleness recant your errors of opinion while proving your patriotism. Do justice then to your own as well as to the Union Party."[53]

Whether from policy or principle, Simms seems to have tried to follow his own advice and do justice to both parties in the 1860 edition of *The History of South Carolina*. There he sympathetically, though in an unsophisticated manner (as perhaps befits a book planned for children), outlined the argument for nullification. South Carolina, he explained, contended that the bond of Union was the Constitution and that the Constitution was "a compact between sovereign equals, in which they pledged themselves to forbear the exercise of their sovereign power over certain defined objects, and to assert jointly their sovereign power over other equally specified objects." That the parties to the compact ceded "power to the general government only in certain respects, which were all declared," while reserving all powers not enumerated. "That, in forming the constitution, the states divested themselves of none of their sovereignty," and only granted powers of attorney to their agent, the federal government. Therefore, since the federal congress is simply an agent of the states, the refusal of any one of the states "to recognize the law passed by the Congress is an inherent right of principal." Furthermore, he claimed it was absurd to speak of a state rebelling against the federal government: "The superior can not rebel against the inferior—the principal against the agent." Each state then had a right to veto or nullify any act of Congress deemed unconstitutional and was duty bound to protect her citizens against usurpations of power.[54]

Yet, Simms admitted, "even in South Carolina there was a large party opposed," to nullification.[55] Both sides were led by able men, and the anti-Nullifiers were in agreement with the majority on the principle of states' rights. The Unionists, though they believed in states' rights and the doctrine of secession, could not see how it was logically possible to nullify a federal law while remaining in the Union. The contest between the two parties in South Carolina "became heated to such a degree as to threaten the country with civil war."[56] When the Nullifiers won at the ballot box, President Jackson threatened to coerce the state—if necessary—to enforce federal law, and preparations were made to repel an invasion. South Carolinians united among themselves and with other southerners against the coercion of a state by the federal government, and a compromise was reached on the tariff. "Free states are not to be cemented into sisterly harmony by blood and fire!" the former Unionist declared.[57]

There is also the possibility that Simms's opposition to nullification is not obvious in the 1860 edition of his *History of South Carolina* because he changed his mind. From 1850 onward, he no longer criticizes nullification when he mentions it in his letters—though he does not exactly recant his previous position either. For example, in a November 1850 letter to Nathaniel Beverley Tucker, Simms writes that the only reason he does not favor immediate secession on the part of South Carolina is because he doubts the rest of the South will stand by her: "None of the South. States stood to the rack in 1833 when S. C. threw herself into the breach—and owing to the same cause—the faithlessness & selfishness of trading politicians."[58] And in a December 12, 1860, letter, later published in the Charleston *Mercury,* he explains that nullification is a conservative doctrine. South Carolinians loved the Union, he wrote, and *"Had their great men been listened to, they would have saved the Union!"*[59]

With both the worsening sectional conflict and the young readers for whom he wrote *The History of South Carolina* undoubtedly in mind, Simms closed the 1860 edition by noting that South Carolina had never lacked men equal to the challenge of leading her through any trial. "We have every reason to hope and believe," he confidently wrote, "that she will never be deficient in the men who are to wield her power, assert and maintain her arguments, and defend her rights."[60] South Carolina's citizens had always been one of her greatest resources, and he felt this would continue to be true.

Yet, with more than a hint of foreboding he listed in the 1860 edition those leaders his state had recently lost.

It is with a mournful pride that we refer to the great names, in recent periods, which she has possessed and lost. [John C.] Calhoun, [George] McDuffie, [Langdon] Cheves, [Robert Y.] Hayne, [James] Hamilton [Jr.], [Thomas] Cooper, [William] Drayton, [Hugh Swinton] Legaré, [Thomas S.] Grimké, [Stephen] Elliot[t]—these are names of men equal to all the exigencies of a people, and capable of conferring fame upon any annals. They are gone! and South Carolina stands upon the threshold of a new era, and, we trust in God, a yet superior progress! Let us hope that each season shall produce its proper men.[61]

The talent and character possessed by these men, who inherited a tradition of patriotism and public service passed down through the Pinckneys, Rutledges, Gadsdens, Moultrie, Marion, Sumter, Laurens, and Pickens proved the worth of studying history and "that the example of the past has not been chronicled in vain," he wrote in the first edition.[62] Perhaps one day, surely Simms hoped, some of his young readers' names could be added to the list.

Much to Simms's disappointment, *The History of South Carolina* was not adopted by the legislature for use in schools. This is not to say he was dissatisfied with his work, only with the legislature's failure to adopt it for public schools. He believed it was as "necessary to the public man, as to the pupil." Certainly he would be satisfied to know that in 1917, long after his death, his granddaughter Mrs. Mary C. Simms Oliphant heavily revised the book and, in this form, won its adoption for use in public schools. *The New Simms History of South Carolina* went through multiple printings and editions, and remained in use by schools into the latter twentieth century.[63]

SIX

Simms as a Presenter of History through Fiction

Simms has often been compared to that better known American master of the historical romance, James Fenimore Cooper.[1] Like Simms, Cooper wrote history as well as fiction, and both wrote popular historical romances about Native Americans set in colonial America. The two certainly had much in common, yet in the end we must conclude with Vernon Parrington that their differences are as striking as their similarities.[2] One important difference is in their approaches to the historical content of their romances. Whereas Simms uniformly claims authenticity for his historical romances, Cooper is at pains to explain that his historical romances are works of fiction, not bound by the conventions of history. Though his works are indispensable to historians, Cooper explained to readers that he believed a "rigid adhesion to truth . . . destroys the charm of fiction."[3]

The opposite is the case with Simms, who believed that his historical fiction was more truthful than other people's history. Because fiction is usually more character-driven than history, in his fiction Simms carefully delineated character and motivation. This, for Gore Vidal, is the chief attraction of the historical novel: "that one can be as meticulous (or as careless!) as the historian and yet reserve the right . . . to attribute motive—something the conscientious historian or biographer ought never do."[4] Romance, Simms recognized, was better suited to the creation of living and breathing characters than history. "The warm atmosphere of present emotions, and present purposes, belongs to the dramatis personae of art; and she is never so well satisfied in showing us human performances, as when she betrays the passions and affections by which they were dictated and endured," he claimed.[5] However Simms saw this as a responsibility, not a liberty. If free to attribute motive, he was constrained to attribute only motives that were consistent with what was known of a character and that readers would find believable. Though both the historian and the writer of romances had to be careful with their facts and just in their judgments, Simms, like Gore Vidal, found the latter's task more attractive. Its appeal was that

> it admits of so much more of that detail, in the affairs of a favourite, which brings us to a familiar acquaintance with the graces of the family circle, the nice sensibilities of the heart, the growth of the purest affections, and those more ennobling virtues of the citizen, which, as they are seldom suffered to show

themselves beyond the sphere of domestic privacy, and not often permitted to glide into, and relieve the uniform majesty of, history.[6]

For a writer, like Simms, interested in morally edifying his readers, the freedom to probe a character's heart and assign motive was of no little importance.

Simms also believed that his historical fiction was truer than standard histories because establishing verisimilitude in fiction required attention to the details of everyday life that were commonly overlooked by historians. Fiction, in his estimation, sometimes exceeded history in truthfulness "because she supplies those details which the latter, unwisely as we think, but too commonly, holds beneath her regard."[7]

In the dedication to the Redfield edition of *The Wigwam and the Cabin*, Simms wrote, "I need not apologize for the endeavor to cast over the actual that atmosphere from the realms of the ideal, which, while it constitutes the very element of fiction, is neither inconsistent with intellectual truthfulness, nor unfriendly to the great policies of human society."[8] This blending of the actual and the ideal, of history and fiction, is perhaps best illustrated in the collection's final story, "Lucas de Ayllon. A Historical Nouvellette," a tale of an unsuccessful Spanish attempt at colonization, set in what Simms called the first period of American history. The long footnote that begins the story claims "the essential facts"—which are supported with quotations from Simms's own *History of South Carolina*—are "all historical . . . enlivened only by the introduction of persons of whom history says nothing in detail."[9]

Simms believed the highest goal to which an author could aspire was the moral elevation of his readers. In a letter to Philip Pendleton, editor of the *Magnolia*, dated August 12, 1841, he revealed how he thought an author could reach this goal. An author could only hope to elevate the moral character of his readers when he presented them with a story of the ultimate triumph of virtue over vice. Simms voiced this view in defending another story from *The Wigwam and the Cabin*, "Caloya; or the Loves of the Driver," against the charge of immorality. Writers have a responsibility to show their readers the whole truth he claimed. They must not make vice attractive. Furthermore, the author "is and cannot but be, immoral, whose truth is partial and one-sided; who shows the sweets of vice, without their bitterness; who depicts the successes, while he hides or softens the defeats, the shame and suffering of the criminal."[10] Simms thus hoped to improve the moral character of his readers by showing them the criminal receiving his just punishment.

Except for the manner of Ayllon's death, Simms adhered faithfully to the essential facts in "Lucas de Ayllon." The two main characters, Chiquola and Lucas de Ayllon, were both historical figures. While exploring the eastern coast of North America in the early sixteenth century, Ayllon came ashore at the mouth of a river somewhere between the Savannah and the Potomac Rivers, and left with Chiquola and scores of captive Native Americans, whom he intended to sell as slaves. Whether Chiquola went willingly is not known. As Simms recounts, Ayllon later returned to the mouth of the river. There one of his ships ran aground and sank, and although no one is exactly certain how, Ayllon and most of his companions perished.[11]

Although in "Lucas de Ayllon" Simms generously blessed the Native Americans with virtues such as hospitality and courage, he did not portray them unrealistically. "Fierce valour and generous hospitality were the natural virtues of the Southern Indians," wrote Simms. It was this valor that enabled them to attack the Spanish ships in their canoes, armed only with bows and "their strength, and skill and courage," to attempt a rescue of Chiquola. Their downfall, however, was their naïveté. "The natives were a race as unconscious of guile as they were fearless of danger," and thus fell victim to the wily Spaniard.[12]

Simms's description of Chiquola's tribe bears a striking similarity to his description of Native American character in his essay "Literature and Art among the American Aborigines," found in *Views and Reviews,* where he described the North American Indians as "proud, . . . generous, and capable of the most magnanimous actions;—you shall share his bread and salt to his own privation;—loves liberty with a passion that absorbs almost all others—and brave—rushing into battle with the phrenzy of one who loves it—he prolongs the conflict, unhappily, long after mercy entreats to spare."[13] Simms wrote more, and more realistically, about Indians than any other nineteenth-century American fictionist. Native Americans figure prominently in at least seventy-four of his novels, stories, and poems. In this body of writing he realistically portrayed, according to the best sources available at the time, sixty different Native American linguistic, social, or cultural groups.[14] To a greater degree than George Bancroft, Richard Hildreth, and many later historians, he recognized the centrality of the dispossession of Indians to the American narrative.

Simms's Indians are not caricatures. They live and love like everyone else. He recognizes that they are "human; having . . . the same vital passions, . . . the hopes, the fears, the loves and the hates, which establish the humanity of the whites."[15] Consequently, they are more complex characters than the typical brutish or noble savages of American literature. In the dedication to *The Yemassee,* he explained that his goal was a "just delineation" of Native American character that could serve as a corrective to "the rude portraits of the red man, as given by those who see him in degrading attitudes only, and in humiliating relation with the whites."[16] It is surely no exaggeration to point out, as John Guilds has done, that Simms produced the most realistic treatment of American Indians in nineteenth-century American literature. "An early and strong sympathy with the subject of the Red Men, in moral and literary points of view, have rendered me in some degree a fit person to insist upon their original claims and upon what is still due them by our race," Simms wrote to Henry Rowe Schoolcraft.[17]

In contrast to the virtuous Native Americans, Simms described the Spaniards as possessing the vices of greed and cunning. Lucas Velasquez de Ayllon, we are told, was a criminal, who corrupted the New World Eden when he "brought cunning" with him to the shores of Carolina: "Having the narrow contracted soul of a miser, he was incapable of noble thoughts or generous feelings. The love of gold was the settled passion of his heart, as it was too much the passion of his countrymen." This harmonizes with Simms's assessment of the Spanish adventurers in his reviews of Prescott's histories of the conquest of Mexico and Peru. Indeed, it was Ayllon's greed that brought him to Carolina. So covetous was Ayllon that he forbore firing on the Indians when they attacked his ship for fear that he might thereby diminish his profits. "I see not present enemies but future slaves in all these assailants," Simms has him explain to his crew.[18]

Simms's Spaniards are technologically advanced, but morally bankrupt. They lack all the generous tendencies that Simms hoped to awaken in his readers. The conflict between the two societies, Indian and Spanish, provides a good illustration of a recurring theme in Simms's work: the contrast between moral and material (or technological) progress. This theme figures prominently in his *Egeria* and *Poetry and the Practical.*

Simms abandons the historical record in his description of Ayllon's death. Although no one is certain exactly how he died, no account fully supports Simms's version of events. Most historians have attributed the failure of Ayllon's second expedition and his death to a number of factors including a lack of discipline and preparedness, hostile natives, the foundering of one of his ships, disease, and other natural causes. Simms, in *The History of South Carolina,* tells of the Spaniards suffering a shipwreck when they returned to the Combahee River, whereupon they were massacred by the Indians and "fell victim to the cannibal propensities of the savages."[19] In "Lucas de Ayllon," he has the Spaniards burnt by the Indians as a human sacrifice to "warm the bones" of Chiquola, who had earlier drowned in the cold ocean. "At all events," wrote Simms in *Views and Reviews,* "whatever may have been the manner of his death, it is involved in that happy obscurity which leaves the poet at perfect liberty so to shape his catastrophe as to adapt it to the general exigencies of his story."[20]

This is the point at which the *actual* gives way to the *ideal*—the point at which Simms uses fiction to supply the deficiencies or correct the judgments of history.[21] In order to teach a truth, Simms the artist has Ayllon suffer a terrible yet just punishment for his crimes. Yet, Simms does so without obscuring the moral lesson: he refrains from showing Ayllon being cannibalized and becoming a victim himself to a barbaric crime perpetrated by the Indians. In Simms's view, the author who wishes to elevate the moral character of his readers, thereby assisting the cause of moral progress, must show virtue and vice "in contrast and opposition." He must illustrate for his readers "the beauties of the one and the deformities of the other."[22]

In James Kibler's judgment, Simms's dislike for utilitarianism and "his affirmation and demonstration of a fuller way of seeing pervade so many of his poems, stories, novels, and essays as to constitute . . . *the* major theme of his cannon."[23]

Although this may be overstating the case, it is an important theme that runs through much of his writing. The character of Ayllon might have been the perfect personification of the utilitarianism Simms despised, and his distaste for it is most certainly conveyed in "Lucas de Ayllon." He forcefully presented it to his readers by blending the actual and the ideal and by contrasting the virtues of the Indians with the vices of Ayllon.

Simms employed this same method in romances and stories that portrayed American history from the earliest attempts at colonization, through the Revolution, to recent episodes on the frontier. Whether writing about the Spanish and French exploration of America, the English settlers' dispossession of the Indians, the American Revolution, or frontier incidents such as the Kentucky Tragedy or the exploits of John Murrell, the "great western land pirate," he claimed that his romances were faithful to the known facts. He insisted that the historical events depicted in his romances were "strictly true," and that they were "very carefully prepared from and according to the evidence; the art of the romancer being held in close subjection to the historical authorities."[24]

That Simms attempted to be faithful to the *known* history does not mean that his romances are in all respects accurate. As has already been shown, he felt free to fill in gaps in the historical record, provided he remained within the realm of the believable. He, like most historians, was also sometimes misled by inaccurate sources. For instance, he claims that the facts in *Richard Hurdis* and *Border Beagles* are "beyond question" and based on interviews with Virgil Stewart, the man who captured the outlaw John Murrell, and certain other of the dramatis personae. "I can confidently affirm that all the leading characters are drawn from life," he wrote.[25] However, the truth is that Simms and the American public had been duped. According to James Penick Jr., Murrell was in fact a petty criminal whom Stewart hyped as the leader of a vast criminal organization, inciting a panic along the southern frontier.[26]

One of his most unusual experiments at blending history and fiction was *The Lily and the Totem*.[27] Simms intended this book to be more historical than his typical romances. As he explained the project to his publisher, the book would contain "the history of a most exciting and interesting endeavor of the French to colonize Florida with Huguenots, all enveloped in an atmosphere of fiction."[28] As published, the book contained an "Epistle Dedicatory" to James H. Hammond explaining the author's technique, twenty-five chapters with chapters 10, 13, 18, and 21 being historical summaries, and "a religious narrative poem on the subject of the preceeding history" as an appendix.[29] In the historical summaries he revealed where the narrative might or might not be relied upon as history. Here also he outlined facts essential to the completeness and truthfulness of his story, the introduction of which would ordinarily have disrupted the narrative flow of the romance.

In the dedication, he explained that "the design of the narrative which follows contemplates, in nearly equal degree, the picturesque and the historical." Whereas the author of a historical romance typically uses history "as a mere loop, upon which to hang his lively fancies and audacious inventions," Simms sought to reverse the process in *The Lily and the Totem*. Fancy would be employed for the sake of history instead of vice versa. "The romance here is not suffered to supersede the history," he wrote. "On the contrary, the design of the writer has been simply to supply the deficiencies of the record."[30]

Simms professed devotion to the historical facts uncovered by his careful research. He ventured to graft fiction upon history only in areas where details were sparse, "and seemed to demand the helping agency of art." Yet even here he was bound by truthfulness. In "helping" history he merely supplied "from the *probable*, the apparent deficiencies of the *actual*."[31] The finished product was not romance, but history enlivened or made dramatic by art.

This claim could be made for most of Simms's historical fiction, especially "Lucas de Ayllon" and his Revolutionary War romances. But *The Lily and the Totem* was unique in that the blending of history and fiction was less subtle. In it the lines between history and fiction were drawn more cleanly. In his historical summaries and footnotes, Simms told precisely how far the historical record supported his narrative. He also advised readers where his sources were questionable or disagreed with each other. "I have been at no . . . pains to disguise the chronicle, as will prevent the reader from separating,—should he desire to do so,—the *certain* from the *conjectural;* and yet, I trust, that I have succeeded in so linking the two together, as to prevent the lines of junction from obtruding themselves offensively upon his consciousness," he wrote.[32]

As was common for Simms's historical writings, *The Lily and the Totem* was designed to serve the purpose of moral instruction. To this end he showed how the Huguenot colonists—like Lucas de Ayllon—were excessively materialistic. Nicholas Meriwether has justly remarked that "their fatal mistake is in not recognizing the falseness of their values."[33] They would rather search for gold than raise provisions.[34]

Simms's most ambitious foray into the field of historical romance as well as into writing the history of the American Revolution was his series of eight Revolutionary War romances. These novels, originally published between 1835 and 1867, together constitute the most extensive treatment of the Revolutionary War in nineteenth-century American literature. They are a "remarkable achievement," in the words of Simms's biographer John C. Guilds, forming "by far the most illuminating portrayal of the American Revolution in fiction."[35] Noted South Carolina historian George C. Rogers Jr. found that the Revolutionary War romances "actually give a better picture of the times than do the history books."[36] And John Esten Cooke called the Revolutionary romances "the best histories that exist anywhere," of the Revolution in South Carolina.[37] Consequently, these novels deserve consideration in any study of how the history of the Revolution has been written and especially in a study of Simms's accomplishments as a historian, despite being fiction and not traditional history.

The Revolutionary romances also deserve significant attention because in them history is the foreground, whereas in *The Yemassee* and some of the border romances history serves more as a colorful background. In other words, history provides the setting for *The Yemassee* and the border romances, while history is the story in the Revolutionary romances.[38] It is also important to note that in the border romances Simms is often portraying recent events. The action in many of the border romances takes place too recently to have been studied with the same degree of historical detachment that is evident in the Revolutionary romances.

In order of publication, the Revolutionary romances are *The Partisan: A Tale of the Revolution* (1835); *Mellichampe: A Legend of the Santee* (1836); *The Kinsmen; or, The Black Riders of Congaree* (1841), revised and retitled *The Scout; or, The Black Riders of Congaree* (1854); *Katharine Walton; or, The Rebel of Dorchester: An Historical Romance of the Revolution in South Carolina* (1850); *The Sword and the Distaff; or, "Fair, Fat and Forty," A Story of the South, at the Close of the Revolution* (1852), revised and retitled *Woodcraft; or, Hawks about the Dovecote: A Story of the South, at the Close of the Revolution* (1854); *The Forayers; or, The Raid of the Dog-Days* (1855); *Eutaw: A Sequel to The Forayers; or, The Raid of the Dog-Days: A Tale of the Revolution* (1856); and *Joscelyn: A Tale of the Revolution* (1867). Each of these novels was popular enough to be reprinted. *The Partisan* was one of Simms's most popular romances, while *Woodcraft* is considered by many critics to be his finest novel, and its protagonist, Captain Porgy, is generally recognized as Simms's most memorable and well-drawn character. The last written novel, *Joscelyn,* was originally published serially in the New York monthly the *Old Guard,* and only in 1975 was it published in book form by the University of South Carolina Press. It, along with the seven other books, was reprinted in 1976 by the Reprint Company.

Read in order of publication, the novels do not chronologically follow the events of the Revolution, but they do chronicle the war in South Carolina from the late summer of 1775 (in *Joscelyn*) through the British evacuation of Charleston in December 1782 (in *Woodcraft*). The eight novels portray the war in backcountry forests, swamps, and Charleston, and give attention to both minor skirmishes and major battles, such as those at Camden, Ninety Six, and Eutaw Springs.

Simms's goal in writing these books was simple. He wanted to describe the Revolution in South Carolina, as he understood it, in a lively narrative. Such a history, he hoped, would be widely read and would both inform and help to form good morals and patriotism while it entertained. He "particularly intended to do honor to the resolute and hardy patriotism of the scattered bands of patriots," who carried on the fight for independence "among the swamps and thickets, . . . keeping alive the spirit of the country."[39]

As he understood it, the Revolution in South Carolina was a civil war between Whigs and Tories.[40] With the state divided into almost equal factions of Whigs and Tories, the war quickly degenerated into a brutal conflict with neighbor fighting against neighbor. Raids carried out by small, loosely organized bands of partisans occurred far more often than large pitched battles between professional armies.

Throughout this series of novels, as in all his history, Simms strove both to be accurate and to tell a good tale. He clearly states his devotion to historical veracity in the introduction to *The Partisan:* "In this romance, even where the written history has not been found, tradition and the local chronicles preserved as family records, have furnished adequate authorities."[41] Simms's familiarity with published, manuscript, and oral sources served as a solid historical foundation upon which to build with fiction.

Something has already been said of Simms's access to extensive manuscript collections. Exactly what he knew of oral tradition, and from whom he learned it, is difficult to ascertain. Fortunately, he has left some clues. For instance, in a review of Elizabeth Ellet's *Women of the Revolution,* he relates how, as a boy, he learned much local history "at the knees of those who were young spectators in the grand panorama of our Revolution. . . . This was their favourite topic; and each had details of the local struggle which were as interesting as they were veracious."[42] This is likely how he learned the story of Frampton told in *The Partisan.*[43] Whenever he undertook a new work of history or historical fiction, he familiarized himself with the setting and actively sought the counsel of anyone who could enlighten him as to local history and lore. In *Joscelyn,* Simms tells us that he gathered much "old local tradition . . . and little snatches of anecdote, dimly remembered details of domestic strife and excitement" of the Revolutionary War in and around Augusta from James H. Hammond, John Bones, "and subsequently by others who I sought for information."[44]

In the dedication to *The Forayers,* Simms acknowledges borrowing freely from the notes of his neighbor General David Flavel Jamison, who owned a large library and was knowledgeable in the history and legends of Orangeburg District.[45] Joseph Johnson, author of *Traditions and Reminiscences Chiefly of the American Revolution in the South* (1851), receives the author's thanks in the dedication to *Woodcraft* for sharing his "communications" and "researches."[46] William Peterfield Trent, who, writing in 1892, had access to people who knew Simms, reports that Simms interviewed still-living members of Francis Marion's brigade.[47] We also know from Simms's own notes that he interviewed an eyewitness to Isaac Hayne's hanging, an event he made good use of in *Katharine Walton.*[48]

Simms was also familiar with all the important published sources on the Revolution in South Carolina. Among those sources that he relied heavily upon for his Revolutionary War novels are Alexander Garden's *Anecdotes of the Revolutionary War in America;* Lt. Colonel Henry Lee's *The Campaign of 1781 in the Carolinas;* General William Moultrie's *Memoirs of the American Revolution;* David Ramsay's *History of South Carolina* and *History of the Revolution of South Carolina;* and Lt. Colonel Banastre Tarleton's *History of the Campaigns of 1780 and 1781, in the Southern Provinces of North America.*

As a result of his diligent research, Simms's Revolutionary novels are generally accurate in their details. They are usually organized around an actual event, and most of the major and many of the minor characters are historical personages—or at least based upon real people. He deviates from the strictest standards of historical accuracy most frequently in the invention of conversations or in "changing of dates by a few days or the condensing of separate but similar events into one to achieve economy and to heighten the dramatic impact."[49]

Like other romantic historians, Simms, of course, romanticized history. The heroes in his novels were invariably of sterling character, and his villains were quite often very bad. For example, he describes the "sinister" British Colonel Banastre Tarleton's pursuit of the fleeing Americans after the battle of Camden thus: "Tarleton, with his eye kindled with fight, and a lip that seemed quivering with its pleasurable convulsions, led his cavalry in pursuit of the fugitives, marking his progress for twenty-two miles from the field of battle with proofs of that sanguinary appetite for blood, which formed the leading feature of his character, according to history and tradition, in all the fields of Carolina."[50] Taking advantage of the greater license afforded the writer of fiction, his dramatization of the past sometimes took on an aspect of the sensational.

Be that as it may, the chief value of Simms's Revolutionary novels lies not in the historical details, but in the overall picture they paint of Carolina society at war. Novelists often surpass historians in the creation of authentic settings and lifelike characters with believable motivations.[51] Through his novels Simms paints a more realistic, and certainly more memorable, picture of revolutionary South Carolina than have many historians who have tackled the same subject. One has only to reflect on the great mass of South Carolinians, who are invisible in most histories. Poor whites, yeomen, women, and African Americans frequently remain nameless in the pages of histories of the Revolution, but in Simms's novels, characters such as yeoman Jack Bannister, "Thumbscrew," Millhouse, the widow Eveleigh, Janet Berkeley, and the slaves Scipio, Benny Bowlegs, and Tom are among the most interesting and heroic, and are indispensable to the narrative.[52] One critic charged that the "low" characters in *The Partisan* were too many and too prominent. Simms countered that low characters "predominate in all warfare, and in all times of warfare."[53] For the writer to paint a contrary picture would be dishonest. Most readers and critics seem to side with Simms on this point: during their author's lifetime the Revolutionary novels won the praise of astute reviewers, who recognized that through fiction Simms was able to convey historical truth.[54]

As Simms understood and portrayed the Revolution in his novels, it originated in social forces, in ideology mingled with practical considerations, and in the burgeoning American nationalism. But his romances are about individuals, and individuals play the decisive roles in his history of the Revolution. Though influenced by social forces, his characters weigh arguments for and against independence when deciding whether to back the rebellion. Anticipating twentieth-century intellectual historians who found the justification for rebellion in republican ideology, he placed great importance on talk about rights and their defense against corrupt governments. Simms has William Henry Drayton make the colonists' case at a 1775 backcountry public gathering in *Joscelyn.* "He proceeded to show," Simms wrote, "what were the rights of the people under the British Constitution; in what manner these rights had been invaded, and what would be the dangers to American and even British liberty, if the aggressions of Parliament and the Crown were permitted to continue and grow."[55]

In another instance, Simms describes how an unschooled boy came to understand the issues at stake. "The furious popular discussions of the five preceeding years [1775–80] had not been unheard by the youthful soldier; and its appeals were not lost upon" him. Through the opinions of friends and neighbors, not the tracts of Tom Paine, he "acquired some knowledge of the abstract question upon which [the Revolution] depended; and though his thoughts were all vague and indistinct on the subject, the rights of man, the freedom of the citizen, and the integrity of his country, he had learned to feel should all be among the first considerations, as their preservation was always the first care, of the true patriot."[56] The protection of self and home mingled with love of country and defense of her rights to produce strong feelings of patriotism. Simms understood both how abstract ideas could play on the feelings as well as the intellect and that ideas were most forceful when they were linked to concrete rather than abstract considerations.

In one of the most memorable scenes of the entire series, Simms expresses the argument for independence in a more earthy manner. In *The Scout,* he has the rustic patriot "Supple" Jack Bannister try to convince one-armed Loyalist tavern keeper Isaac Muggs of the justice of the Whig cause and republican principles.

> "It's agin natur' and reason, and a man's own seven senses," said Supple Jack, "to reckon on any man's right to make laws for another, when he don't live in the same country with him. I say, King George, living in England, never had a right to make John Bannister, living on the Congaree, pay him taxes for tea or anything."
>
> "But it's all the same country, England and America, Jack Bannister," [said Isaac Muggs].
>
> "Jimini!—if that's the how, what makes you give 'em different names, I want to know?"[57]

After failing to persuade Muggs with his less-than-impressive powers of reasoning, Bannister challenges the one-armed Loyalist to a wrestling match to decide the issue. As one would expect Muggs is beaten, then renounces his Loyalist views. There were many more Jack Bannisters in South Carolina than William Henry Draytons, and it is one of the merits of these novels that Simms has given a voice to a class of citizens underrepresented in most histories.

As the colonies matured and no longer needed the protection of the mother country, it was only natural that indigenous nationalism combined with republican sentiments would lead Americans to seek their independence from a distant government that they perceived as a threat to their liberties. "The American colonies have passed through their minority," one of Simms's characters explained. Proof of this could be found in their ability to withstand the British invasion: "The mental and social developments which enable them to defend themselves by arms, are in proof of resources which revolt at foreign dominion. If the American mind is equal to its own necessities, it is adequate to its own rule." The growing American national spirit demanded independence so that it could reach its full potential. Under such circumstances, "the denial of our right . . . is the worst slavery."[58]

But not all Carolinians saw the justice of these claims. As does his *History of South Carolina,* Simms's romances depict the state nearly equally divided between Whigs and Tories. A large number of the Loyalists in Simms's romances were recent immigrants who had not resided in Carolina long enough to develop a preference for her over the British government.[59] Others remained loyal out of resentment against the lowcountry elite, who played leading roles in the independence movement. Most people's loyalties could be accounted for by their particular circumstances and interest: "The revolutionary war, in South Carolina, did not so much divide the people, because of the tendencies to loyalty, or liberty, on either hand, as because of social and other influences—personal and sectional feuds—natural enough to a new country, in which one third of the people were of foreign birth."[60] The charge that the Loyalists in the Revolutionary War novels are all lower-class scoundrels is an old but unjust one.[61] In truth Simms was fairer to the Loyalists than many historians before or since have been. While some of his Tories were indeed scoundrels or were from the lower class, others were local aristocrats or had honorable reasons for loyalty.

"Hell-fire" Dick, one of Simms's most famous Tories, is one of those lower-class scoundrels. An opportunistic bandit, taking advantage of the anarchy occasioned by a guerrilla war, "Hell-fire" Dick is filled with social resentment against the well-bred planter aristocracy. Another Loyalist, Thomas Browne, though a scoundrel and not wellborn, is somewhat more sympathetically portrayed. Browne launches a campaign of vengeance against Whigs after being unjustly tarred and feathered: "In the name of liberty, they subjected the fainting wretch to the scourge, and smeared over with tar and feathers, torn by the lash, he was left fainting."[62] After suffering this abuse at the hands of the Whigs, his subsequent career is understandable if not excusable. Edward Conway, the Tory outlaw of *The Scout,* came from good (or half good) stock: he was the half brother of the Whig hero. Another Tory, Colonel Sinclair from *The Forayers,* is neither lowbred nor a scoundrel. Sinclair, father of the book's hero, is a true gentleman from an old Carolina family. "Never was man more honorable, or more steadfast to the polar star of truth and justice,"[63] but Sinclair simply could not countenance rebellion against his monarch and separation from the mother country. Ella Monckton of *Katharine Walton,* who simply adopted the political inclinations of her father and had a crush on an English soldier, was another respectable Loyalist. Ella possessed "a just, discriminating judgment, high resolves, deliberate thought, and a warm, deeply-feeling, and loving nature."[64] Simms's Loyalists are never heroes, but not all of them are lowbred villains either.

Some of the Loyalists in the novels eventually undergo a change in sympathies. This, he tells us, was not uncommon. Toward the close of the Revolution "many were the tories, converted to the patriot cause, who, at the eleventh hour, displayed the most conspicuous bravery fighting on the popular side. And this must not be suffered to lower them in our opinion."[65]

Perhaps the Loyalists received fairer treatment at Simms's hands than they did from many historians, because he saw the war in Carolina as a civil war, pitting Carolinians against each other, as much as a war against the British.[66] The division of the Sinclair and Conway families was by no means atypical. "These have been . . . miserable years to the country, since the beginning of this war. Neighbor against neighbor, friend against friend, and sometimes even brother arming and going out to battle with his brother." Personal animosities were vented on the battlefield as endless cycles of vengeance played themselves out. The Whig hero Clarence Conway explained, "the strife . . . is of no ordinary character. It is a strife between brothers, all of whom have learned to hate as I do, and to seek to destroy with an appetite of far greater anxiety. The terms between whig and tory, now, are death only. No quarter is demanded—none is given."[67] The severity and personal nature of the war only intensified in the absence of the Continental Army after the surrender of Charleston in May and the defeat of General Gates at Camden in August 1780. The revenge-driven characters—"Goggle" Blonay, the elder Frampton, and Jake Clarkson in *The Partisan, Mellichampe,* and *The Scout*—as well as Thomas Browne (a real figure) powerfully show the ruthlessness of the civil war in South Carolina.

After the Continental Army was driven from the state following the battle of Camden, the defense of South Carolina was left to the badly outnumbered local militia led by partisans such as Generals Marion, Pickens, and Sumter. To compensate for their lack of numbers, the Carolinians resorted to guerrilla tactics. Relying on surprise, ambush, and the advantages which naturally accrue to an army fighting on its own soil, the small bands of patriots kept up a constant harassment of the numerically superior British forces. Attacking the British and their Loyalist allies where they were weak and retreating before larger forces was the policy of the partisans. The partisan forces were always on the move to avoid being surprised themselves: "Their cavalry was kept in motion startling the British with incessant alarms; hovering about their posts, snatching up their convoys, and occasionally cutting off their detachments. In this sort of work, we find all our great captains of partisans equally engaged, Marion, Sumter, Pickens, Lee, Maham, Harden, the two Hamptons, Horry, Taylor, and many others."[68] Sparsely populated South Carolina, with its plentiful swamps and forests to serve as hiding places, proved an ideal theatre for partisan warfare. The Carolinians' guerrilla tactics prevented the British from consolidating their gains in the state and wore them down through attrition.

The partisan forces were citizen militias, not professional armies. Because they were composed of citizen-volunteers, their enrollment fluctuated substantially. "Historians tell you that the men of Marion and Sumter went and came at pleasure," Simms wrote. But, he explained, this was necessitated by their circumstances. "The soldiers were all farmers, interested necessarily in the domestic progress, and required to see, at certain periods, to their families and agricultural interests—to the season of planting, and of harvest, especially." Not only did the citizen-soldiers have farms to tend to and families to feed, which could call them away from camp, they also had to protect their families from the enemy as well as from bands of roving outlaws like the one led by "Hell-fire" Dick. "When, too, it is understood that the country was perpetually traversed by foreign refugees, having no families, no responsibilities to society, and seeking plunder only, it will not be thought surprising if the partisans, having done a severe duty of three months at a spell, found it necessary to hurry home to see that the homestead was kept in order, and made as secure and prosperous as it was possible to be."[69] A strong defender of the militia, Simms wanted readers to understand that cowardice or lack of resolve were not the causes for the frequent delinquency of troops. The militiamen were citizens who had taken up arms in defense of their homes as well as their liberties. It was only natural that they should continue to see to the security of home and family even if it meant temporarily leaving camp.

They excelled at hit-and-run maneuvers, but their methods were unconventional and they were sometimes out of their element in pitched battles. Simms did not fault them for this either. In warfare, results mattered more than methods: "That our backwoods boys bungled frequently in winning their victories, may afford a surly fireside satisfaction to the beaten party. . . . We may leave our enemies this satisfaction surely." While the British might console themselves with the knowledge that they had fought according to the laws of war, Simms was content with victory: "The *laws* of war are, no doubt, very admirable and wholesome provisions; but I confess, with other politicians, that I prefer the *spoils*. Our rangers knew little of the one, but they had an instinctive appreciation of the other; and contrived to get them, by hook and by crook." He little cared that the partisans, without bayonets of their own, fled before the bayonet charges of the British. On the contrary, he faulted the Continental officers who placed them in the front of their battle formations where they were certain to be overrun. Neither did he care if raw, undrilled troops preferred to fire from behind trees than out in the open. "For my own part," Simms wrote, "I shall be very sorry that the day should ever arrive when the good sense of this doctrine shall be subjected to dispute."[70]

Through these unconventional means the Carolina partisans managed, against long odds, to keep forces in the field, thus inspiring their countrymen while steadily thinning the British ranks. Unable to decisively defeat the British and their

Loyalist allies, they were nevertheless able to sufficiently weaken them to prepare the way for their ultimate defeat by the regular forces of the Continental army. "For it is not to be doubted or denied, though the fact has never been honestly asserted by our historians," Simms noted, "that but for the partisan warfare of the South, the regular armies would have taken the field in vain."[71] This was the supreme achievement of the partisans, which Simms thought went unrecognized because of a New England sectional bias that underrated the accomplishments of South Carolinians and of the historians' bias that favored reporting large battles over small skirmishes. "Badly armed and worse clad, fighting for years . . . without pay, and almost without thanks or acknowledgment, their achievements slurred over and disparaged, as they have been too frequently since—while the deeds of others were exaggerated," the Carolina partisans managed to significantly contribute to the American victory while escaping the notice of historians.[72] Simms hoped his Revolutionary novels would help give these men the credit he thought they were due.

Listen to Porgy's defense of the militia after the battle of Eutaw, one of the last major engagements of the war. At Eutaw on September 8, 1781, on the cusp of victory, American forces became disorganized when they discovered a supply of liquor in the camp of the hastily retreating British. In this vulnerable state they suffered heavily from a British counterattack. Back at camp, Porgy explains the day's failure to his comrades: "We poor militiamen, rangers, riflemen, and partisans, as we are called, should lay bare, whenever we can, the vices and the worthlessnesses of these martinets, and regulars, who invariably excuse their own defeats by charging their disasters upon the militia." Militiamen were no less brave than regulars. When militiamen run, it is typically because incompetent generals have placed them, poorly armed and without bayonets, in the first rank to meet British regulars: "They seem to be put forward, as David put forward Uriah, to be slain certainly." A wiser disposition would have employed the militia as skirmishers, or placed them on the flanks of the main force to serve as sharpshooters, or intermingled veteran militiamen with regular troops. The fighting at Eutaw showed that the distinction between the courage and discipline of regular troops and militia is a false one. Militiamen would display admirable courage and discipline if only they were used properly, and at Eutaw it was the Continentals' lack of discipline that deprived the Americans of a complete victory. How was the victory lost? asked Porgy. Not by the militiamen, who fought well and bravely. They were denied victory "by the dispersion of our regulars among the tents; by the mad fury with which they fastened upon the rum and brandy." If Marion had been in charge, he wagers, the British would have been utterly routed.[73]

Not only did Simms hope to bring to light unrecorded deeds of valor, but he also hoped his novels would serve as a means of educating his readers in patriotism and virtue. He always considered the moral elevation of mankind one of the chief duties of artists. This could only be accomplished by painting a true picture. "I am decided that a nation gains only in glory and in greatness, as it is resolute to behold and to pursue the truth," he wrote. The lessons of the Revolutionary heroes should not be neglected. Stories of "that deliberate valour, that unyielding patriotism, which, in a few spirits, defying danger and above the sense of privation, could keep alive the sacred fires of liberty in the thick swamps and gloomy forests of Carolina," he thought could be profitably read.[74]

Simms believed that his novels were truer than standard histories because he attempted to make them a people's history. The story of the Revolution in South Carolina was not just about great (and terrible) generals and decisive battles. It was equally, or perhaps more, the story of the unnamed men and women, black and white, who sacrificed their comfort, their property, and sometimes their lives in the cause of liberty on forgotten battlefields. His depiction of blacks as contented loyal companions of their white masters is likely to offend modern readers, but it is to his credit that he threw light upon elements of society ignored by other historians. We may question his interpretation of the master-slave relationship, but he at least recognized that slaves had a role to play in the Revolution. Too many historians, he thought, were "quite too apt to overlook the best essentials of society . . . —in order to dilate on great events,—scenes in which men are merely massed, while a single favourite overtops all the rest, the Hero . . . absorbing within himself all the consideration which a more veracious and philosophical mode of writing would distribute over states and communities, and the humblest walks of life."[75]

The heroes of the Revolutionary novels were the patriotic citizens of South Carolina, not Generals Marion or Greene. The novel form allowed Simms to address individual characters and their motivations in greater detail than history could. Thus he could more easily dwell on the moral lessons of the Revolution while doing "honor to the resolute and hardy patriotism of the scattered bands of patriots." The historian who reads the novels today is rewarded with a sophisticated portrait of Carolina society at war that cannot be found elsewhere.[76]

Perhaps the greatest value of Simms's historical fiction was that it reached a wider audience than history typically would and it taught readers some history while keeping them entertained. Charles E. A. Gayarré, a historian whose ideas on the relationship between history and fiction paralleled Simms's own, wrote, "When history is not disfigured by inappropriate invention, but merely embellished and made attractive by being set in a glittering frame, this artful preparation honies the cup of useful knowledge, and makes it acceptable to the lips of the multitude." Thus many had learned some history from the novels of Walter Scott and had been provoked to further study, "who, without that tempting bait, would have turned away from what appeared to them to be but a dry and barren field."[77]

Simms himself recognized that this was the chief value of his historical romances. When first published, his Revolutionary romances were "so many new developments and discoveries to our people." Many who would never read David Ramsay first learned the nature of the Revolution in South Carolina through the adventures of Captain Porgy. Simms's romances awakened an interest in history and "opened the way to historical studies among us—they suggested clews to the historian— . . . they showed to succeeding laborers—far abler than myself—what treasures of *material,* lay waiting for the shaping hands of future genius."[78]

| SEVEN |

South Carolina in the Revolution
Simms and the North

The policy in what you do should be drawn from the inscription that met the eyes of Spencer's knight over all the doors (but one) in the enchanted castle—"Be bold! Be bold! Be bold!" It was over one door only that was written—"Be not too bold!"
—Simms to Nathaniel Beverley Tucker, May 30, 1850

In the summer of 1848 Simms published two lengthy reviews of Lorenzo Sabine's *The American Loyalists,* "South Carolina in the Revolution" and "The Siege of Charleston in the American Revolution," in the July and October issues of the *Southern Quarterly Review.* Sabine's book charged that South Carolina was a hotbed of Tory sentiments during the Revolution and that the state owed its independence to the exertions of New England soldiers. Simms considered such charges not only untrue but offensive, and he worked to correct Sabine's misrepresentations in these reviews. Thus began his battle with New Englanders over South Carolina's role in the Revolution, a battle which would last until the Civil War.[1]

Simms was taken aback by the charges Sabine leveled against South Carolina. "In the midst of our serenest sky," Simms later explained, "the bolt has fallen among us!"[2] New Englanders had always written American history as if it were simply New England history writ large,[3] but never before could Simms recall one section actually attacking another. Even during the most bitter sectional disputes South Carolinians never suspected that their history and ancestors might fall under attack. The Revolution, after all, was sacrosanct as the great unifying event in the nation's past.

Well might South Carolinians have been surprised by Sabine's book. The first generation of American historians to write about the Revolution had lived through and often actively participated in the events they wrote about. They were passionately committed to the Revolution and the young republic to which it gave birth. This commitment showed up in their history as a strong sense of nationalism. Dedicated to national unity and cultural independence to go along with America's political independence, they produced for the United States a national history. Well versed in classical history, they knew that republics were fragile creations and large republics were supposed to be untenable. Therefore when diverse conditions within the United States spawned party battles that seemed to threaten their young republic, American historians responded by stressing their nation's unity.[4]

One example of this devotion to national unity is their portrayal of the Loyalists. The generation of historians contemporary with the Revolution were generally predisposed to promote the idea that the Revolution was a unified national movement by treating the Loyalists as a small, unimportant minority. Except for David Ramsay of South Carolina, who dealt with the Loyalists sympathetically, they tended to portray the Loyalists as shortsighted, mean-minded, corrupt men.[5]

Despite the bias toward national unity, the history produced by this generation was colored by localism. The majority of their histories were local histories, partly because of the difficulties involved in research and travel. But it was partly also due to strong local loyalties, whose roots ran deeper than loyalties to the new nation. Indeed "the most cosmopolitan writers commonly used a particular locale as the backdrop for defining the nation's character and past."[6] Their eagerness to demonstrate America's political and cultural unity led them to commit the logical error of generalizing from the specific. They generalized about the national experience from the particular experience of their own specific locale.

Since most early historians were from New England, the history of the Revolution took on a decided Yankee flavor. Even some southern historians, such as David Ramsay and Chief Justice John Marshall of Virginia, were not inclined to rebut the notion of New England's cultural and moral superiority. This reticence may have had to do with both men's Federalist politics. Additionally, Ramsay's New England sympathies were undoubtedly augmented by his membership in Charleston's Congregational Church and the fact that he was born and educated in the North.[7] So, although there was a vigorous tradition of southern historical writing dating back to John Smith and Robert Beverley, no one produced a southern interpretation of national history until George Tucker's four-volume *History of the United States from the Colonization to the End of the Twenty-Sixth Congress, in 1841* (1854–58).[8] As Michael Kammen has correctly observed, "the hegemony of New Englanders over the writing of American history," perpetuated (and perhaps exacerbated) social tensions. New England's hegemony has been resented by midwesterners and New Yorkers, "but nowhere has it been despised so much as in the South."[9] Nevertheless, the work early historians produced was national, not sectional, history since it stressed America's unity. While writers may have displayed local biases, no section was subjected to criticism for not conforming to the nation's ideals or the ideals of the writer's section.

The second generation of American historians did not write in the shadow of the Revolution and of the divisive battles over ratification of the Constitution. Therefore, even though travel was easier and they had better access to sources than earlier historians, they were not as concerned as their predecessors with promoting national unity. These romantic-era historians produced the first sectional, as opposed to regional, American histories. The repudiation of literary nationalism was mirrored in "the changing emphasis of political writing of the period.

During the 1810s and 1820s, statesmen-writers . . . continued to advance the vision of a unified America typical of the colonial and revolutionary periods." By the 1830s however, the increasing sectionalism of literature reflected the changing tone of political discourse.[10] Similarly, their distance from the Revolution made it easier for romantic era historians like Lorenzo Sabine to write sympathetically about the Loyalists.

Like the first generation of historians of the Revolution, Simms was a strong nationalist. This is not to say, however, that his history was not colored by local prejudices. In the introduction to *The Wigwam and the Cabin,* he explained, "to be *national* in literature, one must needs be *sectional.* No one mind can fully or fairly illustrate the characteristics of any great country; and he who shall depict *one section* faithfully, has made his proper and sufficient contribution to the great work of *national* illustration."[11] By faithfully depicting the history of his state, Simms was contributing to a national history, as others had done before him. Yet as national politics became more poisoned by sectionalism, so too did history. Some historians began to stress America's diversity instead of its unity. Local pride began to manifest itself as bitter sectionalism. New Englanders in particular started to view slavery as evidence of the South's deviance. For the first time, the South's role in the Revolution was under attack.

Lorenzo Sabine's *The American Loyalists* was just such a sectional history. An Abolitionist politician from Maine, Sabine berated the South for not contributing its fair share to the struggle for American independence. He argued that South Carolina's revolutionaries were hampered by the existence of slavery in their state. Sabine tallied the number of troops each state contributed to the continental army and found that nearly 68,000 of the over 230,000 men who served were from Massachusetts, while the combined total for all the states south of Pennsylvania was less than 60,000.[12] However, it should be noted that he counted enlistments, not men. If one man enlisted four times, he was counted four times. But according to Sabine's math, South Carolina was full of Loyalists while New England provided more than her share of patriots.

Indeed, according to Sabine, Charleston's surrender to the British was attributable to a lack of commitment to the patriot cause. South Carolina, he claimed, "could not defend herself against her own Tories; and it is hardly an exaggeration to add, that more Whigs of New England were sent to her aid, and now lie buried in her soil, than she sent from it to every scene of strife from Lexington to Yorktown."[13] The southern colonies, and South Carolina especially, according to Sabine, owed their independence to the heroic sacrifices of New England soldiers.

Simms first replied to Sabine's criticism of South Carolina's role in the Revolution in an article for the July 1848 issue of the *Southern Quarterly Review,* which was also published in an 1853 book titled *South-Carolina in the Revolutionary War: Being a Reply to Certain Misrepresentations and Mistakes of Recent Writers, in Relation to the Course and Conduct of this State.* During his northern lecture tour of 1856 and southern lectures of May and June 1857, he again defended South Carolina against Sabine's indictment.

In the *Southern Quarterly Review,* he praised Sabine's historical essay at the beginning of the book for being clearly and forcefully written. Though he doubted the utility of a book on the Loyalists, he was not even "prepared to quarrel with that taste, or passion for novelty, which, of late, seems disposed to busy itself in rescuing the memories of the American Loyalists." Very few of the Loyalists were "distinguished by remarkable endowments," and he questioned the moral object of praising people whom he considered lacking in patriotism. But "many of them, doubtless, were very worthy people," and "some of them had respectable talents," so he could understand the need to study them. "Let the deserving have their dues," he wrote.[14]

His objection was to Sabine's charge that South Carolina was so enfeebled with supporters of the Loyalist cause that it owed its independence to New England soldiers. This error, Simms wrote, sprang from a common fault of Yankee historians and politicians. Long has New England regarded "her children as the saints, to whom the possession of the earth has been finally decreed." Therefore, according to Simms, they naturally assumed that all good deeds were performed by New Englanders: "They have all the talents, all the virtues, and perform all the achievements." Reading only their own historians, they have no reason to believe otherwise.[15]

Simms thought his review might serve as a corrective. If he could not change Yankee minds, he might at least persuade honest people in other sections and provide South Carolinians with the ammunition to defend their ancestors. In 1856 he still believed he might do good by meeting Sabine's charges head on. Just eight days before he first delivered "South Carolina in the Revolution" to a northern audience, Simms optimistically wrote to George Bancroft, William Cullen Bryant, and others that he trusted that through his lectures he would "be able to disabuse the public of the North of many mistaken impressions which do us wrong."[16]

However he greatly underestimated northern resentment against slavery and South Carolina, the hotbed of treason. His proposed route—through Buffalo, Rochester, and Syracuse—took him through the heart of the "Burned-Over District." So named because it had been so hotly evangelized during the Second Great Awakening, the "Burned-Over District" was the epicenter for northern radical reform movements. A quarter century before Simms's tour, Charles Grandison Finney arrived in Rochester to lead an important series of revivals. He preached Arminianism and perfectionism to New Yorkers and "said flatly that if Christians united and dedicated their lives to the task, they could convert the world and bring on the millennium in three months."[17] They became convinced that Christians had it within their power to eradicate sin from the world by perfecting themselves and others, and that by doing so they could hasten Christ's return. High on the list of sins that needed to be eliminated were sloth, intemperance, and slavery. So lazy slavemasters were at least doubly cursed and in need of reforming, by force if necessary, as they stood in the way of the millennium.[18]

Simms expected a more sympathetic hearing from New Yorkers. Simms spent most of his summers in New York and counted New Yorkers James Lawson and Evert Duyckinck among his closest friends, even naming one of his daughters for Lawson's wife, Mary. "I have come to look upon [New York] as my own city," he wrote to Lawson in 1845. Later, after the death of his daughter Valeria, his fourth child to die in a short period of time, he "seriously deliberate[d]" moving to Philadelphia or New York.[19] Indeed, so close was Simms's association with New York that during an 1846 campaign his political opponents accused him of being a northern man and having northern sympathies.[20]

Earlier New York had been aligned with the South and West against Boston's literary and political chauvinism.[21] Under the first party system, Jeffersonians in the middle states, the South, and the West worked together to isolate New England Federalists. This political cooperation continued, though to a lesser extent, into the early years of the second party system. Early on, people of the West and middle states were quite as resentful of New England cultural arrogance as southerners.[22] Simms even thought New Yorkers were closer in temperament to southerners than to New Englanders. When Lawson's wife complained of the coldness of New England hospitality, he explained that they "lack that warmth & eagerness which to a Southron & to you New Yorkers are so essential to the deportment of friends."[23] What is the bond of union between New York, Philadelphia, and Massachusetts, he asked Nathaniel Beverley Tucker in December 1849: "They clash in interest, in character, in almost every thing."[24] Yet the spread of a reforming impulse that considered slavery an abomination and the development of northern nationalism increasingly left the South isolated within the Union.

Another reason he may have expected a warmer reception than awaited him is found in a notice he wrote of the 1844 proceedings of the New-York Historical Society. After praising the New-York Historical Society for its efforts to preserve the state's history, he briefly discusses the Society's dinner and some of the dignitaries in attendance. Then, he says,

> It is a sign not wanting in significance, that, at this dinner, so disgustingly did the New-England orators dilate upon the glories and the greatness of New-England, to the utter exclusion of all other subjects, as to provoke a very manly and spirited speech from Mr. Charles F. Hoffman, in which, while he seeks to repair the slight and injustice, he adroitly reflects on the vanity and the indecency of these self-complacent Yankees, who, as has been shown, have come really to consider the United States as their exclusive possession, to fancy that they have founded it wholly, achieved all its successes, reared up and established its liberties, and, voting themselves the saints, have concluded to take possession of the spoils. Enough;—this impudence will provoke resistance, and finally cure itself.[25]

Knowing that Hoffman, a New York editor and poet who moved in the same literary circle as Simms, Irving, Cooper, Bryant, Paulding, and Duyckinck, had gotten away with criticizing New England historians in New York for their sectionalism undoubtedly encouraged Simms. But, as he would learn, twelve years can make a big difference. Furthermore, Hoffman spoke to an assembly of historians from across the nation. Simms planned to lecture to the New York public, much of it of Yankee origin. And Hoffman was not a slaveowner from South Carolina.

Charges such as those issued by Sumner and Sabine came as a shock to Simms. "In the midst of a serene period," he said, ". . . suddenly . . . it is charged against us that we are living upon a spurious reputation—that the ancestors of whom it has been our pride to boast, were, in fact, false to their duties and their country—recreant to their trusts—heedless of their honour—faithless to their bretheren—traitors in the cabinet and cowards in the field!"[26] Such bitterly sectional history was something new that caught South Carolinians by surprise.

"It will be permitted to a son of Carolina to assert her character;—to reassert her history;—and endeavor to maintain her argument," said Simms.[27] It was true that South Carolina had contributed few men to the continental army compared to Massachusetts. This was not, however, indicative of a lack of patriotic zeal. Rather, it was because South Carolinians preferred to serve in their militia or as irregular partisans while the majority of Massachusetts' soldiers enlisted in the continental army. Taking this into consideration, in Simms's estimation South Carolina furnished 35,000 soldiers out of a white population of 80,000. Massachusetts, he pointed out by way of comparison, furnished a total of only 88,000 soldiers out of a population of 352,000.[28]

Furthermore, Simms asserted that South Carolina was not saved by the exertions of New England troops. Although South Carolina received assistance, most of it came from Georgia, North Carolina, Virginia, and Maryland. Never, did she receive "any assistance, whatsoever, from her States North of the Hudson."[29] Yet, South Carolina sent one thousand troops to join the northern army at Philadelphia after the fall of Charleston—when they were most needed at home. According to Simms, the fact of the matter was that "the South sent a hundred men East of the Hudson, during the revolution, for every one that ever came South of it, except at the single siege of York."[30]

Simms freely admitted Sabine's claim that a large portion of South Carolina's population remained loyal to the crown. In fact, he had often before acknowledged that his state had possessed a substantial and active Loyalist population and that the war there more closely resembled a civil war than a war for independence. These had long been themes of his work. Therefore, though Simms's treatment of the Loyalists is not approving, it is much more sophisticated and sympathetic than most of the revolutionary historians'. This is not to say that Simms portrayed the Loyalists as being as high-minded as the patriots. Nor could he even think of a good reason to resuscitate their names as Sabine had done.

The Loyalists were motivated by the "natural jealousies" of the poor interior settlements toward the affluent coastal settlements: "The common appeal of the loyalist leaders was to the vulgar prejudices against rank and wealth, the haughty assumptions of the citizens and planters of the seaboard, and their free expenditure of the public money."[31] Even in this description of the Loyalists, we see that Simms credited them with more than purely selfish motives.

Simms's Loyalists were distinguished by more than just their "natural jealousies." They were also distinguished from the patriots geographically and ethnically. According to Simms, Loyalists normally lived in the backcountry and were often of English, Scottish, or German descent. In their defense, Simms wrote: "They had their arguments for Loyalty, and these were founded equally in reason and in natural sympathies." They were not small-minded men. "They were faithful to their old traditions;—faithful to the laws and the authorities;—faithful to every sentiment in which their childhood had been trained; and were, accordingly, incapable of seeing with the eyes of the natives, the same degree of provocation or wrong which they felt, or the propriety of that revolution which they held to be the proper remedy."[32] Additionally, Simms reminded his readers that South Carolina contained a Quaker population, whose religious devotion to pacifism accounted for their hostility to the revolutionaries and *de facto* put them in the Loyalist camp.[33] Many of the Loyalists, under other circumstances, would have been good citizens of whom any community could be proud. But in these circumstances, "praise is out of the question."[34]

That South Carolina possessed a large number of Loyalists was not a matter of shame in Simms's opinion. On the contrary, it increased the honor of South Carolina's patriots.

> In fact, so far from disparaging her claims, this serves to make them brighter and more glorious. Her fame is the greater, in degree with the numbers who were thus, within her own bowels, laboring at her destruction. The more you increase the numbers of the foreign Loyalists in her domain, the more you heighten the merits of those who braved them from the first, nor shrunk beneath the conflict, when these were openly arrayed beneath the banner of Britain and sustained by British & Hessian Legionaires.[35]

It was a matter of pride among South Carolinians that their ancestors had been able to achieve so much against such great odds.

Sabine's most censorious accusation, though, was that loyalty to the crown ran so strong in Charleston that the city needlessly surrendered, after offering only token resistance to the British, in hopes of rejoining the empire. Charleston, Simms rebutted, resisted as long as possible against a superior force. Five thousand troops heroically held Charleston for six weeks against the combined might of the Royal Navy and 12,000 British regulars. In the end, "she succumbed, to famine, only; though her batteries, and one half of her houses were in ruins! And this defence was made wholly by the troops of the two Carolinas & Virginia, behind mere field works which the French engineers pronounced untenable from the beginning!" At the very least, Simms told his audience, Charleston put up more of a fight than many other cities. If Charleston should be scolded, "what shall we say of those bigger, braver cities, who never stood siege a moment?"[36]

He closed the lecture by reminding his audience that Massachusetts and South Carolina had cooperated in the cause of independence. Their common heritage ought to be celebrated: "The Past of both regions ought to be secure. Let the strifes of the Present be what they may, neither party gains by the brutal defamation of the other." He could see no reason for denouncing his state's past unless it was to isolate her "by odium, that she may be more easily offered up at the altar, without sympathy or succour." South Carolina would not peacefully submit to the defamation of her ancestors or her isolation within the Union. Such a course could only lead to civil war and the destruction of the Union. Simms considered himself "on a purely Literary Mission," appealing to the calm reason of an impartial audience.[37] But in 1856 everything was subsumed in politics.

Simms's northern lecture tour "proved a failure." He later confided to James Chesnut Jr. that, after delivering his lecture defending South Carolina's role in the Revolution three times, "my Committee reported to me that such was the public hostility, such the rancour occasioned by my revelations, . . . that they— the Committee—could neither sell nor give away the Tickets."[38] For the sake of his friends on the Committee, who would lose money if he continued the lectures to empty halls, he canceled the rest of his engagements. When Sabine revised his book in 1864, interestingly enough he conceded that no New England troops actually saw service below the James River in Virginia. He reaffirmed, however, that Charleston's surrender was attributable to its citizens' loyalty to the crown. Not only that, but then-current circumstances led Sabine to make the further claim that the surrender of Charleston constituted an early attempt at secession from the American Union.[39]

Simms had rushed to the defense of his state when he felt it was threatened by an outsider. This was precisely the lesson he hoped to teach in his *History of South Carolina*. He had perhaps spoken more "warmly" than was politically wise. But he believed his course was justified "in the assertion of a Mother's honour."[40] At home, however, he did not hesitate to criticize his fellow South Carolinians.

Back in South Carolina he delivered a series of lectures in May 1857 on the "social moral," in which he tried to explain the reasons for his northern lecture tour's failure. He warned his audience of northern hostility to the South. Carolinians should, he advised, "calmly and resolutely prepare themselves for every issue, and . . . deliberately study all those signs in the sky which seem to be the harbingers of convulsion." He went North to attempt to correct "slanders" against Carolina's past that he thought could easily be refuted "in a fair field." "There are thousands," he thought, "who will gladly listen to the truth—nay, be glad of a case made out, for them, in defence of a section with which they are closely connected by ties of blood, trade and habitual association." Simms hoped to persuade these thousands who, having read only New England histories, were hostile to the South merely through ignorance.[41]

But South Carolinians bore some of the blame for the North's ignorant hostility. Southerners were too neglectful of their own history. They had not actively engaged New Englanders in historical debate to refute their errors. "In South Carolina, as in all the purely agricultural states, the public mind has seldom addressed itself to the preservation of the public records"; whereas in the commercial states, "they have been perpetually busy in the assertion of their local claims. Sedulously devoted to this object, they have as sedulously ignored the services of all other regions."[42] South Carolinians did not know enough of their own history to set the record straight. They could not, therefore, expect New Yorkers to be able to see through what he considered the deceptions of New England histories.

In New York Simms's lectures were assailed by the press. Yankees "are the most intolerant people in the world, and have been so from the days of Cotton Mather. They have never shown indulgence to any who oppose their vanities or will," he told Carolinians.[43] All this he knew before he began his lecture tour. But he hoped that if he avoided politics and the subject of slavery, "I should have toleration."[44] Therefore, intent on not sitting idly by while his state was slandered, he set off to try correcting historical errors. "Do you not agree with me that I had no alternative" but to go North? he asked James Henry Hammond.[45] Hammond gracefully avoided answering his friend's question directly. "To be explicit," he wrote, "so far as I can learn, it is thought that your attempt to take the North by the nose, in its state of highest excitement and utmost exasperation, and to subdue it to your will by rhetoric and argument and even odd fact, was a little Quixotic." His retreat, however, Hammond called "masterly."[46]

Notwithstanding his claim to have avoided politics, his New York lecture did contain thinly veiled references to Senator Sumner that he probably knew a more prudent speaker would have left unsaid. However, this indiscretion likely mattered little. Talking about the Revolution was an inherently political act. It always has been and always will be in our self-created republic. How Americans interpret the Revolution is an important part of how we define who we are. Especially was this the case in 1856. George Orwell taught us that who controls the past controls the future. In the rancorous atmosphere of 1856 it mattered very much who could lay claim to the Revolutionary heritage.

EIGHT

Conclusion

At the end of *Woodcraft* (first published in 1852 as *The Sword and the Distaff*) Simms describes how Porgy, with his plantation now secure and under the able management of his brother-in-arms-turned-overseer Millhouse, transformed Glen-Eberly into "a sort of centre for the parish civilization." With no more danger to threaten them from without, peace reigned in the neighborhood. "Free of anxiety, Porgy resumed his ancient spirit," Simms wrote. The genial society of Porgy and the boys was frequently sought by the surrounding gentry who, we can be sure, enjoyed evenings filled with food, fun, and philosophy. On such occasions, the master of Glen-Eberly entertained guests by narrating "the experiences through which he had gone, delivering history and biography, anecdote and opinion, with the ease of a well-bred gentleman over his wine and walnuts." "Thus the days glided by as if all were winged with sunshine."[1]

One day Simms hoped to record these happy times—the "Humors of Glen-Eberly."[2] He never managed to though because he never enjoyed the same repose as Porgy. His financial situation was often tenuous. He was, therefore, always in a hurry when writing and frequently had to write with an eye on the market. Also his own neighborhood was increasingly threatened from without. Northern attacks goaded Simms to defend South Carolina and the South against a North that was increasingly hostile to slavery and the South. Instead of recording Porgy's retirement or enjoying repose at Woodlands while relating history, biography, and anecdote, he was drawn more and more into the sectional controversy.

The cancellation of Simms's 1856 lecture tour did not mark the end of his work as a historian. He continued writing history for periodicals until the end of his life in 1870. *The Cassique of Kiawah,* a novel some readers consider his finest historical romance, was published in 1859. The next year he published a revised and expanded edition of his *History of South Carolina.* He published *Sack and Destruction of the City of Columbia, S.C.* in 1865, a work rather more journalistic than historical. In 1866 he published his selection of James Henry Hammond's letters and speeches. And 1867 saw the publication of *The Army Correspondence of Colonel John Laurens* and the appearance, serially, of *Joscelyn,* one of the better —though unfinished—of his Revolutionary War romances.

Simms was quite busily engaged writing history in the period between 1856 and 1870. However, the difficulties of publishing in the South during and for a while following the Civil War and the destruction of his home and library placed enormous strains upon him as a writer. Also, his northern lectures on "South Carolina in the Revolution" were really the summation of a life's work devoted to preserving and publishing as much of his state's traditions and lore as possible. They therefore mark a fitting conclusion to our study of Simms as a historian.

Simms's contribution to American historiography was fivefold. First, he was actively engaged in collecting and preserving historical records. His library housed one of the most important private collections of historical manuscripts in America. Not only did he preserve important material, such as the Laurens family papers and portions of Peter Horry's memoir, he vigorously encouraged others to do likewise.

Second, he was a prominent and influential advocate of well-written histories as a means of making history more accessible. History, he believed, was the best teacher of morals and virtue. Simms was part of the republican tradition that considered virtue a necessary component of citizenship.[3] Because the people governed themselves, the government would be as virtuous or corrupt as its citizens. In America's increasingly democratic society it was all the more important that the people should be familiar with their history and its lessons in patriotism and virtue.

History should also be accessible to the young. Simms believed that children were the future and strength of a nation. They "must learn to dwell often upon the narratives of the brave fathers who first broke ground in the wilderness, who fought or treated with the red men, and who, finally, girded themselves up for the greater conflict with the imperious mother who had sent them forth."[4] Such histories would make a lasting impression on young minds, teach them patriotism and virtue, and help raise up sons of whom the nation could be proud.

But if he hoped to be read, the historian must be an artist. Here he stood with the great American romantic historians: Bancroft, Cooper, Gayarré, Motley, Parkman, and Prescott.[5] The historian must, without violating truth, enliven his history with art by imaginatively recreating the past. All the great historians from Livy to Gibbon "were artists of singular ability" in the arrangement of facts "and in the delineation of action," Simms wrote.[6] He articulated the defense of romantic history better and more extensively than most. And among Americans only Cooper can come close to matching him when it comes to applying romantic notions of history to the writing of fiction.

Third, it should be understood that his belief in democracy was based in his religious belief in free will. Because he believed man had been divinely blessed with free will and because he regarded "democracy as the principle which lifts man into *responsibility* & trust," Simms regarded his attachment to democracy as "rather a religious sentiment than a principle in politics."[7] To help his fellow citizens develop virtue to better exercise their responsibility and trust, he espoused what he thought of as a democratic history—a history that emphasized individual decisions and taught lessons about character—as a matter of faith.

Though he was influenced both by Carlylean notions of the role of great men and by romantic historicist schools of thought, his desire to teach virtue as a result of his religious faith in free will and democracy placed him between the two camps. National spirit influences people in Simms's writing, but his actors are always autonomous individuals, not impersonal forces. Forces may be influential, but they are never deterministic. Though Simms was associated with the romantic-nationalist Young America movement, he did not fully embrace romantic nationalism. He was an exponent of the literary, not the political, form of romantic nationalism. For Simms, the Young America movement was a vehicle for promoting the creation of a distinctively American literature. Simms had no interest in aggressive political or military nationalism. He was a nationalist in the same way that his fellow Young American, Edgar Allen Poe, was a nationalist. What often passes for nationalism in Simms's thought is more accurately understood as patriotism. This is an important distinction because patriotism and nationalism are sometimes antagonistic sentiments.

Much has been learned from scholars who have studied nationalism as a process of national self-construction, or of self-identification.[8] Simms and his approach to history are better understood, however, if we keep in mind George Orwell's definitions of nationalism and patriotism. Orwell defined patriotism as "devotion to a particular place and a particular way of life, which one believes to be the best in the world, but has no wish to force upon other people. Patriotism is of its nature defensive, both militarily and culturally. Nationalism, on the other hand, is inseparable from the desire for power." "Nationalism is power-hunger tempered by self-deception," wrote Orwell.[9] The farmer-poet Wendell Berry has also noted the important difference between nationalism and patriotism. Patriotism, he explains, is the love of one's community or country, as opposed to love of the state. Unlike patriotism, nationalism "is oblivious of local differences and therefore destructive of communities."[10] "It is patriotism in the abstract—nationalism—that is most apt to be fanatic or brutal or arrogant," writes Berry.[11] Viewed in this light, even Simms's so-called literary nationalism is better understood as a defensive literary patriotism. He wanted American—not English—books in the hands of American readers. He did not wish to force American novels upon unwilling English readers. Nor did he desire a national literature that was oblivious to local differences. On the contrary, he believed that a truly national American literature could only be produced by vibrant regional literary cultures.

We know that Simms was certainly familiar with the important German historians. Yet Simms's historical thinking more closely resembled that of English and French historians, such as Hume, Carlyle, and Michelet. The German historians tended to be less literary than some of their English and French counterparts. The Germans were also too fond of constructing scientific systems for Simms's taste. Their historical systems implied an inevitable progress that Simms simply could not accept.

James Warley Miles, who briefly held a chair of the History of Intellectual Philosophy and Greek Literature at the College of Charleston and had traveled extensively throughout Europe and Mesopotamia, provides an interesting contrast with Simms. Unlike Simms, Miles was "deeply influenced by Hegel's German disciples," and was something of an aberration among Charleston's intellectual elite.[12] Writing in March 1863, in the midst of the Civil War, Miles found unsatisfying "the contemplation of history, as a congeries of events springing from the arbitrary acts of men, where the ambition of a conqueror, or the arts of a demagogue, or the subtlety of a politician, or the policy of a nation, or the combination of various external circumstances are alone assumed as the explanation of historical events." Like Hegel, Miles was a progressive determinist who believed that "history is no mass of arbitrary, disorganized events" but saw "Divine Providence directing with steady and intelligent hand the development of its plan."[13]

Miles struggled to reconcile his view of history as being providentially predetermined with a belief in free will. When looking at the providential plan, he conceded, there will probably "always remain a certain residuum which we cannot perfectly co-ordinate and explain" because man is a "free agent" with unpredictable passions. Nevertheless, Miles believed that "although it requires long and laborious induction to arrive at a perception of the plan, yet, when it is once conceived, it sheds wonderful light, beauty, and unity upon all the various phenomena which it embraces." Once the divine plan has been discerned, all that remains for man is to "accept it as an ultimate fact for us, and not vainly speculate as to why the law is so and not otherwise." Miles, like Abraham Lincoln and many others, found comfort in a philosophy of history that left so little to chance and gave meaning to his country's suffering. "And amid the bitter trials with which this war has afflicted us, it may be regarded as one ground of resignation that they have been no arbitrary inflictions of mere Omnipotent will, but the necessary results of the wise law whereby God is working out our destiny," Miles mused.[14] Such a fatalistic faith in a predetermined divine plan of history left too little room for potentiality to suit Simms.

Contemplating fate, Simms asked, "Is man thus subject to each wind's caprice, / Day's and night's changes? Hath he then no power / To will above the winds? . . . In this, Religion and Philosophy— / The best possessions of his mortal state— / Both tutor him, and happily agree: / Soul-will and manly purpose baffle fate."[15] Good history was the story of soul will and manly purpose wrestling with contingency, not of the inevitable march of fate or progress. Unlike Miles's, Simms's romanticism is derived more from Scott, Wordsworth, Carlyle, Coleridge, and Byron than from German models. Like Francis Parkman, William H. Prescott, and James Fenimore Cooper, Simms was more interested in portraying the clash—and sometimes the decline—of civilizations than in writing progressive nationalist narratives like those of George Bancroft.

Being a novelist, it is perhaps appropriate that he should focus on names instead of numbers; on people instead of impersonal forces. As Shelby Foote,

Gore Vidal, Herbert Butterfield, John Lukacs, and many others have claimed, it is in the delineation of character that novelists best historians. "The novelist looking at a historic figure sees personality where the scientific historian is tempted to see only the incarnation of a policy," wrote Butterfield.[16] Belief in free will effectively negates any tendency toward historical determinism.

But on the other hand, Simms's celebration of autonomous individuals does not quite make him a Carlylean hero worshiper. Since he regarded teaching patriotism and virtue as the main purpose of history, his heroes had to be virtuous. It would not do for them to simply be what Hegel called world-historical individuals, who played a big role on the world's stage without regard to morality. Moreover, Simms was as interested in the common man and woman as he was in the great men of history.

Fourth, Simms focused attention on some of the groups traditionally neglected in American history. He actively encouraged Elizabeth Ellet's pioneering work on women in the Revolution. He also wrote more, more sympathetically, and more realistically about Native Americans than most of his contemporaries.[17] Simms also stands out as one of the few nineteenth-century American historians who recognized the centrality of the Indians' dispossession to America's history.

Also, the Loyalists occupy an important position in Simms's accounting of American history. Loyalists are prominent in his writings because he treated the Revolution in South Carolina as a civil war. But he also treated them with remarkable sympathy considering his proximity to the Revolution. Indeed, as Robert Calhoon has noted, it was through the works of writers like Simms and James Fenimore Cooper that the Loyalists entered American literary consciousness.[18]

Fifth, Simms was the preeminent historian working in the Old South. He encouraged and influenced almost every other contemporary historian working in or on the region.

Despite his importance to other historians and to the writing of history, Simms is still more likely to be read today for what he can tell us about his own time. Through his writings, we see a South struggling to define itself and its place in the nation. Feeling themselves a besieged minority within the Union, it was important for southerners to be able to lay claim to the Revolutionary heritage.[19] Through his historical writings Simms gave southerners a solid historical basis for countering the New England version of America's founding at Boston in 1630. He also showed them their ancestors' successful resistance to oppression and their separation from England. Southerners paid attention. Indeed, by 1861 they believed that in separating from the Union they reenacted the Revolution.[20]

NOTES

Introduction

1. See Jay B. Hubbell, *The South in American Literature, 1607–1900* (Durham, N.C.: Duke University Press, 1954), 572.

2. Drew Gilpin Faust, "The Peculiar South Revisited: White Society, Culture, and Politics in the Antebellum Period, 1800–1860," in *Interpreting Southern History: Historiographical Essays in Honor of Sanford W. Higginbotham,* ed. John B. Boles and Evelyn Thomas Nolen (Baton Rouge: Louisiana State University Press, 1987), 99.

3. Michael O'Brien, *Rethinking the South: Essays in Intellectual History* (Baltimore: Johns Hopkins University Press, 1988), 19.

4. William W. Freehling, *Prelude to Civil War: The Nullification Controversy in South Carolina, 1816–1836* (New York: Harper and Row, 1965); Steven A. Channing, *Crisis of Fear: Secession in South Carolina* (New York: Simon and Schuster, 1970).

5. William L. Barney, *The Road to Secession: A New Perspective on the Old South* (New York: Praeger Publishers, 1972), 5. Note the irony of Barney's subtitle.

6. Representative works include Richard Beale Davis, *Intellectual Life in Jefferson's Virginia, 1790–1830* (Knoxville: University of Tennessee Press, 1972); Eugene D. Genovese, *The Slaveholders' Dilemma: Freedom and Progress in Southern Conservative Thought, 1820–1860* (Columbia: University of South Carolina Press, 1992); Genovese, *The World the Slaveholders Made: Two Essays in Interpretation* (Middletown, Conn.: Wesleyan University Press, 1988); Michael O'Brien, ed., *All Clever Men, Who Make Their Way: Critical Discourse in the Old South* (Fayetteville: University of Arkansas Press, 1982); O'Brien, *A Character of Hugh Legaré* (Knoxville: University of Tennessee Press, 1985); O'Brien, *Rethinking the South;* O'Brien, "On the Writing of History in the Old South," in *Rewriting the South,* ed. Lothar Honnighausen and Valeria Gennaro Lerda, 141–66 (Tübingen: Francke, 1993); David Moltke-Hansen, "Southern Genesis: Regional Identity and the Rise of the Capital of Southern Civilization, 1760–1860" (Ph.D. diss., University of South Carolina, 2000); and Moltke-Hansen and O'Brien, eds., *Intellectual Life in Antebellum Charleston* (Knoxville: University of Tennessee Press, 1986).

7. John Rushing Welsh, *The Mind of William Gilmore Simms: His Social and Political Thought: A Summary of a Thesis Presented to the Faculty of the Graduate School of Vanderbilt University in Partial Fulfillment of the Requirements for the Degree of Doctor of Philosophy* (Nashville, Tenn.: Joint University Libraries, 1951) and "William Gilmore Simms, Critic of the South," *Journal of Southern History* 26 (May 1960): 201–14.

ONE *Art, Patriotism, and Moral Progress*

1. Examples of books on American historians that scarcely mention Simms's contributions include Michael Kraus, *A History of American History* (New York: Farrar and Rinehart,

1937); David Levin, *History as Romantic Art: Bancroft, Prescott, Motley, and Parkman* (New York: AMS Press, 1967); the final chapter of Arthur H. Shaffer, *The Politics of History: Writing the History of the American Revolution, 1783–1815* (Chicago: Precedent Publishing, 1975); and David D. Van Tassel, *Recording America's Past: An Interpretation of the Development of Historical Studies in America, 1607–1884* (Chicago: University of Chicago Press, 1960).

2. John Caldwell Guilds's fine biography, *Simms: A Literary Life* (Fayetteville: University of Arkansas Press, 1992); Mary Ann Wimsatt, *The Major Fiction of William Gilmore Simms: Cultural Traditions and Literary Form* (Baton Rouge: Louisiana State University Press, 1989); Jon L. Wakelyn, *The Politics of a Literary Man: William Gilmore Simms* (Westport, Conn.: Greenwood Press, 1973); and Charles S. Watson, *From Nationalism to Secessionism: The Changing Fiction of William Gilmore Simms* (Westport, Conn.: Greenwood Press, 1993). Even one of the best articles on Simms's historianship deals almost exclusively with his fiction: David Moltke-Hansen, "Ordered Progress: The Historical Philosophy of William Gilmore Simms," in *Long Years of Neglect: The Work and Reputation of William Gilmore Simms,* ed. John C. Guilds, 126–47 (Fayetteville: University of Arkansas Press, 1988). Another example of a treatment of Simms as a historian that concentrates upon his fiction can be found in Michael Kammen, *A Season of Youth: The American Revolution and the Historical Imagination* (New York: Alfred A. Knopf, 1978). William Peterfield Trent's biography is *William Gilmore Simms* (Boston: Houghton, Mifflin and Company, 1892). On Trent, see John McCardell, "Trent's *Simms:* The Making of a Biography," in *A Master's Due: Essays in Honor of David Herbert Donald,* ed. William J. Cooper Jr., Michael F. Holt, and John McCardell, 179–203 (Baton Rouge: Louisiana State University Press, 1985); and Franklin T. Walker, "William Peterfield Trent—A Critical Biography" (Ph.D. diss., George Peabody College for Teachers, 1943).

3. See J. B. Black, *The Art of History: A Study of Four Great Historians of the Eighteenth Century* (New York: F. S. Crofts and Co., 1926); Lionel Gossman, *Between History and Literature* (Cambridge, Mass.: Harvard University Press, 1990); O'Brien, *Rethinking the South,* 8–15 and 27–28.

4. On the historianship of Homer and Shakespeare, see James Ford Rhodes, *Historical Essays* (New York: Macmillan Company, 1909), 1–2.

5. Adam Smith, *Lectures on Rhetoric and Belles Lettres,* ed. J. C. Bryce (Indianapolis, Ind.: Liberty Classics, 1985), 117.

6. Another significant statement of this position can be found in Sir Philip Sidney, *Defence of Poesy,* ed. Dorothy M. Macardle (London: Macmillan, 1968), 3–5.

7. William Gilmore Simms, "Headley's Life of Cromwell," *Southern Quarterly Review* 14 (October 1848): 510.

8. Perhaps the most famous "scientific" historian was Leopold von Ranke. Ironically, Ranke first became interested in history through his reading of the historical romances of Sir Walter Scott. On Ranke, see Anthony Grafton, *The Footnote: A Curious History* (Cambridge, Mass.: Harvard University Press, 1997), 34–93. Grafton questions whether Ranke should more properly be considered the first scientific or the last romantic historian. Notable examples of "history as science" arguments include John Emerich Edward Dalberg-Acton [Lord Acton], "German Schools of History," in *Selected Writings of Lord Acton,* ed. J. Rufus Fears, vol. 2, *Essays in the Study and Writing of History* (Indianapolis, Ind.: Liberty Classics, 1986), 325–64; Acton, "The Study of History," in *Selected Writings of Lord Acton,* 2:504–52; J. B. Bury, "The Science of History," in *The Dimensions of History: Readings on the Nature of History and the Problems of Historical Interpretation,* ed. Thomas N. Guinsburg, 23–27 (Chicago: Rand McNally and Company, 1971); Edward

Hallett Carr, *What Is History? The George Macaulay Trevelyan Lectures Delivered in the University of Cambridge, January–March 1961* (New York: Alfred A. Knopf, 1962), 70–112; and R. G. Collingwood, *The Idea of History,* rev. ed., ed. Jan Van Der Dussen (New York: Oxford University Press, Galaxy Books, 1956), 1–13.

9. Simon Schama, *Dead Certainties (Unwarranted Speculations)* (New York: Alfred A. Knopf, 1991), 325. Some other notable examples of arguments for history as a form of literature (or at least, arguments contra "history as science") include Margaret Atwood, "In Search of *Alias Grace:* On Writing Canadian Historical Fiction," *American Historical Review* 103 (December 1998): 1503–16; Black, *The Art of History;* Jacob Burckhardt, *Judgments on History and Historians* (Indianapolis, Ind.: Liberty Fund, 1999), 167–69; Herbert Butterfield, *The Historical Novel: An Essay* (Cambridge: Cambridge University Press, 1924); Mark C. Carnes, ed., *Novel History: Historians and Novelists Confront America's Past (and Each Other)* (New York: Simon and Schuster, 2001); Henry Steele Commager, "Introduction," and "The Search for a Usable Past," in *The Search for a Usable Past, and Other Essays in Historiography* (New York: Alfred A. Knopf, 1967), ix–27; John Demos, "In Search of Reasons for Historians to Read Novels . . . ," *American Historical Review* 103 (December 1998): 1526–29; Shelby Foote, "The Novelist's View of History," *Sewanee Review* 99 (Summer 1991): 439–45; F. A. Hayek, *The Counter-Revolution of Science: Studies on the Abuse of Reason* (Indianapolis, Ind.: Liberty Fund, 1979); John Lukacs, *Historical Consciousness: The Remembered Past* (New Brunswick, N.J.: Transaction Publishers, 1994); Samuel Eliot Morison, "History as a Literary Art," in *Sailor Historian: The Best of Samuel Eliot Morison,* ed. Emily Morison Beck, 383–93 (Boston: Houghton Mifflin Company, 1977); Emery Neff, *The Poetry of History: The Contribution of Literature and Literary Scholarship to the Writing of History since Voltaire* (New York: Columbia University Press, 1947); Michael Oakeshott, *On History and Other Essays* (Indianapolis, Ind.: Liberty Fund, 1999); Simon Schama, *Citizens: A Chronicle of the French Revolution* (New York: Alfred A. Knopf, 1989), xiii–xvi; Thomas P. Slaughter, *The Natures of John and William Bartram* (New York: Alfred A. Knopf, 1996), xix; and Jonathan D. Spence, "Margaret Atwood and the Edges of History," *American Historical Review* 103 (December 1998): 1522–25.

10. Van Tassel, *Recording America's Past,* vii–viii. See also Charles A. Beard, "That Noble Dream," in *American Historians: A Selection,* ed. Harvey Wish, 361–77 (New York: Oxford University Press, 1962); Peter Novick, *That Noble Dream: The "Objectivity Question" and the American Historical Profession* (Cambridge: Cambridge University Press, 1988), 40.

11. Livy, *The Early History of Rome,* trans. Aubrey de Sélincourt (London: Penguin Books, 1971), 33. Benedetto Croce has observed: "It is true that sometimes we hear ignorance of previous historians praised as a fortunate thing, a *felix culpa,* because thus the object is supposed to have been seen with a fresh eye and aspects not previously observed are noticed." Really, the quality they praise is impartiality or "mental liberty," and is not dependent upon ignorance (Croce, *History as the Story of Liberty* [1938; Indianapolis, Ind.: Liberty Fund, 2000], 215–16).

12. The word "historicism" has been used so indiscriminately, to describe so many different ideas, as to become almost useless. However, for present purposes I employ the term in the sense that Karl Popper did, even though Popper's critique oversimplified historicist thought. This, I think, is historicism's most commonly understood meaning. See David Hackett Fischer, *Historians' Fallacies: Toward a Logic of Historical Thought* (New York: Harper and Row, 1970), 156n; and Lukacs, *Historical Consciousness,* 19.

13. One of the most notable exceptions is Francis Fukuyama, *The End of History and the Last Man* (New York: Free Press, 1992). Fukuyama argues for a "directional" history: modern societies evolve towards democracy.

14. Leo Tolstoy, *War and Peace* (New York: Modern Library, n.d.), 1132–33.

15. Karl R. Popper, *The Poverty of Historicism* (London: Routledge and Kegan Paul, 1957), 159. See also, Isaiah Berlin, *Historical Inevitability* (London: Oxford University Press, 1954); Fischer, *Historians' Fallacies,* 155–57; and Hayek, *The Counter-Revolution of Science.*

16. J. G. Herder, *J. G. Herder on Social and Political Culture,* trans. and ed. F. M. Barnard (Cambridge: Cambridge University Press, 1969). John Passmore (*The Perfectibility of Man* [Indianapolis, Ind.: Liberty Fund, 2000], 356–69) provides a good analysis of Herder's historicism. Simms's copy of Herder's *The Spirit of Hebrew Poetry* is in the South Caroliniana Library. On historicism and the German Enlightenment, see Peter Hans Reill, *The German Enlightenment and the Rise of Historicism* (Berkeley: University of California Press, 1975).

17. Georg Wilhelm Friedrich Hegel, *The Philosophy of History,* trans. by J. Sibree (New York: Dover Publications, 1956), 72.

18. The standard work on the transmission of romantic thought from Europe to the Old South is Rollin G. Osterweis, *Romanticism and Nationalism in the Old South* (New Haven, Conn.: Yale University Press, 1949). More recently Osterweis has been revised by Michael O'Brien in *Rethinking the South,* 38–56. O'Brien has found historicists and students of German thought in almost every corner of the Old South. See especially his sketches of Jesse Burton Harrison, Hugh Swinton Legaré, Thomas Roderick Dew, George Frederick Holmes, Henry Augustine Washington, James Warley Miles, John Holmes Bocock, Basil Lanneau Gildersleeve, and James Henley Thornwell in O'Brien*'s All Clever Men,* 55–57, 89–91, 125–27, 177–79, 228–30, 263–66, 357–59, 398–400, and 420–22.

19. Henry Adams, *The Degradation of the Democratic Dogma* (New York: Peter Smith, 1949), 126. See also Lukacs, *Historical Consciousness,* 273–315.

20. On the differences between Simms's and Bancroft's notions of progress, see Carey M. Roberts, "The Mighty River of Providence or the Secrets of Home: The Historical Theories of Simms and Bancroft," in *Simms Review* 6 (Summer 1998): 35–43. Simms to James H. Hammond, December 24, 1847, in *The Letters of William Gilmore Simms,* eds. Mary C. Simms Oliphant, Alfred Taylor Odell, and T. C. Duncan Eaves (Columbia: University of South Carolina Press, 1953), 2:385; Simms to Hammond, November 22, 1847, *Letters,* 2:372. Interested readers may wish to look at John Milton, "The Readie and Easie Way to Establish a Free Commonwealth," in his *Areopagitica and Other Political Writings of John Milton* (Indianapolis, Ind.: Liberty Fund, 1999), 422.

21. For the inevitability of national expansion, see Simms to James Henry Hammond, May 20, 1846, *Letters,* 2:168. Simms denies the perfectibility of mankind in his "The Good Farmer," *Simms Review* 10 (Summer 2002): 12. I am indebted to Mark M. Smith for the rolling hoop analogy.

22. Carey M. Roberts, "Men of Much Faith: Progress and Declension in Jeffersonian Thought, 1787–1800" (Ph.D. diss., University of South Carolina, 1999). See also Jesse Burton Harrison, "English Civilization," in *All Clever Men,* 55–88.

23. Simms, *Charlemont; or, The Pride of the Village. A Tale of Kentucky* (New York: Redfield, 1856), 8, 9.

24. Bury, "The Science of History," 24.

25. Carl L. Becker, "What Are Historical Facts?" in *The Dimensions of History: Readings on the Nature of History and the Problems of Historical Interpretation,* ed. Thomas N. Guinsburg, 29–40 (Chicago: Rand McNally and Company, 1971).

26. Oakeshott, *On History and Other Essays,* 103–4.

27. Cormac McCarthy, *All the Pretty Horses* (New York: Alfred A. Knopf, 1993), 239. William W. Freehling has echoed this idea in "South Carolina's Pivotal Decision for Disunion: Popular Mandate or Manipulated Verdict?" *University South Caroliniana Society:*

Sixty-fifth Annual Meeting (2001): 6. Address originally delivered at the sixty-fourth annual meeting of the University South Caroliniana Society, Columbia, S.C.

28. R. G. Collingwood, *The Idea of History,* 251; Frederic William Maitland, *A Historical Sketch of Liberty and Equality: As Ideals of English Political Philosophy from the Time of Hobbes to the Time of Coleridge* (Indianapolis, Ind.: Liberty Fund, 2000), 185.

29. Oakeshott, *On History and Other Essays,* 103. Cf. Croce, *History as the Story of Liberty,* 134. Croce believes that historians have incorrectly identified as "poetic fancy" what in truth is merely "associative imagination."

30. Simms, *Views and Reviews in American Literature, History, and Fiction: First Series,* ed. C. Hugh Holmann (Cambridge, Mass.: Belknap Press of Harvard University Press, 1961), 35–36. Simms should not be understood as subscribing to the postmodernist belief that narrative meaning is arbitrary or that truth and fiction alike are mere constructs. On the contrary, he believed that even fictionists should be guided by objective truth. For a postmodernist interpretation of an early American view of the relationship between history and fiction, see Mark L. Kamrath, "Charles Brockden Brown and the 'art of the historian': An Essay Concerning (Post)modern Historical Understanding," *Journal of the Early Republic* 21 (Summer 2001): 231–60.

31. An interesting example of Simms weighing historical evidence can be found in Simms, "Michael Ney, Otherwise Michael Rudolph," *Southern Literary Messenger* 13 (January 1847): 17–23.

32. Simms, *Views and Reviews,* 36; Maitland, *A Historical Sketch of Liberty and Equality,* 185; Simms, *Views and Reviews,* 36.

33. Simms to Albert James Pickett, March 18, 1848, *Letters,* 5:399.

34. Simms to Evert A. Duyckinck, February 2, 1847, *Letters,* 2:264, 265.

35. Simms to Albert James Pickett, March 18, 1848, *Letters,* 5:399–400.

36. William H. Prescott, "Chateaubriand's English Literature," in *Biographical and Critical Miscellanies* (New York: Harper and Brothers, 1852), 284, 285.

37. Ibid., 286.

38. Nicholas G. Meriwether, "Simms's *The Lily and the Totem:* 'History for the Purposes of Art,'" in *Long Years of Neglect: The Work and Reputation of William Gilmore Simms,* ed. John C. Guilds (Fayetteville: University of Arkansas Press, 1988), 77. See also, John C. Guilds, "Introduction," in Simms, *Stories and Tales,* ed. John C. Guilds (Columbia: University of South Carolina Press, 1974), xvii.

39. Aristotle, *Poetics,* in *The Complete Works of Aristotle: The Revised Oxford Translation,* ed. Jonathan Barnes (Princeton, N.J.: Princeton University Press, 1984), 2:2323. For an example of a modern scholar who has recognized this difference between history and fiction, see Lukacs, *Historical Consciousness,* 124–28.

40. Simms, *Views and Reviews,* 38.

41. Ibid., 15–17.

42. Quotations from Genovese, *The Slaveholders' Dilemma,* 12, 13. Arthur A. Ekirch Jr. wrote about Simms's ideas of progress more cogently than have most subsequent writers in *The Idea of Progress in America, 1815–1860* (New York: Columbia University Press, 1944), 179, 183–84.

43. Richard M. Weaver, "Two Types of American Individualism," in *The Southern Essays of Richard M. Weaver,* ed. George M. Curtis III and James J. Thompson Jr. (Indianapolis, Ind.: Liberty Fund, 1987), 82.

44. James E. Kibler, "Stewardship and *Patria* in Simms's Frontier Poetry," in *William Gilmore Simms and the American Frontier,* ed. John C. Guilds and Caroline Collins (Athens: University of Georgia Press, 1997), 217.

45. Simms, *Egeria: or Voices of Thought and Counsel, for the Woods and Wayside* (Philadelphia: E. H. Butler and Co., 1853), 202, 203.

46. Simms, *The Social Principle: The True Source of National Permanence. An Oration, Delivered before the Erosophic Society of the University of Alabama, December 13, 1842* (Tuscaloosa: Erosophic Society of the University of Alabama, 1843), 53.

47. Simms, *Poetry and the Practical,* ed. James E. Kibler (Fayetteville: University of Arkansas Press, 1996), 73, 77.

48. James Henry Hammond to William Gilmore Simms, August 17, 1849, Hammond Papers, Library of Congress.

49. "History," in *Encyclopædia Americana. A Popular Dictionary of Arts, Sciences, Literature, History, Politics, and Biography, Brought Down to the Present Time; Including a Copious Collection of Original Articles in American Biography on the Basis of the Seventh Edition of the German Conversations-Lexicon,* ed. Francis Lieber (Philadelphia: Desilver, Thomas, and Co., 1835), 342.

50. Walter H. Conser Jr., *God and the Natural World: Religion and Science in Antebellum America* (Columbia: University of South Carolina Press, 1993), 3–4. On the eighteenth- and early nineteenth-century understanding of history as both a science and an art, see also Laurence L. Bongie, *David Hume: Prophet of the Counter-Revolution,* 2nd ed. (Indianapolis, Ind.: Liberty Fund, 2000), 2–9.

51. Charles A. Beard, "Grounds for a Reconsideration of Historiography," in the Social Science Research Council's Committee on Historiography's *Theory and Practice in Historical Study: A Report of the Committee on Historiography* (New York: Social Science Research Council, 1946), 7.

52. Theodore Roosevelt, *History as Literature* (New York: Charles Scribner's Sons, 1913); Frederick Jackson Turner, "The Significance of History," in *Rereading Frederick Jackson Turner: "The Significance of the Frontier in American History" and Other Essays,* commentary by John Mack Faragher (New York: Henry Holt and Company, 1994), 11–30. For examples of those who criticize Simms for his history's literary merit, see Drew Gilpin Faust, *A Sacred Circle: The Dilemma of the Intellectual in the Old South, 1840–1860* (Baltimore: Johns Hopkins University Press, 1977), 75; and Gloria Jahoda, "Commentary," in *Eighteenth-Century Florida and the Revolutionary South,* ed. Samuel Proctor (Gainesville: University Presses of Florida, 1978), 122–24. Likewise, Don Higginbotham gently chides "the high priest of Charleston literary circles" for over-glamorizing the conflict in the South, in *The War of American Independence: Military Attitudes, Policies, and Practice, 1763–1789* (Boston: Northeastern University Press, 1983), 352. See also, John Lukacs, *At the End of an Age* (New Haven, Conn.: Yale University Press, 2002), 47–48n; and Sean Wilentz's critique of David McCullough's popular biography of John Adams, "America Made Easy," *New Republic* (July 2, 2001): 35–40.

53. Simms to James Lawson, December 29, 1839, *Letters,* 1:159–62.

54. Simms, "Ellet's Women of the Revolution," *Southern Quarterly Review,* n.s., 1 (July 1850): 352. In this respect, Simms was no different from generations of children growing up not just in Charleston, but throughout America. Basil Lanneau Gildersleeve, born twenty-five years after Simms, also recalled hearing from his grandmother tales of the Revolution in Charleston (O'Brien, *All Clever Men,* 399).

55. For some representative examples of Simms claiming historical veracity for his fiction, see *Border Beagles: A Tale of Mississippi,* ed. John Caldwell Guilds (Fayetteville: University of Arkansas Press, 1996), advertisement; *Charlemont,* 7–8; *The Lily and the Totem, or, The Huguenots in Florida. A Series of Sketches, Picturesque and Historical, of the Colonies of Coligni, in North America, 1562–1570* (New York: Baker and Scribner, 1850), iv–v; "Lucas

de Ayllon. A Historical Nouvellette," in *The Wigwam and the Cabin,* new and rev. ed. (New York: Redfield, 1859), 430; *The Partisan: With Introduction and Explanatory Notes* (Spartanburg, S.C.: Reprint Company, 1976), viii; *Richard Hurdis: A Tale of Alabama,* ed. John C. Guilds (Fayetteville: University of Arkansas Press, 1995), xxvii–xxviii; *Southward Ho! A Spell of Sunshine* (New York: Redfield, 1854), 257–58; *Vasconselos: A Romance of the New World* (New York: Redfield, 1853), 1–2; and *The Yemassee: A Romance of Carolina,* ed. John Caldwell Guilds (Fayetteville: University of Arkansas Press, 1994), xxx.

56. Examples of poems with historical notes can be found in *Early Lays* (Charleston, S.C.: A. E. Miller, 1827). The poems in this, Simms's third book, have notes referencing such works as Bartram's *Travels* and Jefferson's *Notes on the State of Virginia.*

57. Simms to Rufus Wilmot Griswold, December 6, 1846, *Letters,* 2:221.

58. Frederick Jackson Turner, *Rise of the New West, 1819–1829* (New York: Harper and Brothers Publishers, 1906). See especially chapters 1 and 19.

59. Simms, "Sonnet—To My Books," in *Selected Poems of William Gilmore Simms,* ed. James Everett Kibler Jr. (Athens: University of Georgia Press, 1990), 3, 314.

60. Simms to James Lawson, October 16, 1841, *Letters,* 1:285. "Oyster Point" likely became the novel *The Cassique of Kiawah,* published in 1859.

61. For example, the very titles of Charles Watson's *From Nationalism to Secessionism: The Changing Fiction of William Gilmore Simms* (Westport, Conn.: Greenwood Press, 1993) and John Higham's "The Changing Loyalties of William Gilmore Simms" (*Journal of Southern History* 9 [1943]: 210–23) imply that nationalism and sectionalism are incompatible, as do the subtitles of Charles M. Wiltse's three-volume biography of John C. Calhoun: *Nationalist, Nullifier,* and *Sectionalist.*

62. Johannes Althusius, *Politica* (Indianapolis, Ind.: Liberty Fund, 1995); Edmund Burke, *Reflections on the Revolution in France* (Indianapolis, Ind.: Liberty Fund, 1999), especially p. 307; John Shelton Reed, *The Enduring South: Subcultural Persistence in Mass Society* (Chapel Hill: University of North Carolina Press, 1974), 35; David Waldstreicher, *In the Midst of Perpetual Fetes: The Making of American Nationalism, 1776–1820* (Chapel Hill: University of North Carolina Press, 1997); David M. Potter, "The Historian's Use of Nationalism and Vice Versa," in *History and American Society: Essays of David M. Potter,* ed. Don E. Fehrenbacher (New York: Oxford University Press, 1973), 60–108.

63. Eugene D. Genovese, *The Political Economy of Slavery: Studies in the Economy and Society of the Slave South* (New York: Vintage Books, 1967), 31.

64. Mark D. Kaplanoff, "How Federalist Was South Carolina in 1787–1788?" in *The Meaning of South Carolina History: Essays in Honor of George C. Rogers Jr.,* ed. David R. Chesnutt and Clyde N. Wilson (Columbia: University of South Carolina Press, 1991), 89.

65. Lukacs, *Historical Consciousness,* 200–201, 382. Edward Shils has also commented on this difference between nationalism and patriotism in *The Virtue of Civility: Selected Essays on Liberalism, Tradition, and Civil Society* (Indianapolis, Ind.: Liberty Fund, 1997), 83. Edward Gibbon, *The History of the Decline and Fall of the Roman Empire* (London: Folio Society, 1983), 1:37.

66. Simms, "South Carolina in the Revolution. The Social Moral. Lecture 1." Charles Carroll Simms Collection, South Caroliniana Library, University of South Carolina, Columbia. The lecture was delivered in Charleston on May 25, 1857.

67. The exception to this rule is his support of an active policy of westward expansion. Simms to James Henry Hammond, May 1, 1847, *Letters,* 2:311.

68. John C. Calhoun, "A Disquisition on Government," in *Union and Liberty: The Political Philosophy of John C. Calhoun,* ed. Ross M. Lence (Indianapolis, Ind.: Liberty Fund, 1992), 88–89.

69. John McCardell, *The Idea of a Southern Nation: Southern Nationalists and Southern Nationalism, 1830–1860* (New York: W. W. Norton and Company, 1979), 5–9. Older, but still useful, works on southern nationalism include Avery O. Craven, *The Growth of Southern Nationalism, 1848–1861* (Baton Rouge: Louisiana State University Press, 1953), and *The Coming of the Civil War*, 2nd ed. (Chicago: University of Chicago Press, 1957); Jesse T. Carpenter, *The South as a Conscious Minority, 1789–1861: A Study in Political Thought* (Columbia: University of South Carolina Press, 1990); and William R. Taylor, *Cavalier and Yankee: The Old South and American National Character* (New York: Oxford University Press, 1993).

70. William Gilmore Simms, "28th June," *Southern Literary Gazette*, n.s., 1, (July 1, 1829): 93. Although published anonymously, Simms acknowledged delivering this Palmetto Day address in a letter to James Lawson dated December 29, 1839. Simms, *Letters*, 1:164.

71. Simms, "28th June," 95.

72. For Simms's contributions to the *Album* and the *Southern Literary Gazette*, see John C. Guilds, "Simms's First Magazine: *The Album*," *Studies in Bibliography* 8 (1956): 169–84; and "Simms and the *Southern Literary Gazette*," *Studies in Bibliography* 21 (1968): 59–92.

73. Simms, "Whom the Coat Fits, Let Him Wear It," *Album* 1 (November 5, 1825): 146.

74. Simms, *Views and Reviews*, 34–35.

75. Ibid., 34.

76. John C. Guilds, "Simms and the *Southern Literary Gazette*," 91; S. Austin Allibone, *A Critical Dictionary of English Literature and British and American Authors* (Philadelphia: J. B. Lippincott Company, 1891), 2:2105; Simms, "The Cypress Swamp," *Southern Literary Gazette*, n.s., 1 (September 15, 1829): 211–12.

77. Simms, "Battle of Fort Moultrie," *Southern Literary Gazette*, n.s., 1 (August 1, 1829): 138.

78. William Crafts, "Address Delivered June 28th, 1825, before the Palmetto Society, in Commemoration of the Defence of the Palmetto Fort, on Sullivan's Island, (June 28, 1776)," in *A Selection, in Prose and Poetry, from the Miscellaneous Writings of the Late William Crafts* (Charleston, S.C.: C. C. Sebring and J. S. Burges, 1828), 72.

79. Johan Huizinga, "The Idea of History," in *The Varieties of History: From Voltaire to the Present*, ed. Fritz Stern (New York: Meridian Books, 1957), 292.

80. Ibid.

TWO   *Simms and Other Historians*

1. Simms to Albert James Pickett, March 18, 1848, *Letters*, 5:399–400; Pickett, *History of Alabama, and Incidentally of Georgia and Mississippi, from the Earliest Periods* (Charleston, S.C.: Walker and James, 1851), dedication, xiv.

2. Representative letters include the following: Simms to George Bancroft, January 15, 1858, *Letters*, 4:4–6; Simms to Evert A. Duyckinck, December 13, 1866, *Letters*, 4:624 (allowing Bancroft access to manuscripts); Simms to James Fenimore Cooper, September 27, 1843, *Letters*, 5:376–77; Simms to Henry B. Dawson, March 15, 1859, *Letters*, 4:135–36; Simms to Dawson, April 23, 1859, *Letters*, 4:148–50 (Simms discusses his relationship with Ellet); Simms to William Porcher Miles, January 25, 1858, *Letters*, 4:10 ("old friend"); and Simms to James Lawson, October 12, 1845, *Letters*, 2:104 (supplying Force books); Simms to Charles E. A. Gayarré, May 17 and July 13, 1849, *Letters*, 6:99–100 and

104; Simms to Gayarré, April 12, 1867, *Letters,* 5:42–44; Simms to Francis Lister Hawks, October 8, 1852, *Letters,* 5:418–19 (Hawks was the author of a *History of North Carolina);* Joel Tyler Headley to Simms, February 21, 1845, *Letters,* 2:19n.; Simms to John Pendleton Kennedy, April 9, 1846, *Letters,* 2:159–61; Simms to Benson Lossing, September 1, 1860, *Letters,* 4:239–40; Simms to Henry Stephens Randall, December 3, 1853, *Letters,* 3:264–65; Simms to William James Rivers, June 13, 1859, *Letters,* 6:199–204 (Rivers wrote *A Sketch of the History of South Carolina to the Close of the Proprietary Government by the Revolution of 1719* [1856]); Simms to James Henry Hammond, September 7, 1856, *Letters,* 3:447 (mentions a letter from Sabine); Simms to William Bacon Stevens, December 30, 1841, *Letters,* 1:295–97 (Stevens wrote *A History of Georgia* [1847]); "William H. Trescot," *Letters,* 1:cxli–cxlii; and "David Flavel Jamison," *Letters,* 1:cxvii.

3. The copy of Gayarré's *History of Louisiana* inscribed to Simms is located in the South Caroliniana Library, University of South Carolina.

4. [Simms,] "Views and Reviews in American History, Literature and Fiction," *Southern Literary Messenger* 13 (April 1847): 250.

5. Shelby Foote, *The Civil War: A Narrative, Fort Sumter to Perryville* (New York: Random House, 1958), 815.

6. On the Revolutionary generation's view of history, see Douglass Adair, "'Experience Must Be Our Only Guide': History, Democratic Theory, and the United States Constitution," in Adair's *Fame and the Founding Fathers,* ed. Trevor Colbourn (Indianapolis, Ind.: Liberty Fund, 1998), 152–75; Trevor Colbourn, *The Lamp of Experience: Whig History and the Intellectual Origins of the American Revolution* (Indianapolis, Ind.: Liberty Fund, 1998), 5–24; and Gordon S. Wood, *The Creation of the American Republic, 1776–1787* (Chapel Hill: University of North Carolina Press, 1969), 3–45.

7. In particular, see Simms, "Domestic Histories of the South," *Southern Quarterly Review,* n.s., 5 (January 1852): 507–35; and "Ellet's Women of the Revolution," 314–54, both of which are discussed below.

8. Simms to Benjamin F. Perry, October 30, 1842, *Letters,* 1:328.

9. Simms, *The Life of Francis Marion* (Philadelphia: Geo. G. Evans, 1860), preface and passim.

10. Van Tassel, *Recording America's Past,* 73. See also Marcus Cunliffe, "Introduction," in *The Life of Washington,* by Mason L. Weems (Cambridge, Mass.: Belknap Press of Harvard University Press, 1962), ix–lxii; Ronald W. Howard, "Mason Locke Weems," in *Dictionary of Literary Biography,* vol. 30, *American Historians, 1607–1865,* ed. Clyde N. Wilson (Detroit: Gale Research Co., 1984), 333–40; and Kraus, *A History of American History,* 159–62.

11. Simms, "Weems, the Biographer and Historian," in *Views and Reviews in American Literature, History and Fiction, Second Series* (New York: Wiley and Putnam, 1845), 123.

12. Ibid., 124.

13. Ibid., 124–25. On Niebuhr, see John Emerich Edward Dalberg-Acton [Lord Acton], "German Schools of History," in *Selected Writings of Lord Acton,* 2:325–64. On Lincoln and Wilson, see Richard M. Weaver, "'Parson' Weems: A Study in Early American Rhetoric," in *In Defense of Tradition: Collected Shorter Writings of Richard M. Weaver, 1929–1963,* ed. Ted J. Smith III (Indianapolis, Ind.: Liberty Fund, 2000), 274.

14. Simms "Weems, the Biographer and Historian," 125–26.

15. Weaver, "'Parson' Weems," 275.

16. Marcus Cunliffe, "Introduction," xxxiv–liii; Ronald W. Howard, "Mason Locke Weems," 30:338–40; and Simms, preface to *The Life of Francis Marion* (New York: Henry G. Langley, 1844).

17. For biographical and historiographical information on Headley, see Owen Connelly and Jesse Scott, "Joel T. Headley," in *Dictionary of Literary Biography,* 30:107–11.

18. Simms, "Headley's Life of Cromwell," 510.

19. Ibid., 520, 538.

20. For biographical and historiographical information on Richard Hildreth, see John Braeman, "Richard Hildreth," in *Dictionary of Literary Biography,* 30:116–33.

21. Simms, "Hildreth's United States," *Southern Quarterly Review* 15 (October 1849): 258.

22. The two pamphlets under consideration were Hon. George R. Gilmer, *The Literary Progress of Georgia, An Address Delivered at the College Chapel, at Athens, before the Society of Alumni, and at Their Request, Thursday, August 7, 1851, Being the Semi-Centennial Anniversary of Franklin College* (Athens, Ga.: White and Brother, 1851); and Hon. John P. Kennedy, *Address Delivered before the Maryland Institute for the Promotion of the Mechanical Arts, on the Occasion of the Opening of the Fourth Annual Exhibition, on the 21st October, 1851, Being the First Exhibition in the New Hall of the Institute* (Baltimore: John Murphy and Co., 1851).

23. Simms, "Domestic Histories of the South," 507, 508.

24. Ibid., 508–10.

25. For biographical and historiographical information on Elizabeth F. Ellet, see Clyde Wilson, "Elizabeth F. Ellet," in *Dictionary of Literary Biography,* 30:84–88.

26. Simms, "Ellet's Women of the Revolution," 318, 319.

27. Ibid., 328, 329.

28. Jared Sparks, ed. *The Writings of George Washington; Being His Correspondence, Addresses, Messages and Other Papers, Official and Private, Selected and Published from the Original Manuscripts; with a Life of the Author, Notes and Illustrations,* 12 vols., (New York: Harper and Brothers, 1848). For biographical and historiographical information on Sparks, see Kraus, *A History of American History,* 199–215; and Michael E. Stevens, "Jared Sparks," in *Dictionary of Literary Biography,* 30:298–310.

29. Simms, "Writings of George Washington," *Southern Quarterly Review* 15 (April 1849): 253.

30. Sparks, ed. *The Writings of George Washington,* 2:xiv–xv.

31. George H. Callcott, *History in the United States, 1800–1860: Its Practice and Purpose* (Baltimore: Johns Hopkins Press, 1970), 129–31. See also Jared Sparks, *A Reply to the Strictures of Lord Mahon and Others, on the Mode of Editing the Writings of Washington* (Cambridge, Mass.: John Bartlett, 1852), especially John Marshall's May 6, 1834, letter to Sparks (10–11).

32. Herbert Baxter Adams, *The Life and Writings of Jared Sparks Comprising Selections from His Journals and Correspondence* (Boston: Houghton, Mifflin and Company, 1893), 1:xxiv. For information on Adams, see Raymond J. Cunningham, "Herbert Baxter Adams," in *Dictionary of Literary Biography,* vol. 47, *American Historians, 1866–1912,* ed. Clyde N. Wilson (Detroit: Gale Research Company, 1986), 28–34.

33. Simms, "Writings of George Washington," 253.

34. The letters were dated January 1, 1778; April 18, 1778; September 12, 1778; and September 29, 1779.

35. Simms to Albert James Pickett, March 18, 1848, *Letters,* 5:399–400. On Prescott, see Levin, *History as Romantic Art.*

36. Simms, "Prescott's Conquest of Peru," pt. 1, *Southern Quarterly Review* 13 (January 1848): 136.

37. Simms, *Southward Ho! A Spell of Sunshine,* 108.

38. Simms, "Prescott's Conquest of Peru," 137–38.

39. Foote, *The Civil War,* 815.

40. William Henry Trescot, *Oration Delivered before the South-Carolina Historical Society, Thursday, May 19, 1859* (Charleston, S.C.: James and Williams, 1859), 23; Benson J. Lossing, *Our Country. A Household History for All Readers, from the Discovery of America to the One Hundredth Anniversary of the Declaration of Independence* (New York: Johnson, Wilson and Co., 1875–78), 1429; Lossing, *The Pictorial Field-Book of the Revolution; or, Illustrations, by Pen and Pencil, of the History, Biography, Scenery, Relics, and Traditions of the War for Independence* (New York: Harper and Bros., 1851–52), 686–87n1; Henry B. Dawson, *Battles of the United States, by Sea and Land: Embracing Those of the Revolutionary and Indian Wars, the War of 1812, and the Mexican War; with Important Official Documents* (New York: Johnson, Fry, and Company, 1858), 601, 611, 712, 713, 715; and William H. Whitmore, *The Cavalier Dismounted: An Essay on the Origin of the Founders of the Thirteen Colonies* (Salem, Mass.: G. M. Whipple and A. A. Smith, 1864), 10–11.

41. William H. Venable, *A School History of the United States* (Cincinnati: Wilson, Hinkle and Co., 1872), 70; George R. Fairbanks, *The History and Antiquities of the City of St. Augustine, Florida, Founded* A.D. 1565: *Comprising Some of the Most Interesting Portions of the Early History of Florida* (New York: Charles B. Norton, 1858), 51–52; and Fairbanks, *History of Florida from Its Discovery by Ponce de Leon, in 1512, to the Close of the Florida War, in 1842* (Philadelphia: J. B. Lippincott and Co., 1871), 63–64.

42. Alexander H. Stephens, *A Constitutional View of the Late War between the States; Its Causes, Character, Conduct and Results Presented in a Series of Colloquies at Liberty Hall* (Philadelphia: National Publishing Co., 1868–70), 766. Stephens also wrote a general survey of American history, *A Comprehensive and Popular History of the United States* (1882), and a school text, *A Compendium of the History of the United States from the Earliest Settlements to 1872* (1872). Charles Sumner, "Reply to Assailants: Oath to Support the Constitution; Weakness of the South from Slavery. Second Speech in the Senate on the Boston Petition for the Repeal of the Fugitive Slave Act, June 28, 1854," in *The Works of Charles Sumner* (Boston: Lee and Shepard, 1875), 3:386n2. Ironically, "Reply to Assailants" was delivered before the speech that earned Sumner his caning at the hands of Preston Brooks.

43. Simms to Simon Gratz, November 20, 1860, *Letters,* 4:271; Lukacs, *Historical Consciousness,* 114.

THREE *Simms as Collector and Publisher of Manuscripts*

1. Simms to William James Rivers, May 31, 1862, *Letters,* 6:233.

2. Ibid.; Charles Lanman, "A Novelist's Plantation," quoted in Simms, *Letters,* 2:405; Simms to William Hawkins Ferris, February 8, 1867, *Letters,* 5:13; Simms to Evert A. Duyckinck, July 28, 1866, *Letters,* 4:584; Simms to James Lawson, November 27, 1833, *Letters,* 1:53.

3. Simms to Evert A. Duyckinck, May 1, 1867, *Letters,* 5:44–46; Laurens, *The Papers of Henry Laurens,* eds. Philip M. Hamer and George C. Rogers Jr. (Columbia: University of South Carolina Press, 1968), 1:xxvi–xxvii; and Stephen Meats, "Artist or Historian: William Gilmore Simms and the Revolutionary South," in *Eighteenth-Century Florida and the Revolutionary South,* ed. Samuel Proctor (Gainesville: University Presses of Florida, 1978), 98–99. Simms to William Hawkins Ferris, February 8, 1867, *Letters,* 5:13; Simms to Evert A. Duyckinck, August 3, 1866, *Letters,* 4:587.

4. Simms to Evert A. Duyckinck, May 1, 1867, *Letters,* 5:44–45.

5. Simms to Evert A. Duyckinck, December 13, 1866, *Letters,* 4:625.

6. Simms to Evert A. Duyckinck, May 1, 1867, *Letters,* 5:45.

7. Simms's collection of Laurens family papers is in the South Caroliniana Library. Another example of a historical manuscript annotated by Simms is the letter of July 22, 1778, from George Washington to "The President of Congress," in the Washington Papers, South Caroliniana Library, University of South Carolina. Simms to Simon Gratz, November 20, 1860, *Letters,* 4:271; and Simms to Edward Herrick Jr., November 2, 1859, *Letters,* 4:208–9. Simms to Leavitt, Strebeigh and Company, October 3, 1866, *Letters,* 4:609. In the letter to Leavitt, Strebeigh and Company, Simms describes Tefft's collection. R. W. Gibbes's collection, which was also burned during Sherman's march through South Carolina, is cited in *The Life of Francis Marion.*

8. Simms to James Henry Hammond, January 2, 1848, *Letters,* 2:388.

9. Ibid. On Gayarré, see Wilbur E. Meneray, "Charles E. A. Gayarré," in *Dictionary of Literary Biography,* 30:97–101; and Alcée Fortier, "Charles Gayarré," in *Library of Southern Literature,* ed. Edwin Anderson Alderman, Joel Chandler Harris, and Charles William Kent (New Orleans: Martin and Hoyt Company, 1909), 4:1773–75.

10. Simms to Armistead Burt, January 26, 1845, *Letters,* 2:24.

11. Russell Blaine Nye, *Society and Culture in America, 1830–1860* (New York: Harper and Row, 1974), 108–9; Shaffer, *The Politics of History,* 174; and Michael Kammen, *Mystic Chords of Memory: The Transformation of Tradition in American Culture* (New York: Alfred A. Knopf, 1991), 76–79.

12. Simms, "South Carolina Just before the Revolution," *Southern Literary Messenger* 11 (March 1845): 138.

13. Callcott, *History in the United States,* 35.

14. Simms to John Pendleton Kennedy, May 25, 1851, *Letters,* 3:125; Simms to Israel Keech Tefft, August 23, 1839, *Letters,* 5:344–45; Simms to Lyman C. Draper, March 20, 1854, *Letters,* 3:291.

15. Peter LeRoy Shillingsburg, "The Use of Sources in Simms's Biography of Francis Marion" (master's thesis, University of South Carolina, 1967); Clyde N. Wilson, "William Gilmore Simms," in *Dictionary of Literary Biography,* 30:283.

16. Simms, "A Sketch of the Life and Public Services of John Rutledge of South Carolina," pts. 1 and 2, *American Whig Review* 5 (August 1847): 125–37 and 5 (September 1847): 277–91; "The Baron de Kalb," *Southern Quarterly Review* 6 (July 1852): 141–203; "Revolutionary Letters," *Historical Magazine* 1 (July 1857): 206–7; 1 (September 1857): 266–70; 1 (October 1857): 289–92; 2 (January 1858): 6–11; 2 (September 1858): 259–61; 2 (November 1858): 321–24; 3 (June 1859): 169–71. Other good examples of documentary material published by Simms, can be found in "South Carolina Just before the Revolution," 138–43; and "Reminiscences of the Revolution," *Russell's Magazine* (October 1859): 59–72.

17. Simms to Benjamin F. Perry, October 13, 1843, *Letters,* 1:371.

18. Simms to John Reuben Thompson, January 16, 1862, *Letters,* 6:223–24; Simms to Harry Hammond, January 24, 1865, *Letters,* 4:482–83; Clyde N. Wilson, introduction to *Selections from the Letters and Speeches of the Hon. James H. Hammond, of South Carolina,* ed. Simms (Spartanburg, S.C.: Reprint Company, 1978), xiii–xiv.

19. More recent studies of John Laurens include Gregory D. Massey, *John Laurens and the American Revolution* (Columbia: University of South Carolina Press, 2000); and Robert M. Weir, "John Laurens: Portrait of a Hero," in *"The Last of American Freemen": Studies in the Political Culture of the Colonial and Revolutionary South* (Macon, Ga.: Mercer University Press, 1986), 89–104.

20. Simms to Evert A. Duyckinck, January 19, 1845, *Letters,* 2:21.

21. Ibid.

22. Simms to William James Rivers, May 31, 1862, *Letters,* 6:233. All of the persons listed were active participants in the Revolution.

23. Simms to William James Rivers, no date, in Anne Blythe Meriwether, "An Unpublished Letter of 1862 from Simms to W. J. Rivers," *Simms Review* 3 (Summer 1995): 3. Though undated this letter is obviously a follow-up to the letter of May 31, 1862.

24. Washington's letter is dated September 4, 1778; Adams's letter is dated November 6, 1782; and Hamilton's letter is dated January 12, 1824.

25. Literally: "it is sweet and fitting to die for the fatherland."

26. Simms, "Memoir," in *The Army Correspondence of Colonel John Laurens, in the Years 1777–8, Now First Printed from Original Letters Addressed to His Father, Henry Laurens, President of Congress, with a Memoir* (New York: Bradford Club, 1867), 39, 27; Weir, "John Laurens," 89–91.

27. Simms, "Memoir," 35, 36; Weir, "John Laurens," 91–92.

28. Simms, "Memoir," 35; Weir, "John Laurens," 104.

29. Simms, "Memoir," 9. As regards Simms letting Bancroft see the letters, see Simms to Evert A. Duyckinck, December 13, 1866, *Letters,* 4:624.

FOUR   *Simms as Biographer*

1. Carr, *What Is History?* 59; R. G. Collingwood, *The Idea of History,* 304.

2. Scott E. Casper, *Constructing American Lives: Biography and Culture in Nineteenth-Century America* (Chapel Hill: University of North Carolina Press, 1999). Other studies of the art of biography in the nineteenth century include Edward H. O'Neill's *A History of American Biography: 1800–1935* (Philadelphia: University of Pennsylvania Press, 1935); and William Francis Cash's "Biography and Southern Culture, 1800–1940" (Ph.D. diss., University of Texas, 1990).

3. Adair, *Fame and the Founding Fathers,* 15–17, 30, 355, 388–98 and 405; Bernard Bailyn, *The Ideological Origins of the American Revolution* (Cambridge, Mass.: Belknap Press of Harvard University Press, 1967), 22–26; Robert M. Calhoon, *Dominion and Liberty: Ideology in the Anglo-American World, 1660–1801* (Arlington Heights, Ill.: Harlan Davidson, 1994), 91–92; Colbourn, *The Lamp of Experience;* Wood, *The Creation of the American Republic,* 51.

4. William H. Prescott, "Sir Walter Scott," in *Biographical and Critical Miscellanies* (London: Richard Bentley, 1845), 155.

5. James Savage [?], "The Architecture of a Great Mind," in *The Federalist Literary Mind: Selections from the "Monthly Anthology and Boston Review," 1803–1811, Including Documents Relating to the Boston Athenaeum,* ed. Lewis P. Simpson (Baton Rouge: Louisiana State University Press, 1962), 79.

6. Edmund Burke, "An Appeal from the New to the Old Whigs," in *Further Reflections on the Revolution in France,* ed. Daniel E. Ritchie (Indianapolis, Ind.: Liberty Fund, 1992), 197; Casper, *Constructing American Lives,* 2. Also see Ralph Waldo Emerson on the importance of individualism in "The American Scholar," in *The Portable Emerson,* ed. Mark Van Doren (New York: Viking Press, 1946), 38–46.

7. Callcott, *History in the United States,* 98; Jacob Burckhardt, *Reflections on History* (Indianapolis, Ind.: Liberty Fund, 1979), 292.

8. On the portrayal of Revolutionary heroes, see Casper, *Constructing American Lives;* Kammen, *Mystic Chords of Memory* and *A Season of Youth;* William C. Dowling, foreword to *An Essay on the Life of the Honourable Major-General Israel Putnam: Addressed to the State Society of the Cincinnati in Connecticut and Published by Their Order,* by David

Humphreys (Indianapolis, Ind.: Liberty Fund, 2000); Christopher Harris, "Character Portraits of American Military Heroes of the Revolution, 1782–1832" (Ph.D. diss., Brown University, 1985); James Joseph Schramer, "The Myth of Cincinnatus: The Citizen-Soldier in Early American Literature" (Ph.D. diss., University of Minnesota, 1987); and Edward Tang, "Revolutionary Legacies: History, Literature, and Memory in Nineteenth-Century America, 1820–1880" (Ph.D. diss., New York University, 1996).

9. John Pendleton Kennedy, *Memoirs of the Life of William Wirt, Attorney-General of the United States* (Philadelphia: Lea and Blanchard, 1850), dedication. Casper, *Constructing American Lives,* 179 and 4–10. See also Merrill D. Peterson, *The Jefferson Image in the American Mind* (New York: Oxford University Press, 1960), 112–61.

10. For example, see Wilentz, "America Made Easy," 35–40.

11. Berlin, *Historical Inevitability;* Popper, *The Poverty of Historicism;* Marc Bloch, *The Historian's Craft,* trans. Peter Putnam (New York: Vintage Books, 1953), 47; George C. Rogers Jr., "Names, Not Numbers," *William and Mary Quarterly,* 3rd ser., 45 (1988): 574–79; Lukacs, *Historical Consciousness,* 172.

12. Hayne's biography of Pickens, written in 1864, was never published.

13. Robert Penn Warren, "Biography," in *An Approach to Literature,* 4th ed., ed. Cleanth Brooks, John Thibaut Purser, and Robert Penn Warren (New York: Appleton-Century-Crofts, 1964), 559.

14. Simms to James Lawson, January 2, 1847, *Letters,* 2:250. There is no good modern biography of Marion, but interested readers should find the following reliable sources for background information: John Buchanan, *The Road to Guilford Courthouse: The American Revolution in the Carolinas* (New York: John Wiley and Sons, 1997); George C. Rogers Jr., *Charleston in the Age of the Pinckneys* (Norman: University of Oklahoma Press, 1969); and David Duncan Wallace, *South Carolina: A Short History, 1529–1948* (Chapel Hill: University of North Carolina Press, 1951). Those interested in how Marion has been portrayed over the years should refer to Alexander Moore's brief but informative article "The Swamp Fox in History and Literature: A Select Bibliography of Books about Francis Marion," *Carologue: A Publication of the South Carolina Historical Society* 15 (Winter 1999): 14–15.

15. Simms to Carey and Hart, June 7, 1838, *Letters,* 1:134.

16. Simms, *The Life of the Chevalier Bayard; "The Good Knight," "Sans peur et sans reproche"* (New York: Harper and Brothers, 1847), advertisement. For instance, see the footnotes on page 121 to "Livy," a poem by Macauley, and to Crowe's *History of France.*

17. Simms to James Lawson, April 25, 1840, *Letters,* 1:171; Simms to Lawson, September 15, 1840, *Letters,* 1:188–89; Simms to George Frederick Holmes, October 27, 1843, *Letters,* 1:378–79; Simms to Holmes, January 26, 1844, *Letters,* 1:399; Simms to Holmes, May 14, 1844, *Letters,* 1:417. David Flavel Jamison was a neighbor of Simms who possessed a substantial library and was considered an authority on local history. The letter to Jamison has not been located.

18. Simms, *The Life of Francis Marion* (New York: Henry G. Langley, 1844), 348, 349. Robert Wilson Gibbes took offense at not receiving credit as the possessor of the five volumes of MS. letters. Simms corrected this in later editions by adding that the five volumes of MS. letters are "in the possession of Dr. R. W. Gibbes, of S. Carolina." For an explanation of this matter, see Simms to Robert Wilson Gibbes, December 30, 1844, *Letters,* 5:386–87. Peter LeRoy Shillingsburg, "The Use of Sources in Simms's Biography of Francis Marion."

19. Simms, *The Life of Francis Marion* (Philadelphia: Geo. G. Evans, 1860), 13, 14, passim. All subsequent citations are to this 1860 edition.

20. For Simms's use of oral history, see "Ellet's Women of the Revolution," 351–52; *Katharine Walton: [or, The Rebel of Dorchester:] With Introduction and Explanatory Notes*

(Spartanburg, S.C.: Reprint Company, 1976), 521–22 note 469.20; and Trent, *William Gilmore Simms,* 106.

21. Simms, "Daniel Boon," in *Views and Reviews,* 151n.

22. Simms, *The Life of Francis Marion,* preface, 28n, 46n. Another example of him correcting one of Weems's errors can be found on page 264. An example of Simms pointing out the silence of his sources can be found on page 268.

23. Frederick Wagner, "Simms's Editing of *The Life of Nathanael Greene,*" *Southern Literary Journal* 11 (Fall 1978): 40–43. Simms's copy of Johnson is in Special Collections of the Thomas Cooper Library, University of South Carolina.

24. Simms to Benjamin F. Perry, October 30, 1842, *Letters,* 1:329.

25. Simms to Albert James Pickett, December 4, 1847, *Letters,* 5:397.

26. Simms to Henry B. Dawson, February 21 and March 15, 1859, *Letters,* 4:124–25 and 135–36.

27. Simms, *The History of South Carolina, from Its First European Discovery to Its Erection into a Republic: With a Supplementary Book, Bringing the Narrative Down to the Present Time* (New York: Redfield, 1860), 4.

28. Trent, *William Gilmore Simms,* 139. O'Neill, *A History of American Biography,* 29; Wakelyn, *The Politics of a Literary Man.* John McCardell, "Biography and the Southern Mind: William Gilmore Simms," in *Long Years of Neglect: The Work and Reputation of William Gilmore Simms,* ed. John C. Guilds (Fayetteville: University of Arkansas Press, 1988), 211.

29. Simms to James Lawson, September 15, 1840, *Letters,* 1:188–89.

30. Simms to James Lawson, August 2, 1848, *Letters,* 2:430.

31. The memoirs and histories Simms was referring to probably included the following: William Johnson, *Sketches of the Life and Correspondence of Nathanael Greene, Major General of the Armies of the United States, in the War of the Revolution* (1822); Henry Lee, *Memoirs of the War in the Southern Department of the United States* (1812); David Ramsay, *History of the Revolution of South-Carolina;* William Moultrie, *Memoirs of the American Revolution, So Far as It Related to the States of North and South Carolina, and Georgia* (1802); John Marshall, *Life of George Washington* (1803–7); Banastre Tarleton, *A History of the Campaigns of 1780 and 1781, in the Southern Provinces of North America* (1797); and Alexander Graydon, *Memoirs of a Life, Chiefly Passed in Pennsylvania, within the Last Sixty Years . . .* (1811).

32. Simms, *The Life of Nathanael Greene, Major-General in the Army of the Revolution* (New York: George F. Cooledge and Brother, 1849), advertisement.

33. Lee's book is organized in such a way as to make cross-referencing easy. Henry Lee Jr., *The Campaign of 1781 in the Carolinas: With Remarks Historical and Critical on Johnson's Life of Greene* (1824; repr., Chicago: Quadrangle Books, 1962).

34. M. F. Treacy, *Prelude to Yorktown: The Southern Campaign of Nathanael Greene, 1780–1781* (Chapel Hill: University of North Carolina Press, 1963), 253.

35. John McCardell, "Poetry and the Practical: William Gilmore Simms," in *Intellectual Life in Antebellum Charleston,* eds. Michael O'Brien and David Moltke-Hansen (Knoxville: University of Tennessee Press, 1986), 202; Faust, *A Sacred Circle.*

36. Simms to Evert A. Duyckinck, February 11, 1848, *Letters,* 2:396.

37. Hegel, *The Philosophy of History,* 32.

38. Simms, "Cortés and the Conquest of Mexico," in *Views and Reviews,* 185–87.

39. Simms, "Daniel Boon," in *Views and Reviews,* 150 and 175–76. A good biography of Boone that chronicles his changing reputation is John Mack Faragher, *Daniel Boone: The Life and Legend of an American Pioneer* (New York: Henry Holt and Company, 1992).

40. Simms, "Cortés and the Conquest of Mexico," 186, 185.

41. Simms, *Greene,* 14, 17, 24, 32, 103, 392.

42. Examples of the use of the word "hero": Simms, *The Life of Captain John Smith: The Founder of Virginia* (New York: Perkins Book Company, 1902), 15, 18, 220, and 283.

43. Simms, *Marion,* 12, 347.

44. Simms, *Greene,* 24.

45. Ibid., 116–18. Sources vary as regards the exact number of men in Greene's army, but generally figure the number close to Simms's count. Don Higginbotham places Greene's force at "fewer than 2,000 men" in *War and Society in Revolutionary America: The Wider Dimensions of Conflict* (Columbia: University of South Carolina Press, 1988), 169. John Buchanan, in *The Road to Guilford Courthouse,* numbers Greene's command at 2,307 men. Of those, only 1,482 men were present and fit for duty with a mere 800 properly clothed and equipped. The core of this army was 949 veteran Continental troops of the Maryland and Delaware lines (288). And David Duncan Wallace gives Greene "fewer than 800 men [who] were fit in health and equipment for duty," while numbering the British reinforcements under General Leslie at 2,300 (*South Carolina,* 310).

46. Simms, *The Scout: [or, The Black Riders of Congaree:] With Introduction and Explanatory Notes* (Spartanburg, S.C.: Reprint Company, 1976), 9.

47. Simms, *Greene,* 213–14.

48. Ibid., 120; Higginbotham, *War and Society in Revolutionary America,* 169–70.

49. Simms, *Greene,* 340.

50. John McCardell, in "Biography and the Southern Mind," makes the case that Simms had his own early years in mind when describing Greene's humble beginnings (211).

51. Simms, *Greene,* 31.

52. Ibid., 357.

53. There are few good biographies of the Chevalier Bayard in English. Interested readers could do worse than Samuel Shellabarger's *The Chevalier Bayard: A Study in Fading Chivalry* (New York: Century Co., 1928).

54. Simms, *Bayard,* 396, 2.

55. Ibid., 123.

56. Ibid., 5.

57. Simms, *Life of Captain John Smith,* 2–3.

58. Ibid., 2.

59. O'Neill, *A History of American Biography,* 29; Simms, *Life of Captain John Smith,* 283.

60. Simms, *Marion,* 13, 14.

61. Ibid., 9.

62. Ibid., 25.

63. Ibid., 26.

64. Ibid., 30, 135, 32, 53, 54.

65. Ibid., 128n, 343.

66. Ibid., 60, 113, 134.

67. Ibid., 62.

68. Ibid., 82.

69. Ibid., 189, 162.

70. Ibid., 186, 187.

71. Ibid., 187, 271, 261, 323. William Richardson Davie (1756–1820) led troops in North and South Carolina, served as Greene's commissary general, and later was governor of North Carolina.

72. O'Neill, *A History of American Biography,* 29; Simms, *Marion,* 165, 183–84, 202–3, 208, 246, 183, and 50–52.

73. Simms, *Marion,* 237.

74. Ibid., 347.

75. "The Study of History," in *Southern Quarterly Review* 10 (July 1846): 145.

FIVE *The History of South Carolina*

1. Simms, *History,* 5.

2. Simms, *The Geography of South Carolina: Being a Companion to the History of That State by William Gilmore Simms. Compiled from the Latest and Best Authorities, and Designed for the Instruction of the Young.* (Charleston, S.C.: Babcock and Co., 1843), iii.

3. Wood, *The Creation of the American Republic,* 52. On the importance of education in a republican polity, see Richard D. Brown, *The Strength of a People: The Idea of an Informed Citizenry in America, 1650–1870* (Chapel Hill: University of North Carolina Press, 1996). On early Americans' sense of the value of historical education, see also Adair, "'Experience Must Be Our Only Guide,'" in *Fame and the Founding Fathers,* 152–75.

4. Samuel Langdon, "The Republic of the Israelites an Example to the American States," in Ellis Sandoz, ed., *Political Sermons of the American Founding Era, 1730–1805* (Indianapolis, Ind.: Liberty Fund, 1991), 957.

5. Simms, *History,* 1.

6. Ibid., 2.

7. Ibid., 3.

8. Ibid., 6.

9. Ibid., 3.

10. Ibid., 6.

11. Simms to James Henry Hammond, January 2, 1848, *Letters,* 2:387–88; Simms to James Henry Hammond, February 12, 1848, *Letters,* 2:398–99.

12. For the history and organization of American natural history writing, see Pamela Regis, *Describing Early America: Bartram, Jefferson, Crèvecoeur, and the Influence of Natural History* (Philadelphia: University of Pennsylvania Press, 1999).

13. Simms, *History,* 5.

14. For examples, see Simms, *History,* 199 and 299. In the first example Simms questions estimates of South Carolina's population. In the second he points out what he feels is an error on the part of some historians who have said General Greene was surprised by Lord Rawdon at Hobkirk's Hill in April 1781.

15. Ibid., 6.

16. Ibid., 6.

17. Simms to James Lawson, October 25, 1840, *Letters,* 1:194.

18. Simms to John C. Calhoun, May 21, 1847, *Letters,* 2:318–19.

19. Simms to Benjamin F. Perry, May 20, 1847, *Letters,* 2:317.

20. Simms to James Henry Hammond, July 15, 1847, *Letters,* 2:330; Simms to Benjamin F. Perry, July 15, 1847, *Letters,* 2:333.

21. Simms to William Porcher Miles, January 18, 1860, *Letters,* 4:187.

22. Simms, *History,* 158. It is worth noting that Simms's description of South Carolina's road to independence in *The History of South Carolina* does not differ substantially from the summary of the Revolution written over one hundred years later by George C. Rogers Jr. in *A South Carolina Chronology, 1497–1970,* South Carolina Tricentennial Commission, 11 (Columbia: University of South Carolina Press, 1973), 30.

23. Simms, *History,* 152 and 153.

24. Ibid., 202.

25. Ibid., 181.

26. Ibid., 180.

27. Ibid., 152 and 153.

28. Ibid., 154.

29. Ibid., 148.

30. Ibid., 136.

31. Ibid., 160–61.

32. See, David Ramsay, *The History of the American Revolution,* ed. Lester H. Cohen (Indianapolis, Ind.: Liberty Fund, 1990), 2:625–29. For a modern analysis (that bears some similarity to Simms's and Ramsay's) of how ethnic and religious identities can help to explain Loyalism, see Robert M. Weir, *Colonial South Carolina: A History* (Millwood, N.Y.: KTO Press, 1983), 322.

33. Simms, *History,* 151.

34. Simms, *The Life of Francis Marion,* 134; Simms, "South Carolina in the Revolution. A Lecture," in *Letters,* 3:525.

35. Simms, *History,* 142–43, 183.

36. Ibid., 179–80 and 182.

37. Ibid., 151.

38. Ibid., 181.

39. Ramsay, *History of the American Revolution,* 2:625. See also Weir, *Colonial South Carolina.*

40. Simms, *History,* 181.

41. Ibid., 180.

42. Ibid., 182.

43. Page Smith, *The Historian and History* (New York: Alfred A. Knopf, 1966).

44. Simms, *History,* 297–98 and 216.

45. Ibid., 224.

46. Ibid., 267.

47. Ibid., 256–57 and 325.

48. Simms, *The History of South Carolina, from Its First European Discovery to Its Erection into a Republic: With a Supplementary Chronicle of Events to the Present Time* (Charleston, S.C.: S. Babcock and Co., 1840), 329. Unless otherwise noted, all citations are to the 1860 edition of Simms's *The History of South Carolina.*

49. Ibid. (1840), 319. This section of text also appears in the 1860 edition, on page 391.

50. Robert M. Weir, "'The Harmony We Were Famous For': An Interpretation of Prerevolutionary South Carolina Politics," in *"The Last of American Freemen": Studies in the Political Culture of the Colonial and Revolutionary South* (Macon, Ga.: Mercer University Press, 1986), 30.

51. Simms to Hammond, January 2, 1848, *Letters,* 2:387.

52. James Henry Hammond to Simms, January 14, 1848, James H. Hammond Papers, Library of Congress.

53. Simms to Hammond, February 12, 1848, *Letters,* 2:398–99.

54. Simms, *History* (1860), 416.

55. Ibid., 419.

56. Ibid., 420.

57. Ibid., 422.

58. Simms to Nathaniel Beverley Tucker, November 27, 1850, *Letters,* 3:76.

59. Simms to John Jacob Bockee, December 12, 1860, *Letters,* 4:292.

60. Simms, *History* (1860), 436–37.

61. Ibid., 437. It is interesting to note that Simms once looked forward to Calhoun's passing, thinking that the void he left would be filled by younger men of equal, if not greater, abilities. In fact, many of the men he listed were at one time or another counted among Simms's political opponents.

62. Simms, *History* (1840), 318.

63. Simms to William Porcher Miles, January 18, 1860, *Letters,* 4:186–87. A. S. Salley, *Catalogue of the Salley Collection of the Works of Wm. Gilmore Simms* (1943; repr., New York: Burt Franklin, 1969), 106. Differing definitions of what a "public" school is make satisfactory numbers hard to come by, but according to one estimate there were 746 "public" schools with 9,061 pupils in South Carolina in 1826, and 757 schools with 20,716 pupils in 1860 (Wallace, *South Carolina,* 460, 464).

SIX *Simms as a Presenter of History through Fiction*

1. For such comparisons, see "Table Talk: Death of William Gilmore Simms," *Appleton's Journal: A Magazine of General Literature* 4 (July 9, 1870): 49; C. Hugh Holman, "The Influence of Scott and Cooper on Simms," in *The Roots of Southern Writing: Essays on the Literature of the American South* (Athens: University of Georgia Press, 1972), 50–60; and Wimsatt, *The Major Fiction of William Gilmore Simms,* 35–40.

2. Vernon L. Parrington, *Main Currents in American Thought: An Interpretation of American Literature from the Beginnings to 1920,* vol. 2, *The Romantic Revolution in America* (New York: Harcourt, Brace and Company, 1930), 135.

3. James Fenimore Cooper, introduction to *The Pioneers, or the Sources of the Susquehanna; A Descriptive Tale,* in *The Leatherstocking Tales* (New York: Library of America, 1985), 1:7. See also Cooper's prefaces and introductions to *The Last of the Mohicans* and *The Prairie.* Kay S. House has written a brief study of Cooper's historianship that is worth reading: "Cooper as Historian," in George A. Test, ed. *James Fenimore Cooper: His Country and His Art* (Papers from the 1986 Conference at State University College of New York–Oneonta and Cooperstown), 1–13; available on-line at http://external.oneonta.edu /cooper/articles/suny/1986suny-house.html (accessed September 2004).

4. Gore Vidal, *Burr: A Novel* (New York: Random House, 1973), 429. See also Lukacs, *Historical Consciousness,* 127.

5. Simms, *Vasconselos,* 1.

6. Simms, *Views and Reviews,* 44–45.

7. Simms, *Vasconselos,* 1.

8. Simms, *The Wigwam and the Cabin,* 5 (dedication).

9. Simms, "Lucas de Ayllon," 430.

10. Simms to Philip C. Pendleton, August 12, 1841, *Letters,* 1:259.

11. For historians' accounts of Lucas de Ayllon's voyage to Carolina, see Robert M. Weir, *Colonial South Carolina;* Samuel Eliot Morison, *The European Discovery of America: The Northern Voyages* (New York: Oxford University Press, 1971); and John Fiske, *The Discovery of America: With Some Account of Ancient America and the Spanish Conquest,* vol. 2 (Cambridge, Mass.: Riverside Press, 1894).

12. Simms, "Lucas de Ayllon," 431, 445, 433.

13. Simms, *Views and Reviews,* 135. In *Alternative Americas: A Reading of Antebellum Political Culture* (Chicago: University of Chicago Press, 1986), Anne Norton has

shown that antebellum southerners were viewed by northerners in much the same way as Indians.

14. I am indebted to John C. Guilds and Charles Hudson for some of these observations. See their book *An Early and Strong Sympathy: The Indian Writings of William Gilmore Simms* (Columbia: University of South Carolina Press, 2003).

15. Simms, "Lucas de Ayllon," 455.

16. Simms, *The Yemassee,* xxviii.

17. Guilds, *Simms: A Literary Life,* 60; Simms to Henry Rowe Schoolcraft, March 18, 1851, *Letters,* 3:101.

18. Simms, "Lucas de Ayllon," 431, 432, 433.

19. Simms, *History, 11.*

20. Simms, *Views and Reviews,* 91.

21. Simms, "Lucas de Ayllon," 91.

22. Simms, *Egeria,* 294.

23. Kibler, "Stewardship and *Patria* in Simms's Frontier Poetry," 216.

24. Simms, *The Yemassee,* xxx, and *Charlemont, 7.*

25. Simms, *Richard Hurdis,* xxviii; *Border Beagles,* advertisement. For Simms's treatment of the Murrell story, see Dianne C. Luce, "John A. Murrell and the Imaginations of Simms and Faulkner," in *William Gilmore Simms and the American Frontier,* 237–57.

26. James Lal Penick Jr. *The Great Western Land Pirate: John A. Murrell in Legend and History* (Columbia: University of Missouri Press, 1981).

27. Nick Meriwether has written the most thorough analysis of *The Lily and the Totem:* "Simms's *The Lily and the Totem:* 'History for the Purposes of Art,'" in *Long Years of Neglect,* 76–105.

28. Simms to Carey & Hart, *Letters,* 4:93.

29. Simms, *The Lily and the Totem,* 463.

30. Ibid., iv.

31. Ibid., iv, v.

32. Ibid., v.

33. Meriwether, "Simms's *The Lily and the Totem,*" 97.

34. Simms, *The Lily and the Totem,* 315.

35. John C. Guilds, "Simms's Use of History: Theory and Practice," *Mississippi Quarterly: Journal of Southern Culture* 30 (Fall 1977): 505.

36. Rogers, *Charleston in the Age of the Pinckneys,* 48.

37. John Esten Cooke, *Charleston (S.C.) Mercury,* July 16, 1859. On the novels' value as history, see also William Gordon Belser Jr., "William Gilmore Simms: Fictionist as Military Historian of the Revolution" (Ph.D. diss., St. John's University, 1977).

38. For the difference between history as foreground and history as background, see John Lukacs, *A Thread of Years* (New Haven, Conn.: Yale University Press, 1998), 6.

39. Simms, *The Forayers: or, The Raid of the Dog-Days: With Introduction and Explanatory Notes* (Spartanburg, S.C.: Reprint Company, 1976), 4.

40. For Simms's portrayal in fiction of the Revolution as a civil war, see Belser, "William Gilmore Simms: Fictionist as Military Historian of the Revolution"; and C. Hugh Holman, "William Gilmore Simms's Picture of the Revolution as a Civil War," in *The Roots of Southern Writing,* 35–49.

41. Simms, *The Partisan,* viii. For similar assertions of the historical accuracy of the Revolutionary novels, see *The Partisan,* 483; *Mellichampe: With Introduction and Explanatory Notes* (Spartanburg, S.C.: Reprint Company, 1976), 1–8; *Katharine Walton,* 2–3, 295, 329, 474; *Joscelyn: With Introduction and Explanatory Notes* (Spartanburg, S.C.: Reprint Company, 1976), 5–6.

42. Simms, "Ellet's Women of the Revolution," 351–52.

43. Simms, *The Partisan*, viii.

44. Simms, *Joscelyn*, 5. John Bones was a friend of Hammond's and a resident of Augusta.

45. Simms, *The Forayers*, 1, 563.

46. Simms, *Woodcraft: [or, Hawks about the Dovecote:] With Introduction and Explanatory Notes* (Spartanburg, S.C.: Reprint Company, 1976), 4.

47. Trent, *William Gilmore Simms*, 106. Unfortunately, Trent only sparsely footnoted his sources.

48. Simms, *Katharine Walton*, 521–22, n.469.20.

49. Stephen Meats, "Artist or Historian," 101. Meats prepared an introduction and explanatory notes for *Joscelyn* and compiled Simms's *The Revolutionary War in South Carolina: An Anthology* (Columbia: Southern Studies Program, University of South Carolina, 1975).

50. Simms, *The Partisan*, 474.

51. Foote, "The Novelist's View of History," 439–45; Butterfield, *The Historical Novel*; Gore Vidal, "First Note on Abraham Lincoln," "Lincoln, *Lincoln*, and the Priests of Academe," and "Last Note on Lincoln," in *United States: Essays, 1952–1992* (New York: Random House, 1993), 664–707; Eugene Genovese, "William Styron's *The Confessions of Nat Turner*: A Meditation on Evil, Redemption, and History," in *Novel History*, 209–20.

52. Jacob F. Rivers III, "Prominent Female Characters in the Revolutionary War Novels of William Gilmore Simms" (master's thesis, University of South Carolina, 1987). Rivers concludes that "Simms drew the portraits of a great number and variety of remarkable women in his eight narratives of South Carolina in the Revolution" (91).

53. Simms, *Mellichampe*, 7.

54. Review of *Mellichampe*, *Godey's* 48 (June 1854): 558; review of *Katharine Walton*, *Godey's* 49 (August 1854): 179; review of *Mellichampe*, *Charleston (S.C.) Weekly News*, April 6, 1854, 2; notice of *The Forayers*, *Graham's*, 48 (January 1856): 83.

55. Simms, *Joscelyn*, 54.

56. Simms, *The Partisan*, 398.

57. Simms, *The Scout*, 142–43.

58. Simms, *The Forayers*, 152–53.

59. Simms, *Joscelyn*, 53.

60. Simms, *The Scout*, 159.

61. Parrington, *Main Currents in American Thought*, 2:128.

62. Simms, *Joscelyn*, 82. See also *Mellichampe*, 2.

63. Simms, *The Forayers*, 147.

64. Simms, *Katharine Walton*, 194.

65. Simms, *The Scout*, 159.

66. Robert M. Calhoon, "The Reintegration of the Loyalists and the Disaffected," in *The American Revolution: Its Character and Limits*, ed. Jack P. Greene (New York: New York University Press, 1987), 67–68.

67. Simms, *Mellichampe*, 68, 199.

68. Simms, *The Forayers*, 7. The partisan leaders referred to are Francis Marion, Thomas Sumter, Henry "Light-Horse Harry" Lee, Hezekiah Maham, William Harden, Wade and Henry Hampton, Peter (or perhaps his brother Hugh) Horry, and Thomas Taylor.

69. Simms, *Eutaw: With Introduction and Explanatory Notes* (Spartanburg, S.C.: Reprint Company, 1976), 99–100.

70. Simms, *Mellichampe*, iv–v.

71. Simms, *The Partisan*, viii.

72. Simms, *Woodcraft*, 47.

73. Simms, *Eutaw*, 528–33. In *The History of South Carolina*, Simms records that "the partisans of the South were especially dissatisfied with the reports of the affair. That they did their duty well is undeniable. They make, however, an unfavorable report of the performances of other parties of whom the official report speaks favorably" (345).

74. Simms, *The Partisan*, x, 17.

75. Ibid., ix.

76. Simms, *The Forayers*, 4. On Simms's novels as social history, see Watson, *From Nationalism to Secessionism*, 78; Wimsatt, *The Major Fiction of William Gilmore Simms*, 69–70; and Rivers, "Prominent Female Characters in the Revolutionary War Novels of William Gilmore Simms." On the novels as military history, see Belser, "William Gilmore Simms: Fictionist as Military Historian of the Revolution."

77. Charles E. A. Gayarré, *Romance of the History of Louisiana. A Series of Lectures* (New York: D. Appleton and Company, 1848), 16–17.

78. Simms, *Katharine Walton*, 3.

SEVEN *South Carolina in the Revolution*

1. Simms's dispute with Lorenzo Sabine and his northern lecture tour of 1856 have received coverage in Miriam J. Shillingsburg, "Simms's Failed Lecture Tour of 1856: The Mind of the North," in *Long Years of Neglect: The Work and Reputation of William Gilmore Simms*, ed. John C. Guilds (Fayetteville: University of Arkansas Press, 1988), 183–201; James Perrin Warren, *Culture of Eloquence: Oratory and Reform in Antebellum America* (University Park: Pennsylvania State University Press, 1999); and Clyde N. Wilson, "Tiger's Meat: William Gilmore Simms and the History of the Revolution," *Simms Review* 8 (Winter 2000): 22–31.

2. Simms, "South Carolina in the Revolution. The Social Moral. Lecture 1." Charles Carroll Simms Collection, South Caroliniana Library, University of South Carolina, Columbia. The lecture was delivered in Charleston on May 25, 1857.

3. On New Englanders' sectional nationalism and their bid for hegemony, see Susan-Mary Grant, *North over South: Northern Nationalism and American Identity in the Antebellum Era* (Lawrence: University Press of Kansas, 2000); Joanne Pope Melish, "The 'Condition' Debate and Racial Discourse in the Antebellum North," *Journal of the Early Republic* 19 (Winter 1999): 670–72; Harlow W. Sheidley, *Sectional Nationalism: Massachusetts Conservative Leaders and the Transformation of America, 1815–1836* (Boston: Northeastern University Press, 1998); and Paul E. Teed, "The Politics of Sectional Memory: Theodore Parker and the *Massachusetts Quarterly Review*, 1847–1850," *Journal of the Early Republic* 21 (Summer 2001): 301–29.

4. Arthur H. Shaffer, *To Be an American: David Ramsay and the Making of the American Consciousness* (Columbia: University of South Carolina Press, 1991), 109.

5. Shaffer, *The Politics of History*, 120.

6. Ibid., 15.

7. Ibid., 19. For an alternative reading of Ramsay, see Karen O'Brien, "David Ramsay and the Delayed Americanization of American History," *Early American Literature* 29, no. 1 (1994): 1–18. According to O'Brien, Ramsay's *History of the American Revolution* should be welcomed as a counterbalance to New England's hegemony over national history.

8. Davis, *Intellectual Life in Jefferson's Virginia*, 278.

9. Michael Kammen, "Challenges and Opportunities in Writing State and Local History," in *Selvages and Biases: The Fabric of History in American Culture* (Ithaca, N.Y.: Cornell University Press, 1987), 158.

10. Craig Werner, "The Old South, 1815–1840," in *The History of Southern Literature*, ed. Louis D. Rubin Jr. et al. (Baton Rouge: Louisiana State University Press, 1985), 84.

11. Simms, *The Wigwam and the Cabin*, 4.

12. Lorenzo Sabine, *The American Loyalists or Biographical Sketches of Adherents to the British Crown in the War of the Revolution; Alphabetically Arranged; with a Preliminary Historical Essay* (Boston: Charles C. Little and James Brown, 1847), 30.

13. Ibid., 32.

14. Simms, "South Carolina in the Revolution," *Southern Quarterly Review* (July 1848): 44, 38, 39.

15. Ibid., 45.

16. Simms to George Bancroft, William C. Bryant, and others, November 3, 1856, *Letters*, 3:454.

17. Paul E. Johnson, *A Shopkeeper's Millennium: Society and Revivals in Rochester, New York, 1815–1837* (New York: Hill and Wang, 1978), 3–4.

18. Ernest Lee Tuveson, *Redeemer Nation: The Idea of America's Millennial Role* (Chicago: University of Chicago Press, 1968); and Richard Franklin Bensel, *Yankee Leviathan: The Origins of Central State Authority in America, 1859–1877* (Cambridge: Cambridge University Press, 1990).

19. Simms to James Lawson, August 11, 1845, *Letters*, 2:100; Simms to Lawson, October 23, 1846, *Letters*, 2:196.

20. Simms to Lawson, October 9, 1846, *Letters*, 2:191.

21. On the Young America movement that united Simms with New York, see John Stafford, *The Literary Criticism of "Young America": A Study in the Relationship of Politics and Literature, 1837–1850*, University of California Publications, English Studies, no. 3 (Berkeley: University of California Press, 1952); and Edward L. Widman, *Young America: The Flowering of Democracy in New York City* (New York: Oxford University Press, 1999).

22. H. Arthur Scott Trask, "The Constitutional Republicans of Philadelphia, 1818–1848: Hard Money, Free Trade, and State Rights" (Ph.D. diss., University of South Carolina, 1998); Richard Lyle Power, *Planting Corn Belt Culture: The Impress of the Upland Southerner and Yankee in the Old Northwest* (Indianapolis: Indiana Historical Society, 1953).

23. Simms to Lawson, August 5, 1845, *Letters*, 2:92–93.

24. Simms to Nathaniel Beverley Tucker, December 17, 1849, *Letters*, 2:574.

25. Simms, "Proceedings of the New-York Historical Society—1844," *Southern and Western Magazine and Review* 2 (July 1845): 63.

26. Simms, "South Carolina in the Revolution. The Social Moral. Lecture 1," 1.

27. Simms, "South Carolina in the Revolution. A Lecture," in *Letters*, 3:523. This lecture was first delivered in Buffalo, N.Y., on November 11, 1856.

28. Ibid., 524.

29. Ibid., 528.

30. Ibid., 543.

31. Simms, *History*, 179.

32. Simms, "South Carolina in the Revolution. A Lecture," in *Letters*, 3:525.

33. Ibid. For a modern analysis (that bears some similarity to Simms's) of how ethnic and religious identities can help to explain Loyalism in South Carolina, see Weir, *Colonial South Carolina*, 322.

34. Simms, "South Carolina in the Revolution," *Southern Quarterly Review* 14 (July 1848): 39.

35. Simms, "South Carolina in the Revolution. A Lecture," in *Letters*, 3:528–29.

36. Ibid., 543.

37. Ibid., 548.

38. Simms to James Chesnut Jr., December 16, 1856, *Letters,* 3:472.

39. Lorenzo Sabine, *Biographical Sketches of Loyalists of the American Revolution, with an Historical Essay* (Boston: Little, Brown and Company, 1864), 1:38–45.

40. Simms, "South Carolina in the Revolution. A Lecture," in *Letters,* 3:549.

41. Simms, "Antagonisms of the Social Moral. North and South," 2, 5. Charles Carroll Simms Collection, South Caroliniana Library, University of South Carolina.

42. Ibid., 7.

43. Ibid., 54.

44. Ibid., 56.

45. Simms to James Henry Hammond, January 23, 1857, *Letters,* 3:493.

46. James Henry Hammond to William Gilmore Simms, January 31, 1857, in Carol Bleser, ed., *The Hammonds of Redcliffe* (New York: Oxford University Press, 1981), 25.

EIGHT *Conclusion*

1. Simms, *Woodcraft,* 508–9.

2. Ibid., 509.

3. On the necessity of virtue to a free people, see H. Lee Cheek Jr., *Calhoun and Popular Rule: The Political Theory of the "Disquisition" and "Discourse"* (Columbia: University of Missouri Press, 2001); and Jean M. Yarborough, *American Virtues: Thomas Jefferson on the Character of a Free People* (Lawrence: University Press of Kansas, 1998).

4. Simms, *Views and Reviews,* 16–17.

5. Levin, *History as Romantic Art;* Gayarré, *Romance of the History of Louisiana;* Prescott, "Chateaubriand's English Literature," in *Biographical and Critical Miscellanies,* 284–86.

6. Simms, *Views and Reviews,* 42.

7. Simms to Nathaniel Beverley Tucker, September 6, 1849, *Letters,* 2:554.

8. For example, see Grant, *North over South;* Potter, "The Historian's Use of Nationalism and Vice Versa," 60–108; and Waldstreicher, *In the Midst of Perpetual Fetes.* Grant notes a shift from a romantic-iiberal to an imperialist-Darwinian nationalism in the antebellum United States.

9. George Orwell, "Notes on Nationalism," in *Essays,* ed. John Carey (New York: Everyman's Library, 2002), 866, 867.

10. Wendell Berry, *Sex, Economy, Freedom and Community: Eight Essays* (New York: Pantheon Books, 1993), 148.

11. Wendell Berry, *The Long-Legged House* (New York: Harcourt, Brace and World, 1969), 49.

12. O'Brien, *All Clever Men,* 264.

13. James Warley Miles, *God in History. A Discourse Delivered before the Graduating Class of the College of Charleston on Sunday Evening, March 29, 1863* (Charleston, S.C.: Evans and Cogswell, 1863), 5, 30.

14. Ibid., 8, 9, and 30.

15. Simms, "The Close of the Year 1861," in *Selected Poems of William Gilmore Simms,* 216–17.

16. Butterfield, *The Historical Novel,* 74. See also Foote, "The Novelist's View of History," 439–45; Vidal, "Lincoln and the Priests of Academe," in *United States: Essays, 1952–1992,* 675; and Lukacs, *Historical Consciousness,* 127, 252–62.

17. Guilds and Hudson, *An Early and Strong Sympathy.*

18. Calhoon, "The Reintegration of the Loyalists," 67.

19. On southerners' attempts to define themselves and the rest of the nation's perceptions of them, see Norton, *Alternative Americas*. On southerners' recognition of their minority status in the Union and attempts to develop a separate nationalism, see Carpenter, *The South as a Conscious Minority;* Craven, *The Growth of Southern Nationalism;* McCardell, *The Idea of a Southern Nation;* and Charles S. Sydnor, *The Development of Southern Sectionalism, 1819–1848* (Baton Rouge: Louisiana State University Press, 1948).

20. Norton, *Alternative Americas,* 112; George C. Rable, *The Confederate Republic: A Revolution against Politics* (Chapel Hill: University of North Carolina Press, 1994), 46–47; Michael A. Morrison, *Slavery and the American West: The Eclipse of Manifest Destiny and the Coming of the Civil War* (Chapel Hill: University of North Carolina Press, 1997), 260–63.

BIBLIOGRAPHY

Manuscript Collections

University of South Carolina, South Caroliniana Library. Columbia, South Carolina.
James Henry Hammond Papers
Laurens Family Papers
Charles Carrol Simms Collection
William Gilmore Simms Papers
George Washington Papers
Library of Congress
Hammond Papers

Simms's Works

Books

The Army Correspondence of Colonel John Laurens, in the Years 1777–8, Now First Printed from Original Letters Addressed to His Father, Henry Laurens, President of Congress, with a Memoir. New York: Bradford Club, 1867.

As Good as a Comedy; or, The Tennesseean's Story. Edited by James B. Meriwether. Columbia: University of South Carolina Press, 1972.

Beauchampe; or, The Kentucky Tragedy. A Sequel to Charlemont. New York: Redfield, 1856.

Border Beagles: A Tale of Mississippi. Edited by John Caldwell Guilds. Fayetteville: University of Arkansas Press, 1996.

The Cassique of Kiawah: A Colonial Romance. New York: Redfield, 1859.

Charlemont; or, The Pride of the Village. A Tale of Kentucky. New York: Redfield, 1856.

Charleston, and Her Satirists; A Scribblement. Charleston, S.C.: James S. Burges, 1848.

The Cub of the Panther: A Hunter Legend of the "Old North State." Edited by Miriam Jones Shillingsburg. Fayetteville: University of Arkansas Press, 1997.

Early Lays. Charleston, S.C.: A. E. Miller, 1827.

Egeria: or Voices of Thought and Counsel, for the Woods and Wayside. Philadelphia: E. H. Butler and Co., 1853.

Essays on the Literary and Intellectual History of South Carolina from "The XIX Century," 1869–1870. Columbia: Southern Studies Program, University of South Carolina, 1977.

Eutaw: With Introduction and Explanatory Notes. Spartanburg, S.C.: Reprint Company, 1976.

The Forayers: or, The Raid of the Dog-Days: With Introduction and Explanatory Notes. Spartanburg, S.C.: Reprint Company, 1976.

The Geography of South Carolina: Being a Companion to the History of That State by William Gilmore Simms. Compiled from the Latest and Best Authorities, and Designed for the Instruction of the Young. Charleston, S.C.: Babcock and Co., 1843.

The Golden Christmas: A Chronicle of St. John's, Berkeley. Compiled from the Notes of a Brief- less Barrister. Charleston, S.C.: Walker, Richards and Co., 1852.

Guy Rivers: A Tale of Georgia. Edited by John Caldwell Guilds. Fayetteville: University of Arkansas Press, 1993.

The History of South Carolina, from Its First European Discovery to Its Erection into a Republic: With a Supplementary Book, Bringing the Narrative Down to the Present Time. New York: Redfield, 1860.

The History of South Carolina, from Its First European Discovery to Its Erection into a Republic: With a Supplementary Chronicle of Events to the Present Time. Charleston, S.C.: S. Babcock and Co., 1840.

Joscelyn: With Introduction and Explanatory Notes. Spartanburg, S.C.: Reprint Company, 1976.

Katharine Walton: [or, The Rebel of Dorchester:] With Introduction and Explanatory Notes. Spartanburg, S.C.: Reprint Company, 1976.

The Letters of William Gilmore Simms. Edited by Mary C. Simms Oliphant, Alfred Taylor Odell, and T. C. Duncan Eaves. 6 vols. Columbia: University of South Carolina Press, 1952–82.

The Life of Captain John Smith: The Founder of Virginia. New York: Perkins Book Company, 1902.

The Life of Francis Marion. New York: Henry G. Langley, 1844; Philadelphia: Geo. G. Evans, 1860.

Editor. *The Life of Nathanael Greene, Major-General in the Army of the Revolution.* New York: George F. Cooledge and Brother, 1849.

The Life of the Chevalier Bayard; "The Good Knight," "Sans peur et sans reproche." New York: Harper and Brothers, 1847.

The Lily and the Totem, or, The Huguenots in Florida. A Series of Sketches, Picturesque and Historical, of the Colonies of Coligni, in North America, 1562–1570. New York: Baker and Scribner, 1850.

Mellichampe: With Introduction and Explanatory Notes. Spartanburg, S.C.: Reprint Company, 1976.

Paddy McGann; or, The Demon of the Stump. Edited by James B. Meriwether. Columbia: University of South Carolina Press, 1972.

The Partisan: With Introduction and Explanatory Notes. Spartanburg, S.C.: Reprint Company, 1976.

Poetry and the Practical. Edited by James E. Kibler. Fayetteville: University of Arkansas Press, 1996.

The Revolutionary War in South Carolina: An Anthology. Compiled, with a preface by Stephen Meats. Columbia: Southern Studies Program, University of South Carolina, 1975.

Richard Hurdis: A Tale of Alabama. Edited by John Caldwell Guilds. Fayetteville: University of Arkansas Press, 1995.

Sack and Destruction of the City of Columbia, S.C. To Which Is Added a List of the Property Destroyed. Columbia, S.C.: Power Press of the Daily Phoenix, 1865.

The Scout: [or, The Black Riders of Congaree:] With Introduction and Explanatory Notes. Spartanburg, S.C.: Reprint Company, 1976.

Selected Poems of William Gilmore Simms. Edited by James Everett Kibler Jr. Athens: University of Georgia Press, 1990.

[Editor.] *Selections from the Letters and Speeches of the Hon. James H. Hammond, of South Carolina.* With an introduction and notes by Clyde N. Wilson. Spartanburg, S.C.: Reprint Company, 1978.

The Sense of the Beautiful. Charleston: Walker, Evans and Cogswell, 1870.

Slavery in America: Being a Brief Review of Miss Martineau on That Subject. Richmond: Thomas W. White, 1838.

The Social Principle: The True Source of National Permanence. An Oration, Delivered before the Erosophic Society of the University of Alabama December 13, 1842. Tuscaloosa: Erosophic Society of the University of Alabama, 1843.

The Sources of American Independence. An Oration, on the Sixty-Ninth Anniversary of American Independence; Delivered at Aiken, South-Carolina, before the Town Council and Citizens Thereof. Aiken, S.C.: Published by Council, 1844.

South-Carolina in the Revolutionary War: Being a Reply to Certain Misrepresentations and Mistakes of Recent Writers, in Relation to the Course and Conduct of This State. Charleston, S.C.: Walker and James, 1853.

Southward Ho! A Spell of Sunshine. New York: Redfield, 1854.

Stories and Tales. Edited by John C. Guilds. Columbia: University of South Carolina Press, 1974.

The Tri-Color; or, The Three Days of Blood, in Paris. With Some Other Pieces. London: Wigfall and Davis, 1830.

Vasconselos: A Romance of the New World. New York: Redfield, 1853.

Views and Reviews in American Literature, History, and Fiction: First Series. Edited by C. Hugh Holmann. Cambridge, Mass.: The Belknap Press of Harvard University Press, 1962.

Views and Reviews in American Literature, History and Fiction, Second Series. New York: Wiley and Putnam, 1845.

Voltmeier or the Mountain Men. Edited by James B. Meriwether. Columbia: University of South Carolina Press, 1969.

Editor. *War Poetry of the South.* New York: Richardson and Company, 1867.

The Wigwam and the Cabin. New and revised edition. New York: Redfield, 1859.

Woodcraft: [or, Hawks about the Dovecote:] With Introduction and Explanatory Notes. Spartanburg, S.C.: Reprint Company, 1976.

The Yemassee: A Romance of Carolina. Edited by John Caldwell Guilds. Fayetteville: University of Arkansas Press, 1994.

Selected Articles, Reviews, and Miscellany

"The Baron de Kalb." *Southern Quarterly Review* 6 (July 1852): 141–203.

"Battle of Fort Moultrie." *Southern Literary Gazette*, n.s., 1 (August 1, 1829): 137–42.

"Chi Lo Sa? or What You Will, an You Like It." Pt. 2. *Philadelphia Saturday Express* 1 (January 4, 1851): 1.

"The Cypress Swamp." *Southern Literary Gazette*, n.s., 1 (September 15, 1829): 211–12.

"Domestic Histories of the South." *Southern Quarterly Review*, n.s., 5 (January 1852): 507–35.

"Ellet's Women of the Revolution." *Southern Quarterly Review*, n.s., 1 (July 1850): 314–54.

"The Good Farmer." *Simms Review* 10 (Summer 2002): 12.

"Guizot's Democracy in France." *Southern Quarterly Review* 15 (April 1849): 114–65.

"Headley's Life of Cromwell." *Southern Quarterly Review* 14 (October 1848): 506–38.

"The Hermitage." *Simms Review* 2 (Spring 1994): 21–26.

"Hildreth's United States." *Southern Quarterly Review* 15 (October 1849): 258.

"History of Georgia." *Southern Quarterly Review* 13 (April 1848): 470–501.

"Kennedy's Life of Wirt." *Southern Quarterly Review*, n.s., 1 (April 1850): 192–236.

Letter dated November 9, 1854. In *Semi-Centennial Celebration. Fiftieth Anniversary of the Founding of the New York Historical Society. Monday, November 20, 1854,* page 87. New York: New-York Historical Society, 1854.

"Life of De Witt Clinton." *Southern Quarterly Review* 15 (July 1849): 537–40.

"Marion, the Carolina Partisan." Pts. 1 and 2. *Russell's Magazine* 4 (October 1858): 1–16; (November 1858): 113–28.

"Michael Ney, Otherwise Michael Rudolph." *Southern Literary Messenger* 13 (January 1847): 17–23.

"Mrs. Trollope and the Americans." In *American Criticisms on Mrs. Trollope's "Domestic Manners of the Americans,"* 2nd ed., 1–25. London: O. Rich, 1833. Reprinted from *Amerian Quarterly Review* 12 (September 1832): 109–33.

"The Philosophy of the Omnibus." *Simms Review* 6 (Winter 1998): 13–23.

"Pickett's History of Alabama." *Southern Quarterly Review,* n.s., 5 (January 1852): 182–209.

"Prescott's Conquest of Peru." Pts. 1 and 2. *Southern Quarterly Review* 13 (January 1848):136–87; (April 1848): 273–330.

"Proceedings of the New-York Historical Society—1844." *Southern and Western Magazine and Review* 2 (July 1845): 63.

"Reminiscences of the Revolution." *Russell's Magazine* (October 1859): 59–72.

"Revolutionary Letters." *Historical Magazine* 1 (July 1857): 206–7; 1 (September 1857): 266–70; 1 (October 1857): 289–92; 2 (January 1858): 6–11; 2 (September 1858): 259–61: 2 (November 1858): 321–24; and 3 (June 1859): 169–71.

"The Siege of Charleston in the American Revolution." *Southern Quarterly Review* 14 (October 1848): 261–337.

"A Sketch of the Life and Public Services of John Rutledge of South Carolina." Pts. 1 and 2. *American Whig Review* 5 (August 1847): 125–37; 5 (September 1847): 277–91.

"South Carolina in the Revolution." *Southern Quarterly Review* 14 (July 1848): 37–77.

"South Carolina in the Revolution. The Social Moral." Charles Carroll Simms Collection, South Caroliniana Library, University of South Carolina, Columbia.

"South Carolina Just before the Revolution." *Southern Literary Messenger* 11 (March 1845): 138–43.

"28th June." *Southern Literary Gazette,* n.s., 1 (July 1, 1829): 93.

"Whom the Coat Fits, Let Him Wear It." *Album* 1 (November 5, 1825): 145–46.

"Writings of George Washington." *Southern Quarterly Review* 15 (April 1849): 253–57.

Secondary Sources

Books

Acton, John Emerich Edward Dalberg-Acton, Lord. *Selected Writings of Lord Acton.* Edited by J. Rufus Fears. Vol. 2, *Essays in the Study and Writing of History.* Indianapolis, Ind.: Liberty Fund, 1986.

Adair, Douglass. *Fame and the Founding Fathers.* Edited by Trevor Colbourn. Indianapolis, Ind.: Liberty Fund, 1998.

Adams, Henry. *The Degradation of the Democratic Dogma.* New York: Peter Smith, 1949.

Adams, Herbert Baxter. *The Life and Writings of Jared Sparks Comprising Selections from His Journals and Correspondence.* 2 vols. Boston: Houghton, Mifflin and Company, 1893.

Allibone, S. Austin. *A Critical Dictionary of English Literature and British and American Authors.* 3 vols. Philadelphia: J. B. Lippincott Company, 1891.

Althusius, Johannes. *Politica.* Indianapolis, Ind.: Liberty Fund, 1995.

American Criticisms on Mrs. Trollope's "Domestic Manners of the Americans." 2nd ed. London: O. Rich, 1833.

Aristotle. *The Complete Works of Aristotle: The Revised Oxford Translation*, 2 vols., edited by Jonathan Barnes. Princeton, N.J.: Princeton University Press, 1984.

Bailyn, Bernard. *The Ideological Origins of the American Revolution*. Cambridge, Mass.: Belknap Press of Harvard University Press, 1967.

Baldwin, Joseph Glover. *Party Leaders; Sketches of Thomas Jefferson, Alex'r Hamilton, Andrew Jackson, Henry Clay, John Randolph, of Roanoke, Including Notices of Many Other Distinguished American Statesmen*. New York: D. Appleton and Company, 1855.

Barney, William L. *The Road to Secession: A New Perspective on the Old South*. New York: Praeger Publishers, 1972.

Barzun, Jacques, and Henry F. Graff. *The Modern Researcher*. 3rd ed. New York: Harcourt Brace Jovanovich, 1977.

Bassett, John Spencer. *The Middle Group of American Historians*. New York: MacMillan, 1917.

Beidler, Philip D. *First Books: The Printed Word and Cultural Formation in Early Alabama*. Tuscaloosa: University of Alabama Press, 1999.

Bensel, Richard Franklin. *Yankee Leviathan: The Origins of Central State Authority in America, 1859–1877*. Cambridge: Cambridge University Press, 1990.

Berlin, Isaiah. *Historical Inevitability*. London: Oxford University Press, 1954.

Berry, Wendell. *The Long-Legged House*. New York: Harcourt, Brace and World, 1969.

———. *Sex, Economy, Freedom and Community: Eight Essays*. New York: Pantheon Books, 1993.

Black, J. B. *The Art of History: A Study of Four Great Historians of the Eighteenth Century* New York: F. S. Crofts and Co., 1926.

Bleser, Carol, ed. *The Hammonds of Redcliffe*. New York: Oxford University Press, 1981.

Bloch, Marc. *The Historian's Craft*. Translated by Peter Putnam. New York: Vintage Books, 1953.

Boles, John B., and Evelyn Thomas Nolen, eds. *Interpreting Southern History: Historiographical Essays in Honor of Sanford W. Higginbotham*. Baton Rouge: Louisiana State University Press, 1987.

Bongie, Laurence L. *David Hume: Prophet of the Counter-Revolution*. 2nd ed. Indianapolis, Ind.: Liberty Fund, 2000.

Bradford, M. E. *Against the Barbarians: And Other Reflections on Familiar Themes*. Columbia: University of Missouri Press, 1992.

Brooks, Cleanth, John Thibaut Purser, and Robert Penn Warren, eds. *An Approach to Literature*. 4th ed. New York: Appleton-Century-Crofts, 1964.

Brown, Richard D. *The Strength of a People: The Idea of an Informed Citizenry in America, 1650–1870*. Chapel Hill: University of North Carolina Press, 1996.

Buchanan, John. *The Road to Guilford Courthouse: The American Revolution in the Carolinas*. New York: John Wiley and Sons, 1997.

Burckhardt, Jacob. *Judgments on History and Historians*. Indianapolis, Ind.: Liberty Fund, 1999.

———. *Reflections on History*. Indianapolis, Ind.: Liberty Fund, 1979.

Burke, Edmund. *Further Reflections on the Revolution in France*. Edited by Daniel E. Ritchie. Indianapolis, Ind.: Liberty Fund, 1992.

———. *Reflections on the Revolution in France*. Edited by Daniel E. Ritchie. Indianapolis, Ind.: Liberty Fund, 1999.

Bury, J. B. *The Idea of Progress: An Inquiry into Its Growth and Origin*. Introduction by Charles A. Beard. New York: Dover Publications, 1960 [1932].

Butterfield, Herbert. *The Historical Novel: An Essay.* Cambridge: Cambridge University Press, 1924.

———. *The Whig Interpretation of History.* New York: W. W. Norton and Company, 1965.

Butterworth, Keen, and James E. Kibler Jr. *William Gilmore Simms: A Reference Guide.* Boston: G. K. Hall and Co., 1980.

Calhoon, Robert M. *Dominion and Liberty: Ideology in the Anglo-American World, 1660–1801.* Arlington Heights, Ill.: Harlan Davidson, 1994.

Calhoun, John C. *Union and Liberty: The Political Philosophy of John C. Calhoun.* Edited by Ross M. Lence. Indianapolis, Ind.: Liberty Fund, 1992.

Callcott, George H. *History in the United States, 1800–1860: Its Practice and Purpose.* Baltimore: Johns Hopkins Press, 1970.

Carnes, Mark C., ed. *Novel History: Historians and Novelists Confront America's Past (and Each Other).* New York: Simon and Schuster, 2001.

Carpenter, Jesse T. *The South as a Conscious Minority, 1789–1861: A Study in Political Thought.* Columbia: University of South Carolina Press, 1990.

Carr, Edward Hallett. *What Is History? The George Macaulay Trevelyan Lectures Delivered in the University of Cambridge, January–March 1961.* New York: Alfred A. Knopf, 1962.

Caruthers, William A. *The Kentuckian in New-York. Or, the Adventures of Three Southerns.* Ridgewood, N.J.: Gregg Press, 1968.

Cash, W. J. *The Mind of the South.* New York: Alfred A. Knopf, 1941.

Casper, Scott E. *Constructing American Lives: Biography and Culture in Nineteenth-Century America.* Chapel Hill: University of North Carolina Press, 1999.

Channing, Steven A. *Crisis of Fear: Secession in South Carolina.* New York: Simon and Schuster, 1970.

Chapin, Sallie F. *Fitz-Hugh St. Clair, The South Carolina Rebel Boy; or, It Is No Crime to Be Born a Gentleman.* Philadelphia: Claxton, Remsen and Haffelfinger, 1872.

Chaplin, Joyce E. *An Anxious Pursuit: Agricultural Innovation and Modernity in the Lower South, 1730–1815.* Chapel Hill: University of North Carolina Press, 1993.

Cheek, H. Lee, Jr. *Calhoun and Popular Rule: The Political Theory of the "Disquisition" and "Discourse."* Columbia: University of Missouri Press, 2001.

Cohen, Lester H. *The Revolutionary Histories: Contemporary Narratives of the American Revolution.* Ithaca, N.Y.: Cornell University Press, 1980.

Colbourn, Trevor. *The Lamp of Experience: Whig History and the Intellectual Origins of the American Revolution.* Indianapolis, Ind.: Liberty Fund, 1998.

Collingwood, R. G. *The Idea of History.* Rev. ed., edited by Jan Van Der Dussen. New York: Oxford University Press, Galaxy Books, 1956.

Collini, Stefan, Donald Winch, and John Burrow. *That Noble Science of Politics: A Study in Nineteenth-Century Intellectual History.* Cambridge: Cambridge University Press, 1984.

Commager, Henry Steele. *The Nature and the Study of History.* Columbus, Ohio: Charles E. Merrill Publishing Company, 1965.

———. *The Search for a Usable Past, and Other Essays in Historiography.* New York: Alfred A. Knopf, 1967.

Conser, Walter H., Jr. *God and the Natural World: Religion and Science in Antebellum America.* Columbia: University of South Carolina Press, 1993.

Cooper, James Fenimore. *The Leatherstocking Tales.* Vol. 1, *The Pioneers, or the Sources of the Susquehanna; The Last of the Mohicans; The Prairie.* New York: Library of America, 1985.

Coulter, E. Merton. *The Confederate States of America, 1861–1865.* Baton Rouge: Louisiana State University Press, 1950.

———. *The South during Reconstruction, 1865–1877*. Baton Rouge: Louisiana State University Press, 1947.

Crafts, William. *A Selection, in Prose and Poetry, from the Miscellaneous Writings of the Late William Crafts*. Charleston, S.C.: C. C. Sebring and J. S. Burges, 1828.

Craven, Avery O. *Civil War in the Making, 1815–1860*. Baton Rouge: Louisiana State Univeristy Press, 1959.

———. *The Coming of the Civil War*. 2nd ed. Chicago: University of Chicago Press, 1957.

———. *The Growth of Southern Nationalism, 1848–1861*. Baton Rouge: Louisiana State University Press, 1953.

Croce, Benedetto. *History as the Story of Liberty*. 1938. Indianapolis, Ind.: Liberty Fund, 2000.

Dabney, William M., and Marion Dargon. *William Henry Drayton and the American Revolution*. Albuquerque: University of New Mexico Press, 1962.

Davidson, Donald. *The Attack on Leviathan: Regionalism and Nationalism in the United States*. Chapel Hill: University of North Carolina Press, 1938.

Davis, Richard Beale. *Intellectual Life in Jefferson's Virginia, 1790–1830*. Knoxville: University of Tennessee Press, 1972.

Dawson, Henry B. *Battles of the United States, by Sea and Land: Embracing Those of the Revolutionary and Indian Wars, the War of 1812, and the Mexican War; with Important Official Documents*. New York: Johnson, Fry, and Company, 1858.

Ekirch, Arthur Alphonse, Jr. *The Idea of Progress in America, 1815–1860*. New York: Columbia University Press, 1944.

Fairbanks, George R. *The History and Antiquities of the City of St. Augustine, Florida, Founded A.D. 1565: Comprising Some of the Most Interesting Portions of the Early History of Florida*. New York: Charles B. Norton, 1858.

———. *History of Florida from Its Discovery by Ponce de Leon, in 1512, to the Close of the Florida War, in 1842*. Philadelphia: J. B. Lippincott and Co., 1871.

Faragher, John Mack. *Daniel Boone: The Life and Legend of an American Pioneer*. New York: Henry Holt and Company, 1992.

Faust, Drew Gilpin. *A Sacred Circle: The Dilemma of the Intellectual in the Old South, 1840–1860*. Baltimore: Johns Hopkins University Press, 1977.

Fischer, David Hackett. *Historians' Fallacies: Toward a Logic of Historical Thought*. New York: Harper and Row, 1970.

Fiske, John. *The Discovery of America: With Some Account of Ancient America and the Spanish Conquest*. 2 vols. Cambridge, Mass.: Riverside Press, 1894.

Foote, Shelby. *The Civil War: A Narrative, Fort Sumter to Perryville*. New York: Random House, 1958.

Ford, Lacy K., Jr. *Origins of Southern Radicalism: The South Carolina Upcountry, 1800–1860*. New York: Oxford University Press, 1988.

Freehling, William W. *Prelude to Civil War: The Nullification Controversy in South Carolina, 1816–1836*. New York: Harper and Row, 1965.

Fukuyama, Francis. *The End of History and the Last Man*. New York: Free Press, 1992.

Gallagher, Gary W. *The Confederate War: How Popular Will, Nationalism, and Military Strategy Could Not Stave Off Defeat*. Cambridge, Mass.: Harvard University Press, 1997.

Gay, Peter. *Style in History*. New York: Basic Books, 1974.

Gayarré, Charles E. A. *Romance of the History of Louisiana. A Series of Lectures*. New York: D. Appleton and Company, 1848.

Genovese, Eugene D. *The Political Economy of Slavery: Studies in the Economy and Society of the Slave South*. New York: Vintage Books, 1967.

———. *The Slaveholders' Dilemma: Freedom and Progress in Southern Conservative Thought, 1820–1860.* Columbia: University of South Carolina Press, 1992.

———. *The Southern Front: History and Politics in the Cultural War.* Columbia: University of Missouri Press, 1995.

———. *The World the Slaveholders Made: Two Essays in Interpretation.* Middletown, Conn.: Wesleyan University Press, 1988.

Gibbon, Edward. *The History of the Decline and Fall of the Roman Empire.* London: Folio Society, 1983.

Gossman, Lionel. *Between History and Literature.* Cambridge, Mass.: Harvard University Press, 1990.

Grafton, Anthony. *The Footnote: A Curious History.* Cambridge, Mass.: Harvard University Press, 1997.

Grant, Susan-Mary. *North over South: Northern Nationalism and American Identity in the Antebellum Era.* Lawrence: University Press of Kansas, 2000.

Grayson, William J. *Witness to Sorrow: The Antebellum Autobiography of William J. Grayson.* Edited by Richard J. Calhoun. Columbia: University of South Carolina Press, 1990.

Greene, Jack P. *The Intellectual Construction of America: Exceptionalism and Identity from 1492 to 1800.* Chapel Hill: University of North Carolina Press, 1993.

Guilds, John C., ed. *Long Years of Neglect: The Work and Reputation of William Gilmore Simms.* Fayetteville: University of Arkansas Press, 1988.

———. *Simms: A Literary Life.* Fayetteville: University of Arkansas Press, 1992.

Guilds, John C., and Caroline Collins, eds. *William Gilmore Simms and the American Frontier.* Athens: University of Georgia Press, 1997.

Guilds, John C., and Charles Hudson. *An Early and Strong Sympathy: The Indian Writings of William Gilmore Simms.* Columbia: University of South Carolina Press, 2003.

Hayek, F. A. *The Counter-Revolution of Science: Studies on the Abuse of Reason.* Indianapolis, Ind.: Liberty Fund, 1979.

Hegel, Georg Wilhelm Freidrich. *The Philosophy of History.* Translated by J. Sibree. New York: Dover Publications, 1956.

Herder, J. G. *J. G. Herder on Social and Political Culture.* Translated and edited by F. M. Barnard. Cambridge: Cambridge University Press, 1969.

Heyrman, Christine. *Southern Cross: The Beginnings of the Bible Belt.* New York: Alfred A. Knopf, 1997.

Higginbotham, Don. *War and Society in Revolutionary America: The Wider Dimensions of Conflict.* Columbia: University of South Carolina Press, 1988.

———. *The War of American Independence: Military Attitudes, Policies, and Practice, 1763–1789.* Boston: Northeastern University Press, 1983.

Hoffer, Peter Charles. *Revolution and Regeneration: Life Cycle and the Historical Vision of the Generation of 1776.* Athens: University of Georgia Press, 1983.

Holman, C. Hugh. *The Roots of Southern Writing: Essays on the Literature of the American South.* Athens: University of Georgia Press, 1972.

Holman, David Marion. *A Certain Slant of Light: Regionalism and the Form of Southern and Midwestern Fiction.* Baton Rouge: Louisiana State University Press, 1995.

Hubbell, Jay B. *The South in American Literature, 1607–1900.* Durham, N.C.: Duke University Press, 1954.

Huizinga, Johan. *The Varieties of History: From Voltaire to the Present.* Edited by Fritz Stern. New York: Meridian Books, 1957

Jameson, J. Franklin. *The History of Historical Writing in America.* New York: Greenwood Press, 1969.

Johnson, Paul E. *A Shopkeeper's Millennium: Society and Revivals in Rochester, New York, 1815–1837.* New York: Hill and Wang, 1978.

Kammen, Michael. *Mystic Chords of Memory: The Transformation of Tradition in American Political Culture.* New York: Alfred A. Knopf, 1991.

———. *A Season of Youth: The American Revolution and the Historical Imagination.* New York: Alfred A. Knopf, 1978.

———. *Selvages and Biases: The Fabric of History in American Culture.* Ithaca, N.Y.: Cornell University Press, 1987.

Kennedy, John Pendleton. *Memoirs of the Life of William Wirt, Attorney-General of the United States.* Philadelphia: Lea and Blanchard, 1850.

Kraus, Michael. *A History of American History.* New York: Farrar and Rinehart, 1937.

Laurens, Henry. *The Papers of Henry Laurens.* Vol. 1. Edited by Philip M. Hamer and George C. Rogers Jr. Columbia: University of South Carolina Press, 1968.

Lee, Henry, Jr. *The Campaign of 1781 in the Carolinas: With Remarks Historical and Critical on Johnson's Life of Greene.* 1824. Reprint, Chicago: Quadrangel Books, 1962.

Levin, David. *History as Romantic Art: Bancroft, Prescott, Motley, and Parkman.* New York: AMS Press, 1967.

Lieber, Francis, ed. *Encyclopædia Americana. A Popular Dictionary of Arts, Sciences, Literature, History, Politics, and Biography, Brought Down to the Present Time; Including a Copious Collection of Original Articles in American Biography on the Basis of the Seventh Edition of the German Conversations-Lexicon.* New ed., 13 vols. Philadelphia: Desilver, Thomas, and Co., 1835.

Livy. *The Early History of Rome.* Translated by Aubrey de Sélincourt. London: Penguin Books, 1971.

Lossing, Benson J. *Our Country. A Household History for All Readers, from the Discovery of America to the One Hundreth Anniversary of the Declaration of Independence.* New York: Johnson, Wilson and Co., 1875–78.

———. *The Pictorial Field-Book of the Revolution; or, Illustrations, by Pen and Pencil, of the History, Biography, Scenery, Relics, and Traditions of the War for Independence.* New York: Harper and Bros., 1851–52.

Luce, Dianne C. "John A. Murrell and the Imaginations of Simms and Faulkner." In *William Gilmore Simms and the American Frontier,* edited by John C. Guilds and Caroline Collins, 237–57. Athens: University of Georgia Press, 1997.

Lukacs, John. *At the End of an Age.* New Haven, Conn.: Yale University Press, 2002.

———. *Historical Consciousness: The Remembered Past.* With a new introduction by the author and a foreward by Russell Kirk. New Brunswick, N.J.: Transaction Publishers, 1994.

———. *A Thread of Years.* New Haven, Conn.: Yale University Press, 1998.

Luraghi, Raimondo. *The Rise and Fall of the Plantation South.* New York: New Viewpoints, 1978.

Maitland, Frederic William. *A Historical Sketch of Liberty and Equality: As Ideals of English Political Philosophy from the Time of Hobbes to the Time of Coleridge.* Indianapolis, Ind.: Liberty Fund, 2000.

Marshall, John. *The Life of George Washington.* Indianapolis, Ind.: Liberty Fund, 2000.

Massey, Gregory D. *John Laurens and the American Revolution.* Columbia: University of South Carolina Press, 2000.

McCardell, John. *The Idea of a Southern Nation: Southern Nationalists and Southern Nationalism, 1830–1860.* New York: W. W. Norton and Company, 1979.

McCarthy, Cormac. *All the Pretty Horses.* New York: Alfred A. Knopf, 1993.

McCowen, George Smith, Jr. *The British Occupation of Charleston, 1780–82.* Columbia: University of South Carolina Press, 1972.

Meyers, Marvin. *The Jacksonian Persuasion: Politics and Belief.* Stanford, Calif.: Stanford University Press, 1960.

Miles, James Warley. *God in History. A Discourse Delivered before the Graduating Class of the College of Charleston on Sunday Evening, March 29, 1863.* Charleston, S.C.: Evans and Cogswell, 1863.

Milton, John. *Areopagitica and Other Political Writings of John Milton.* Indianapolis, Ind.: Liberty Fund, 1999.

Mizruchi, Susan L. *The Power of Historical Knowledge: Narrating the Past in Hawthorne, James, and Dreiser.* Princeton, N.J.: Princeton University Press, 1988.

Moltke-Hansen, David, and Michael O'Brien, eds. *Intellectual Life in Antebellum Charleston.* Knoxville: University of Tennessee Press, 1986.

Morison, Samuel Eliot. *The European Discovery of America: The Northern Voyages.* New York: Oxford University Press, 1971.

Morrison, Michael A. *Slavery and the American West: The Eclipse of Manifest Destiny and the Coming of the Civil War.* Chapel Hill: University of North Carolina Press, 1997.

Morse, Jedidiah. *Annals of the American Revolution.* Hartford, Conn., 1824.

Moultrie, William. *Memoirs of the American Revolution, So Far as It Related to the States of North and South Carolina, and Georgia.* 2 vols. New York: D. Longworth, 1802.

Neff, Emery. *The Poetry of History: The Contribution of Literature and Literary Scholarship to the Writing of History since Voltaire.* New York: Columbia University Press, 1947.

Nevins, Alan. *The Gateway to History.* Boston: D. C. Heath and Company, 1938.

Norton, Anne. *Alternative Americas: A Reading of Antebellum Political Culture.* Chicago: University of Chicago Press, 1986.

Novick, Peter. *That Noble Dream: The "Objectivity Question" and the American Historical Profession.* Cambridge: Cambridge University Press, 1988.

Nye, Russell Blaine. *Society and Culture in America, 1830–1860.* New York: Harper and Row, 1974.

———. *This Almost Chosen People: Essays in the History of American Ideas.* East Lansing: Michigan State University Press, 1966.

Oakeshott, Michael. *On History and Other Essays.* Indianapolis, Ind.: Liberty Fund, 1999.

O'Brien, Michael, ed. *All Clever Men, Who Make Their Way: Critical Discourse in the Old South.* Fayetteville: University of Arkansas Press, 1982.

———. *A Character of Hugh Legaré.* Knoxville: University of Tennessee Press, 1985.

———. *Rethinking the South: Essays in Intellectual History.* Baltimore: Johns Hopkins University Press, 1988.

O'Neill, Edward H. *A History of American Biography: 1800–1935.* Philadelphia: University of Pennsylvania Press, 1935.

Orwell, George. *Essays.* Edited by John Carey. New York: Everyman's Library, 2002.

Osterweis, Rollin G. *Romanticism and Nationalism in the Old South.* New Haven, Conn.: Yale University Press, 1949.

Ostrander, Gilman M. *Republic of Letters: The American Intellectual Community, 1776–1865.* Madison, Wis.: Madison House Publishers, 1999.

Parks, Edd Winfield. *William Gilmore Simms as Literary Critic.* Athens: University of Georgia Press, 1961.

Parrington, Vernon L. *Main Currents in American Thought: An Interpretation of American Literature from the Beginnings to 1920.* Vol. 2, *The Romantic Revolution in America.* New York: Harcourt, Brace and Company, 1930.

Passmore, John. *The Perfectibility of Man*. Indianapolis, Ind.: Liberty Fund, 2000.

Penick, James Lal, Jr. *The Great Western Land Pirate: John A. Murrell in Legend and History*. Columbia: University of Missouri Press, 1981.

Peterson, Merrill D. *The Jefferson Image in the American Mind*. New York: Oxford University Press, 1960.

Pickett, Albert James. *History of Alabama, and Incidentally of Georgia and Mississippi, from the Earliest Periods*. Charleston, S.C.: Walker and James, 1851.

Popper, Karl R. *The Poverty of Historicism*. London: Routledge and Kegan Paul, 1957.

Potter, David M. *History and American Society: Essays of David M. Potter*. Edited by Don E. Fehrenbacher. New York: Oxford University Press, 1973.

———. *The Impending Crisis, 1848–1861*. New York: Harper and Row, 1976.

Power, Richard Lyle. *Planting Corn Belt Culture: The Impress of the Upland Southerner and Yankee in the Old Northwest*. Indianapolis: Indiana Historical Society, 1953.

Rable, George C. *The Confederate Republic: A Revolution against Politics*. Chapel Hill: University of North Carolina Press, 1994.

Ramsay, David. *The History of the American Revolution*. 2 vols. Edited by Lester H. Cohen. Indianapolis, Ind.: Liberty Classics, 1990.

———. *History of the Revolution of South-Carolina*. Trenton[, N.J.]: Isaac Collins, 1785.

Reed, John Shelton. *The Enduring South: Subcultural Persistence in Mass Society*. Chapel Hill: University of North Carolina Press, 1974.

Regis, Pamela. *Describing Early America: Bartram, Jefferson, Crèvecoeur, and the Influence of Natural History*. Philadelphia: University of Pennsylvania Press, 1999.

Reill, Peter Hans. *The German Enlightenment and the Rise of Historicism*. Berkeley: University of California Press, 1975.

Rhodes, James Ford. *Historical Essays*. New York: Macmillan Company, 1909.

Ridgley, Joseph V. *William Gilmore Simms*. New York: Twayne Publishers, 1962.

Roberts, Kenneth. *The Battle of Cowpens: The Great Morale-Builder*. Garden City, N.Y.: Doubleday and Company, 1958.

Rogers, George C., Jr. *Charleston in the Age of the Pinckneys*. Norman: University of Oklahoma Press, 1969.

———. *A South Carolina Chronology, 1497–1970*. South Carolina Tricentennial Commission, 11. Columbia: University of South Carolina Press, 1973.

Roosevelt, Theodore. *History as Literature*. New York: Charles Scribner's Sons, 1913.

Rose, Anne C. *Voices of the Marketplace: American Thought and Culture, 1830–1860*. New York: Twayne Publishers, 1995.

Sabine, Lorenzo. *The American Loyalists or Biographical Sketches of Adherents to the British Crown in the War of the Revolution; Alphabetically Arranged; with a Preliminary Historical Essay*. Boston: Charles C. Little and James Brown, 1847.

———. *Biographical Sketches of Loyalists of the American Revolution, with an Historical Essay*. Boston: Little, Brown and Company, 1864.

Salley, A. S. *Catalogue of the Salley Collection of the Works of Wm. Gilmore Simms*. 1943. Reprint, New York: Burt Franklin, 1969.

Sandoz, Ellis, ed. *Political Sermons of the American Founding Era, 1730–1805*. Indianapolis, Ind.: Liberty Fund, 1991.

Schama, Simon. *Citizens: A Chronicle of the French Revolution*. New York: Alfred A. Knopf, 1989.

———. *Dead Certainties (Unwarranted Speculations)*. New York: Alfred A. Knopf, 1991.

Shaffer, Arthur H. *The Politics of History: Writing the History of the American Revolution, 1783–1815*. Chicago: Precedent Publishing, 1975.

————. *To Be an American: David Ramsay and the Making of the American Consciousness.* Columbia: University of South Carolina Press, 1991.

Sheidley, Harlow W. *Sectional Nationalism: Massachusetts Conservative Leaders and the Transformation of America, 1815–1836.* Boston: Northeastern University Press, 1998.

Shellabarger, Samuel. *The Chevalier Bayard: A Study in Fading Chivalry.* New York: Century Co., 1928.

Shils, Edward. *The Virtue of Civility: Selected Essays on Liberalism, Tradition, and Civil Society.* Indianapolis, Ind.: Liberty Fund, 1997.

Sidney, Sir Philip. *Defence of Poesy.* Edited by Dorothy M. Macardle. London: Macmillan, 1968.

Simpson, Lewis P. *The Dispossessed Garden: Pastoral and History in Southern Literature.* Athens: University of Georga Press, 1975.

————, ed. *The Federalist Literary Mind: Selections from the "Monthly Anthology and Boston Review," 1803–1811, Including Documents Relating to the Boston Athenaeum.* Baton Rouge: Louisiana State University Press, 1962.

Skotheim, Robert Allen. *American Intellectual Histories and Historians.* Princeton, N.J.: Princeton University Press, 1966.

Slaughter, Thomas P. *The Natures of John and William Bartram.* New York: Alfred A. Knopf, 1996.

Smith, Adam. *Lectures on Rhetoric and Belles Lettres.* Edited by J. C. Bryce. Indianapolis, Ind.: Liberty Classics, 1985.

Smith, Mark M. *Mastered by the Clock: Time, Slavery, and Freedom in the American South.* Chapel Hill: University of North Carolina Press, 1997.

Smith, Page. *The Historian and History.* New York: Alfred A. Knopf, 1966.

Spadafora, David. *The Idea of Progress in Eighteenth-Century Britain.* New Haven, Conn.: Yale University Press, 1990.

Sparks, Jared. *A Reply to the Strictures of Lord Mahon and Others, on the Mode of Editing the Writings of Washington.* Cambridge, Mass.: John Bartlett, 1852.

————, ed. *The Writings of George Washington; Being His Correspondence, Addresses, Messages and Other Papers, Official and Private, Selected and Published from the Original Manuscripts; with a Life of the Author, Notes and Illustrations.* 12 vols. New York: Harper and Brothers, 1848.

Stafford, John. *The Literary Criticism of "Young America": A Study in the Relationship of Politics and Literature, 1837–1850.* University of California Publications, English Studies, no. 3. Berkeley: University of California Press, 1952.

Stephens, Alexander H. *A Constitutional View of the Late War between the States; Its Causes, Character, Conduct and Results Presented in a Series of Colloquies at Liberty Hall.* Philadelphia: National Publishing Co., 1868–70.

Stern, Fritz, ed. *The Varieties of History: From Voltaire to the Present.* Cleveland: World Publishing Company, 1956.

Stern, Madeleine. *Imprints on History: Book Publishers and American Frontiers.* Bloomington: Indiana University Press, 1956. See chapter 4 on John Russell.

Sumner, Charles. *The Works of Charles Sumner.* 15 vols. Boston: Lee and Shepard, 1870–83.

Sydnor, Charles S. *The Development of Southern Sectionalism, 1819–1848.* Baton Rouge: Louisiana State University Press, 1948.

Taylor, William R. *Cavalier and Yankee: The Old South and American National Character.* New York: Oxford University Press, 1993.

Teggart, Frederick J. *Theory and Processes of History*. Berkeley, Calif.: University of California Press, 1960. Originally published as two volumes, *Theory of History* (1925) and *The Processes of History* (1918), by Yale University Press.

Timrod, Henry. *The Essays of Henry Timrod*. Edited by Edd Winfield Parks. Athens: University of Georgia Press, 1942.

Tolstoy, Leo. *War and Peace*. New York: Modern Library, n.d.

Treacy, M. F. *Prelude to Yorktown: The Southern Campaign of Nathanael Greene, 1780–1781*. Chapel Hill: Univeristy of North Carolina Press, 1963.

Trent, William Peterfield. *William Gilmore Simms*. Boston: Houghton, Mifflin Company, 1892.

Trescot, William Henry. *Oration Delivered before the South-Carolina Historical Society, Thursday, May 19, 1859*. Charleston, S.C.: James and Williams, 1859.

Trevor-Roper, H. R. *History: Professional and Lay; an Inaugural Lecture Delivered before the University of Oxford on 12 November 1957*. Oxford: Clarendon Press, 1957.

Turner, Frederick Jackson. *Rereading Frederick Jackson Turner: "The Significance of the Frontier in American History" and Other Essays*. Commentary by John Mack Faragher. New York: Henry Holt and Company, 1994.

———. *Rise of the New West, 1819–1829*. New York: Harper and Brothers Publishers, 1906.

Tuveson, Ernest Lee. *Redeemer Nation: The Idea of America's Millennial Role*. Chicago: University of Chicago Press, 1968.

Van Tassel, David D. *Recording America's Past: An Interpretation of the Development of Historical Studies in America, 1607–1884*. Chicago: University of Chicago Press, 1960.

Venable, William H. *A School History of the United States*. Cincinnati: Wilson, Hinkle and Co., 1872.

Vidal, Gore. *Burr: A Novel*. New York: Random House, 1973.

———. *United States: Essays, 1952–1992*. New York: Random House, 1993.

Vizthum, Richard C. *The American Compromise: Theme and Method in the Histories of Bancroft, Parkman, and Adams*. Norman: University of Oklahoma Press, 1974.

Wakelyn, Jon L. *The Politics of a Literary Man: William Gilmore Simms*. Westport, Conn.: Greenwood Press, 1973.

Waldstreicher, David. *In the Midst of Perpetual Fetes: The Making of American Nationalism, 1776–1820*. Chapel Hill: University of North Carolina Press, 1997.

Wallace, David Duncan. *South Carolina: A Short History, 1520–1948*. Chapel Hill: University of North Carolina Press, 1951.

Warren, James Perrin. *Culture of Eloquence: Oratory and Reform in Antebellum America*. University Park: Pennsylvania State University Press, 1999.

Watson, Charles S. *From Nationalism to Secessionism: The Changing Fiction of William Gilmore Simms*. Westport, Conn.: Greenwood Press, 1993.

Weaver, Richard M. *In Defense of Tradition: Collected Shorter Writings of Richard M. Weaver, 1929–1963*. Edited by Ted J. Smith III. Indianapolis, Ind.: Liberty Fund, 2000.

———. *The Southern Essays of Richard M. Weaver*. Edited by George M. Curtis III and James J. Thompson Jr. Indianapolis, Ind.: Liberty Fund, 1987.

———. *The Southern Tradition at Bay: A History of Postbellum Thought*. Washington, D.C.: Regnery Gateway, 1989.

Weems, Mason L. *The Life of Washington*. Cambridge, Mass.: Belknap Press of Harvard University Press, 1962.

Weigley, Russell F. *The Partisan War: The South Carolina Campaign of 1780–1782*. Columbia: University of South Carolina Press, 1970.

Weir, Robert M. *Colonial South Carolina: A History.* Millwood, N.Y.: KTO Press, 1983.
———. *"The Last of American Freemen": Studies in the Political Culture of the Colonial and Revolutionary South.* Macon, Ga.: Mercer University Press, 1986.
Welsh, John Rushing. *The Mind of William Gilmore Simms: His Social and Political Thought: A Summary of a Thesis Presented to the Faculty of the Graduate School of Vanderbilt University in Partial Fulfillment of the Requirements for the Degree of Doctor of Philosophy.* Nashville, Tenn.: Joint University Libraries, 1951.
Whitmore, William H. *The Cavalier Dismounted: An Essay on the Origin of the Founders of the Thirteen Colonies.* Salem, Mass.: G. M. Whipple and A. A. Smith, 1864.
Widman, Edward L. *Young America: The Flowering of Democracy in New York City.* New York: Oxford University Press, 1999.
Wilson, Edmund. *Patriotic Gore: Studies in the Literature of the American Civil War.* New York: Oxford University Press, 1962.
Wilson, Major L. *Space, Time, and Freedom: The Quest for Nationality and the Irrepressible Conflict, 1815–1861.* Westport, Conn.: Greenwood Press, 1974.
Wiltse, Charles M. *John C. Calhoun: Nationalist, 1782–1828.* Indianapolis, Ind.: Bobbs-Merrill Company, 1944.
———. *John C. Calhoun: Nullifier, 1829–1839.* Indianapolis, Ind.: Bobbs-Merrill Company, 1949.
———. *John C. Calhoun: Sectionalist, 1840–1850.* Indianapolis, Ind.: Bobbs-Merrill Company, 1951.
———. *The New Nation, 1800–1845.* New York: Hill and Wang, 1961.
Wimsatt, Mary Ann. *The Major Fiction of William Gilmore Simms: Cultural Traditions and Literary Form.* Baton Rouge: Louisiana State University Press, 1989.
Wood, Gordon S. *The Creation of the American Republic, 1776–1787.* Chapel Hill: University of North Carolina Press, 1969.
———. *The Radicalism of the American Revolution.* New York: Vintage Books, 1991.
Wright, Esmond. *Fabric of Freedom, 1763–1800.* Rev. ed. New York: Hill and Wang, 1978.
Yarborough, Jean M. *American Virtues: Thomas Jefferson on the Character of a Free People.* Lawrence: University Press of Kansas, 1998.

Articles, Essays, Chapters, Etc.

Atwood, Margaret. "In Search of *Alias Grace:* On Writing Canadian Historical Fiction." *American Historical Review* 103 (December 1998): 1503–16.
Beard, Charles A. "Grounds for a Reconsideration of Historiography." In the Social Science Research Council's Committee on Historiography's *Theory and Practice in Historical Study: A Report of the Committee on Historiography,* 1–14. New York: Social Science Research Council, 1946.
———. "That Noble Dream." In *American Historians: A Selection,* edited by Harvey Wish, 361–77. New York: Oxford University Press, 1962.
Becker, Carl L. "What Are Historical Facts?" In *The Dimensions of History: Readings on the Nature of History and the Problems of Historical Interpretation,* edited by Thomas N. Guinsburg, 29–40. Chicago: Rand McNally and Company, 1971.
Berry, Wendell. "Writer and Region." In *What Are People For? Essays by Wendell Berry,* 71–87. San Francisco: North Point Press, 1990.
Blassingame, John W. "American Nationalism and Other Loyalties in the Southern Colonies, 1763–1775." *Journal of Southern History* 34 (February 1968): 50–75.
Bradford, M. E. "A Teaching for Republicans: Roman History and the Nation's First Identity." In *A Better Guide Than Reason: Federalists and Antifederalists,* 3–28. New Brunswick, N.J.: Transaction Publishers, 1994.

Bresnahan, Roger J. "William Gilmore Simms's Revolutionary War Novels: A Romantic View of Southern History." *Studies in Romanticism* 15 (Fall 1976): 573–87.

Brown, Thomas. "John Pendleton Kennedy's *Quodlibet* and the Culture of Jacksonian Democracy." *Journal of the Early Republic* 16 (Winter 1996): 625–43.

Bury, J. B. "The Science of History." In *The Dimensions of History: Readings on the Nature of History and the Problems of Historical Interpretation*, edited by Thomas N. Guinsburg, 23–27. Chicago: Rand McNally and Company, 1971.

Busick, Sean R. "The Actual and the Ideal: History and Fiction in 'Lucas de Ayllon.'" *Simms Review* 6 (Summer 1998): 29–34.

———. "Nationalism, History, and Moral Progress in Simms's Earliest Writings." *Simms Review* 7 (Winter 1999): 11–15.

Calhoon, Robert M. "The Reintegration of the Loyalists and the Disaffected." In *The American Revolution: Its Character and Limits*, edited by Jack P. Greene, 51–74. New York: New York University Press, 1987.

Cohen, Lester H. "Creating a Usable Future: The Revolutionary Historians." In *The American Revolution: Its Character and Limits*, edited by Jack P. Greene, 309–31. New York: New York University Press, 1987.

Cunliffe, Marcus. "Introduction." In *The Life of Washington*, by Mason L. Weems, ix–lxii. Cambridge, Mass.: Belknap Press of Harvard University Press, 1962.

Demos, John. "In Search of Reasons for Historians to Read Novels. . . ." *American Historical Review* 103 (December 1998): 1526–29.

Doherty, Herbert J., Jr. "The Mind of the Antebellum South." In *Writing Southern History: Essays in Historiography in Honor of Fletcher M. Green*, edited by Arthru S. Link and Rembert W. Patrick, 198–223. Baton Rouge: Louisiana State University Press, 1965.

Dowling, William C. Foreword to *An Essay on the Life of the Honourable Major-General Israel Putnam: Addressed to the State Society of the Cincinnati in Connecticut and Published by Their Order*, by David Humphreys, ix–xxii. Indianapolis, Ind.: Liberty Fund, 2000.

Dye, Renée. "Narrating Social Theory: Simms's *Woodcraft*." *Simms Review* 4 (Summer 1996): 23–45.

Emerson, Ralph Waldo. "The American Scholar." In *The Portable Emerson*, ed. Mark Van Doren, 38–46. New York: Viking Press, 1946.

Faust, Drew Gilpin. "The Peculiar South Revisited: White Society, Culture, and Politics in the Antebellum Period, 1800–1860." In *Interpreting Southern History: Historiographical Essays in Honor of Sanford W. Higginbotham*, edited by John B. Boles and Evelyn Thomas Nolen, 78–119. Baton Rouge: Louisiana State Univeristy Press, 1987.

Feller, Daniel. "Politics and Society: Toward a Jacksonian Synthesis." *Journal of the Early Republic* 10 (Summer 1990): 135–62.

Foote, Shelby. "The Novelist's View of History." *Sewanee Review* 99 (Summer 1991): 439–45.

Ford, Lacy K., Jr. "Inventing the Concurrent Majority: Madison, Calhoun, and the Problem of Majoritarianism in American Political Thought." *Journal of Southern History* 60 (February 1994): 19–58.

Fox-Genovese, Elizabeth. "The Anxiety of History: The Southern Confrontation with Modernity." *Southern Cultures* 1 (1993): 65–82.

Freehling, William W. "South Carolina's Pivotal Decision for Disunion: Popular Mandate or Manipulated Verdict?" *University South Caroliniana Society: Sixty-fifth Annual Meeting* (2001): 3–11. Address originally delivered at the 64th annual meeting of University South Caroliniana Society, Columbia, S.C.

Genovese, Eugene D. "South Carolina's Contribution to the Doctrine of Slavery in the Abstract." In *The Meaning of South Carolina History: Essays in Honor of George C.*

Rogers, Jr., edited by David R. Chesnutt and Clyde N. Wilson, 146–60. Columbia: University of South Carolina Press, 1991.

———. "William Styron's *The Confessions of Nat Turner:* A Meditation on Evil, Redemption, and History." In *Novel History*, edited by Mark C. Carnes, 209–20. New York: Simon and Schuster, 2001

Guilds, John C. "Simms and the *Southern and Western.*" In *South Carolina Journals and Journalists: Proceedings of the Reynolds Conference, University of South Carolina, May 17–18, 1974*, edited by James B. Meriwether, 45–59. Spartanburg, S.C.: Reprint Company, 1975.

———. "Simms and the *Southern Literary Gazette.*" *Studies in Bibliography* 21 (1968): 59–92.

———. "Simms's First Magazine: *The Album.*" *Studies in Bibliography* 8 (1956): 169–84.

———. "Simms's Use of History: Theory and Practice." *Mississippi Quarterly: The Journal of Southern Culture* 30 (Fall 1977): 505–11.

———. "Simms's Views on National and Sectional Literature, 1825–1845." *North Carolina Historical Review* 34 (July 1957): 393–405.

Harrison, Jesse Burton. "English Civilization." In *All Clever Men, Who Make Their Way: Critical Discourse in the Old South*, edited by Michael O'Brien, 55–88. Fayetteville: University of Arkansas Press, 1982.

Hay, Robert P. "The Glorious Departure of the American Patriarchs: Contemporary Reactions to the Deaths of Jefferson and Adams." *Journal of Southern History* 35 (November 1969): 543–55.

Higham, John. "The Changing Loyalties of William Gilmore Simms." *Journal of Southern History* 9 (1943): 210–23.

Horsman, Reginald. "The Dimensions of an 'Empire for Liberty': Expansion and Republicanism, 1775–1825." *Journal of the Early Republic* 9 (Spring 1989): 1–20.

House, Kay S. "Cooper as Historian." In *James Fenimore Cooper: His Country and His Art*, edited by George A. Test, 1–13. Papers from the 1986 Conference at State University College of New York—Oneonta and Cooperstown. Available on-line at http://external.oneonta.edu/cooper/articles/suny/1986suny-house.html (accessed September 2004).

Hunt, Lynn. "'No Longer an Evenly Flowing River': Time, History, and the Novel." *American Historical Review* 103 (December 1998): 1517–21.

Jahoda, Gloria. "Commentary." In *Eighteenth-Century Florida and the Revolutionary South*, edited by Samuel Proctor, 122–25. Gainesville: University Presses of Florida, 1978.

Jarrell, Hampton M. "William Gilmore Simms—Almost A Historian." In *Proceedings of the South Carolina Historical Association* (1947), edited by Robert D. Ochs, 3–8. Columbia: South Carolina Historical Association, 1947.

Kamrath, Mark L. "Charles Brockden Brown and the 'art of the historian': An Essay Concerning (Post)modern Historical Understanding." *Journal of the Early Republic* 21 (Summer 2001): 231–60.

Kaplanoff, Mark D. "How Federalist Was South Carolina in 1787–1788?" In *The Meaning of South Carolina History: Essays in Honor of George C. Rogers Jr.*, edited by David R. Chesnutt and Clyde N. Wilson, 67–103. Columbia: University of South Carolina Press, 1991.

Kibler, James Everett, Jr. "Simms' Editorship of the Columbia *Phoenix* of 1865." In *South Carolina Journals and Journalists: Proceedings of the Reynolds Conference, University of South Carolina, May 17–18, 1974*, edited by James B. Meriwether, 61–75. Spartanburg, S.C.: Reprint Company, 1975.

———. "Stewardship and *Patria* in Simms's Frontier Poetry." In *William Gilmore Simms and the American Frontier*, edited by John C. Guilds and Caroline Collins, 209–20. Athens: University of Georgia Press, 1997.

———. "William Gilmore Simms." In *Dictionary of Literary Biography*. Vol. 73, *American Magazine Journalists, 1741–1850*, edited by Sam G. Riley, 275–92. Detroit: Gale Research Co., 1988.

Langdon, Samuel. "The Republic of the Israelites an Example to the American States." In *Political Sermons of the American Founding Era, 1730–1805*, edited by Ellis Sandoz, 941–67. Indianapolis, Ind.: Liberty Fund, 1991.

Maier, Pauline. "The Road Not Taken: Nullification, John C. Calhoun and the Revolutionary Tradition in South Carolina." *South Carolina Historical Magazine* 82 (January 1981): 1–19.

Mayfield, John. "'The Soul of a Man!': William Gilmore Simms and the Myths of Southern Manhood." *Journal of the Early Republic* 15 (Fall 1995): 477–500.

McCardell, John. "Poetry and the Practical: William Gilmore Simms." In *Intellectual Life in Antebellum Charleston*, edited by Michael O'Brien and David Moltke-Hansen, 186–210. Knoxville: University of Tennessee Press, 1986.

———. "Trent's *Simms:* The Making of a Biography." In *A Master's Due: Essays in Honor of David Herbert Donald*, edited by William J. Cooper Jr., Michael F. Holt, and John McCardell, 179–203. Baton Rouge: Louisiana State University Press, 1985.

Meats, Stephen. "Artist or Historian: William Gilmore Simms and the Revolutionary South." In *Eighteenth-Century Florida and the Revolutionary South*, edited by Samuel Proctor, 94–109. Gainesville: University Presses of Florida, 1978.

Melish, Joanne Pope. "The 'Condition' Debate and Racial Discourse in the Antebellum North." *Journal of the Early Republic* 19 (Winter 1999): 651–72.

Meriwether, Anne Blythe. "An Unpublished Letter of 1862 from Simms to W. J. Rivers." *Simms Review* 3 (Summer 1995): 1–4.

Miles, Edwin. "The Old South and the Classical World." *North Carolina Historical Review* 48 (July 1971): 258–75.

Moltke-Hansen, David. "Ordered Progress: The Historical Philosophy of William Gilmore Simms." In *Long Years of Neglect: The Work and Reputation of William Gilmore Simms*, edited by John C. Guilds, 126–47. Fayetteville: University of Arkansas Press, 1988.

———. "Protecting Interests, Maintaining Rights, Emulating Ancestors: U.S. Constitution Bicentennial Reflections on 'The Problem of South Carolina,' 1787–1860." *South Carolina Historical Magazine* 89 (July 1988): 160–82.

Moore, Alexander. "The Swamp Fox in History and Literature: A Select Bibliography of Books about Francis Marion." *Carologue: A Publication of the South Carolina Historical Society* 15 (Winter 1999): 14–15.

Moore, Rayburn. "Simms's Literary Reputation since the 1930s: Some Personal Reminiscences." *Simms Review* 8 (Summer 2000): 27–34.

Morison, Samuel Eliot. "History as a Literary Art." In *Sailor Historian: The Best of Samuel Eliot Morison*, ed. Emily Morison Beck, 383–93. Boston: Houghton Mifflin Company, 1977.

O'Brien, Karen. "David Ramsay and the Delayed Americanization of American History." *Early American Literature* 29, no. 1 (1994): 1–18.

O'Brien, Michael. "On the Writing of History in the Old South." In *Rewriting the South*, edited by Lothar Honnighausen and Valeria Gennaro Lerda, 141–66. Tübingen: Francke, 1993.

———. Reviews of *William Gilmore Simms and the American Frontier*, edited by John C. Guilds and Caroline Collins and *From Nationalism to Secessionism: The Changing Fiction of William Gilmore Simms*, by Charles S. Watson. *Southern Cultures* (Summer 1999): 107–12.

Odell, Alfred T. "William Gilmore Simms in the Post-War Years." *Bulletin of Furman University* 29 (May 1946): 5–20.

Oliphant, Mary C. Simms. "William Gilmore Simms—Historical Artist." University South Caroliniana Society, Report of the Secretary and Treasurer for 1942, 16–29.

Potter, David M. "The Historian's Use of Nationalism and Vice Versa." In *History and American Society: Essays of David M. Potter,* edited by Don E. Fehrenbacher, 60–108. New York: Oxford University Press, 1973.

Roberts, Carey M. "The Mighty River of Providence or the Secrets of Home: The Historical Theories of Simms and Bancroft." *Simms Review* 6 (Summer 1998): 35–43.

Rogers, George C., Jr. "Names, Not Numbers." *William and Mary Quarterly,* 3rd ser., 45 (1988): 574–79.

Savage, James [?]. "The Architecture of a Great Mind." In *The Federalist Literary Mind: Selections from the "Monthly Anthology and Boston Review," 1803–1811, Including Documents Relating to the Boston Athenaeum,* edited by Lewis P. Simpson, 79–81. Baton Rouge: Louisiana State University Press, 1962.

Sellers, Charles G., Jr. "The American Revolution: Southern Founders of a National Tradition." In *Writing Southern History: Essays in Historiography in Honor of Fletcher M. Green,* edited by Arthur S. Link and Rembert W. Patrick, 38–66. Baton Rouge: Louisiana State University Press, 1965.

Shillingsburg, Miriam J. "The Influence of Sectionalism on the Revisions in Simms's Revolutionary Romances." *Mississippi Quarterly* 29 (Fall 1976): 526–38.

———. "Simms's Failed Lecture Tour of 1856: The Mind of the North." In *Long Years of Neglect: The Work and Reputation of William Gilmore Simms,* edited by John C. Guilds, 183–201. Fayetteville: University of Arkansas Press, 1988.

———. "'South Carolina in the Revolution': The Charleston Series with an Addendum to the Manuscript." *Simms Review* 3 (Winter 1995): 1–4.

Spence, Jonathan D. "Margaret Atwood and the Edges of History." *American Historical Review* 103 (December 1998): 1522–25.

"The Study of History." *Southern Quarterly Review* 10 (July 1846): 145.

"Table Talk: Death of William Gilmore Simms." *Appleton's Journal: A Magazine of General Literature* 4 (July 9, 1870): 49

Teed, Paul E. "The Politics of Sectional Memory: Theodore Parker and the *Massachusetts Quarterly Review,* 1847–1850." *Journal of the Early Republic* 21 (Summer 2001): 301–29.

Wagner, Frederick. "Simms's Editing of *The Life of Nathanael Greene.*" *Southern Literary Journal* 11 (Fall 1978): 40–43.

Warren, Robert Penn. "Biography." In *An Approach to Literature,* 4th ed., edited by Cleanth Brooks, John Thibaut Purser, and Robert Penn Warren, 559–61. New York: Appleton-Century-Crofts, 1964.

Watson, Charles S. "Simms and the American Revolution." *Mississipi Quarterly* 29 (Fall 1976): 498–500.

Weir, Robert. "John Laurens: Portrait of a Hero." In *"The Last of American Freemen": Studies in the Political Culture of the Colonial and Revolutionary South,* 89–104. Macon, Ga.: Mercer University Press, 1986.

Welsh, John Rushing. "William Gilmore Simms, Critic of the South." *Journal of Southern History* 26 (May 1960): 201–14.

Werner, Craig. "The Old South, 1815–1840." In *The History of Southern Literature,* edited by Louis D. Rubin Jr. et al., 81–91. Baton Rouge: Louisiana State University Press, 1985.

Wilentz, Sean. "America Made Easy." *New Republic,* July 2, 2001, 35–40.

Wilson, Clyde N. Foreword to *Dictionary of Literary Biography*. Vol. 30, *American Historians, 1607–1865*, edited by Clyde N. Wilson, xi–xiii. Detroit: Gale Research Co., 1984.

———. Foreword to *Dictionary of Literary Biography*. Vol. 47, *American Historians, 1866–1912*, edited by Clyde N. Wilson, xi–xii. Detroit: Gale Research Co., 1986.

———. "The Jeffersonian Conservative Tradition." *Modern Age: A Quarterly Review* 14 (Winter 1969–70): 36–48.

———. "Tiger's Meat: William Gilmore Simms and the History of the Revolution." *Simms Review* 8 (Winter 2000): 22–31.

Wilson, Major L. "The 'Country' Versus the 'Court': A Republican Consensus and Party Debate in the Bank War." *Journal of the Early Republic* 15 (Winter 1995): 619–48.

———. "'Liberty and Union': An Analysis of Three Concepts Involved in the Nullification Controversy." *Journal of Southern History* 33, no. 3 (1967): 331–55.

Theses and Dissertations

Belser, William Gordon, Jr. "William Gilmore Simms: Fictionist as Military Historian of the Revolution." Ph.D. diss., St. John's University, 1977.

Busick, Sean R. "South Carolinians' Attitudes toward the European Revolutions of 1848." Master's thesis, University of South Carolina, 1995.

Cash, William Francis. "Biography and Southern Culture, 1800–1940." Ph.D. diss., University of Texas, 1990.

Click, Benjamin A. L., III. "A Rhetoric of Humor: Towards an American Identity as Revealed through the Southwest Humorists." Ph.D. diss., Pennsylvania State University, 1994.

Crocker, William Lee Thomas. "Richard Yeadon." Master's thesis, University of South Carolina, 1927.

Harris, Christopher. "Character Portraits of American Military Heroes of the Revolution, 1782–1832." Ph.D. diss., Brown University, 1985.

McDowell, David Archibald. "The Place of William Gilmore Simms's Fiction in American Literature: A History of the Criticism from 1833 through 1965." Ph.D. diss., Vanderbilt University, 1966.

Moltke-Hansen, David. "Southern Genesis: Regional Identity and the Rise of the Capital of Southern Civilization, 1760–1860." Ph.D. diss., University of South Carolina, 2000.

Rivers, Jacob F., III. "Prominent Female Characters in the Revolutionary War Novels of William Gilmore Simms." Master's thesis, University of South Carolina, 1987.

Roberts, Carey M. "Men of Much Faith: Progress and Declension in Jeffersonian Thought, 1787–1800." Ph.D. diss., University of South Carolina, 1999.

Rogers, Jeffery J. "William Gilmore Simms and Woodlands Plantation." Master's thesis, University of South Carolina, 1998.

Schramer, James Joseph. "The Myth of Cincinnatus: The Citizen-Soldier in Early American Literature." Ph.D. diss., University of Minnesota, 1987.

Shillingsburg, Peter LeRoy. "The Use of Sources in Simms's Biography of Francis Marion." Master's thesis, University of South Carolina, 1967.

Sullivan, Daniel Joseph, Jr. "Social Criticism in the Revolutionary Romances of William Gilmore Simms." Ph.D. diss., University of Notre Dame, 1972.

Tang, Edward. "Revolutionary Legacies: History, Literature, and Memory in Nineteenth-Century America, 1820–1880." Ph.D. diss., New York University, 1996.

Trask, H. Arthur Scott. "The Constitutional Republicans of Philadelphia, 1818–1848: Hard Money, Free Trade, and State Rights." Ph.D. diss., University of South Carolina, 1998.

Walker, Franklin T. "William Peterfield Trent—A Critical Biography." Ph.D. diss., George Peabody College for Teachers, 1943.